Global Interests

PICTURING HISTORY

Series Editors
Peter Burke, Sander L. Gilman, Ludmilla Jordanova,
Roy Porter, †Bob Scribner (1995–8)

In the same series

Global Interests

Renaissance Art between
East and West

Lisa Jardine and Jerry Brotton

REAKTION BOOKS

Published by Reaktion Books Ltd
79 Farringdon Road, London ECIM 3JU, UK

www.reaktionbooks.co.uk

First published 2000

Series design by Humphrey Stone
Colour printed by Balding & Mansell Limited, Norwich
Printed and bound in Great Britain by
Biddles Limited, Guildford and King's Lynn

British Library Cataloguing in Publication Data

Jardine, Lisa
 Global interests: renaissance art between east and west. – (Picturing history)
 1. Art, Renaissance – Europe 2. Art, Ottoman 3. Art, European
 I. Title II. Brotton, Jerry
 709´.031

ISBN 1 86189 079 6

Contents

Preface

This is a book about two-way material exchange across geographical and ideological boundaries, during the period conventionally known as the Renaissance, and its enduring influence on European cultural identity. The book began as a series of heated discussions while each of us was engaged in writing a book of our own. We noticed that the material and the grounding arguments that led us separately to write *Worldly Goods* and *Trading Territories* overlapped at a number of crucial points. We could hardly help exchanging views and arguing over possible alternative interpretations. In the process, we discovered the luxury of conversation with another person equally well informed in your chosen field, and equally willing to rush off and pursue lines of inquiry which both of you are impatient to follow in search of further answers. Although we occasionally set off along individual paths to new archival material, at the end of the day we sat down and wrote the book together, at adjacent, networked computers – such is the luxury of writing in the age of the PC. We can no longer remember which of us wrote which portions of *Global Interests*, or who had the crucial ideas at turning points in our explorations.

We point out here, at the outset, probably pointlessly, that this is not a 'history' in the conventional sense. Often, when we told people what we were working on, they would volunteer the helpful information that 'so-and-so is writing a history of horses', or of tapestries or of portrait medals. Whilst work in those fields has assisted us significantly in filling out the contours of our broad-brush argument, this book tries to look over the shoulders of the concrete examples to the cultural formations that shaped the detailed developments in dressage, tapestry-series composition and the like. It is a historical pursuit of ideas and representations across disciplinary and geographical boundaries. Sometimes, we are persuaded that ours is a new kind of 'cultural history', unrestricted by nation or moment. Sometimes, we think that we are, instead, working in the history of objects, or of design. Whatever we decide, it does not take long before we find that the topic on which we are working takes us beyond the conventional boundaries of named disciplines. That is one of the difficulties with having global interests.

The present work is only a small beginning in what both authors believe to be a much larger project, to be undertaken by all those who, like ourselves, are committed to understanding the origins in the Renaissance of that rich culture which remains our shared European heritage. It has become increasingly clear to us as this enterprise has progressed that what we are looking at in this book is merely the tip of a very large iceberg. Once it is recognized that for purposes of artistic and other material transaction, the boundaries between what we will refer to here as East and West were thoroughly permeable in the Renaissance, and that even in situations of conflict, mutual recognition of icons and images could be used adversarially with creative verve, fresh possibilities for cultural cross-fertilization and a two-way traffic in influence open up at every turn. With these possibilities and their implications comes the inevitable recognition that cultural histories apparently utterly distinct, and traditionally kept entirely separate, are ripe to be rewritten as shared East/West undertakings.

At the end of 1999, for example, the curators of an exhibition in Istanbul on the topic of Mehmet II, to whose Muslim might Constantinople/Istanbul fell in 1453, set out to look westwards, in order to present the great military leader in an unfamiliar light – that of Renaissance patron, art connoisseur, philosopher and linguist. A report of the exhibition in the *New York Times* suggested that this European image of the great Ottoman leader might serve as an appropriate focus for modern Turkey's desire to retrieve some of its European roots and influences in its 'new turn toward Europe'.[1]

The centrepiece of the exhibition was a painting borrowed from the National Gallery in London: the Venetian Gentile Bellini's portrait of Mehmet II (illus. 1). Its return to Istanbul was a cause for general celebration of a key moment in Turkey's past – an artistic and cultural flowering with shared roots in the Italian and Northern European Renaissances. 'We have seen this picture so many times, in so many schoolbooks and on so many walls over so many years that it's really imprinted on our brains,' commented one visitor to the exhibit. 'Now it's finally here, the real thing. Hard to believe.' Yet this is a painting that used to be identified by the National Gallery simply as 'an oriental figure', 'possibly by Bellini'. As recently as 1991, it was referred to in the Gallery's own published catalogue as some kind of copy, 'which may have originated in a likeness made by the Venetian artist Gentile Bellini'.[2]

1 Gentile Bellini, *Portrait of Mehmet II*, 1479, oil on canvas. National Gallery, London.

Secure attribution, in other words, has depended on a restored Western understanding of the time spent by Bellini in Istanbul as one of the Sultan's court artists, on loan from the Venetian Senate, in whose employ he officially was, in 1479. On these kinds of foundations, no doubt, further important collaborative investigations will be built to expand our shared understanding of artistic ventures embarked upon together by Muslim Ottomans and Christian Venetians at the end of the fifteenth century.

From the West, looking eastwards, we offer a single example of the potential impact on our outlook, crying out for further intercultural investigation of this kind of 'cultural mobility'.[3]

In a series of letters written around 1484 and preserved in one of his many notebooks, Leonardo da Vinci reports to someone he calls 'Devatdar Kait-Bai' on the findings of a lengthy scientific mission conducted along the politically contested Turkish coast, in the aftermath of some kind of natural disaster there (an earthquake or catastrophic series of storms). Leonardo's most recent biographer, Michael White, follows his predecessors in pronouncing this 'a singular work of fiction' written to 'a fictitious governor of Cairo'. As recently as twenty years ago, it seemed inconceivable to European scholars that fifteenth-century artists had moved freely between Christian and Muslim cultural centres, and consequently unlikely that Leonardo was doing anything other than fantasizing from an Italian location.[4]

But Qaitbay was in fact the cultivated and culturally ambitious Mamluk Sultan at this date. Following the scrupulous work of contemporary oriental scholars such as Julian Raby and Gülru Necipoğlu, we now have properly documented accounts of the way in which individuals like Bellini, Costanzo da Ferrara and Matteo de' Pasti were sent on extended artistic 'exchanges' to the East by their patrons in this period.[5]

It seems clear that further investigation is needed to find out whether Leonardo really did visit southern Turkey, doing the same kind of surveying or engineering work for which his then-current employer Ludovico Sforza of Milan used him at home and, if so, what impact these encounters had on other aspects of his oeuvre.

Who knows what unfamiliar cultural identities we will discover upon which to ground a future, enriched understanding of ourselves once we have breached the boundaries of our own historical prejudice?

We have incurred, as always, numerous debts to others. The most obvious is to the many scholars acknowledged in our text and references, without whose meticulous work we could never have made our own discoveries and connections. At a more personal level, Peter Barber, Warren Boutcher, Denis Cosgrove, John Elliott, Rachel Holmes, Rachel Jardine, Anthony Pagden, Alan Stewart and Luke Syson have all made important contributions. Toby Mundy found us our subtitle. Michael Leaman helped us enormously with calm encouragement. Our errors, on the other hand, are entirely our own.

1 Exchanging Identity: Breaching the Boundaries of Renaissance Europe

> Ciriac of Ancona (d. 1457) travelled, not only through Italy, but through other countries of the old world, and brought back with him countless inscriptions and sketches. When asked why he took all this trouble, he replied, To wake the dead.
> JACOB BURCKHARDT, *The Civilisation of the Renaissance in Italy*[1]

> Daily [the Ottoman Sultan Mehmet II] has Roman and other historical works read to him by a companion named Ciriac of Ancona and another Italian. He has them read Laertius, Herodotus, Livy, Quintus Curtius, the chronicles of the popes, the emperors, the kings of France, and the Lombards.
> FRANZ BABINGER, *Mehmed the Conqueror and His Time*[2]

In this work, we examine the conceptual boundaries that frame cultural identity, and their location on the map of modern Europe. Specifically, we look at the way in which, historically and in a climate of commercial and political competitiveness, Europeans looked outwards for aesthetic confirmation of who they were – what defined them as 'civilized' – and met the steady returning gaze of the non-European. What, we ask, happened as a result of that encounter? Only as we try to answer this question, we suggest, can we begin the painstaking process of bridging the historiographical gap between our two epigraphs. The first is reassuringly within the Western European classical tradition, whilst the second is strangely exotic, a claim to that same heritage made by the cultural élite of the fifteenth century Islamic orient unfamiliar to us. But that, we shall argue, is *our* problem, as Europeans.

I

Writing in 1930, in *Civilisation and Its Discontents*, Freud characterized the achievements of the Renaissance and the civilization it ushered in in terms intended to recall Jacob Burckhardt's *The Civilisation of the Renaissance in Italy*:

Beauty, cleanliness and order obviously occupy a special position among the requirements of civilisation. No one will maintain that they are as important for life as control over the forces of nature or as some other factors with which we shall become acquainted. And yet no one would care to put them in the background as trivialities ... No feature, however, seems better to characterise civilisation than its esteem and encouragement of man's higher mental activities – his intellectual, scientific and artistic achievements – and the leading role that it assigns to ideas in human life.[3]

Steeped in nineteenth-century admiration for classical antiquity, Burckhardt had set out to show how European culture had evolved by direct descent from Greek and Roman roots. His heavily moralized narrative argued that an antique tradition, retrieved by scholars of humane learning in Italy in the fifteenth century, had given rise to an idealized and aesthetically pure fine art, and to an intellectually abstract framework for thought. These were, he claimed, the enduring triumphs of Western civilization.

Burckhardt's argument had a corollary. The civilized values handed down from antiquity had to be retrieved from amid the social and intellectual debris of late Medieval barbarism. In order for this to happen, Renaissance individuals had for the first time to recognize their identity as separate from visible civic forms, and to shape themselves consciously to the new social world they aspired to inhabit. For Burckhardt as for Freud, Renaissance civilization required men to limit their natural urges in the interests of an urbane mode of living, or humanity (for both, also, secular humanism replaced religion as the cohesive force within civilized society).[4]

As Freud took it over in *Civilisation and Its Discontents*, the point in recalling this idealized moment in human development was to understand the predicament of contemporary Western society. It was here that the struggle of the individual with the restrictions imposed on instinctual (above all sexual) drives had reached a point of crisis:

If the development of civilisation has such a far-reaching similarity to the development of the individual and if it employs the same methods, may we not be justified in reaching the diagnosis that, under the influence of cultural urges, some civilisations, or some epochs of civilisation – possibly the whole of mankind – have become neurotic?[5]

Because Freud here articulates a perceived struggle between dirt, anal and sexual drives, and a communal commitment to aesthetic beauty and intellectual truth, Renaissance Man is established by antithesis as a necessary construct, at once an anterior reality and an impossible dream. He is psychically whole, clean, possessed of integrity and essentially humane.

II

In our own time, the project of excavating the origins of the conte
porary crisis in Western selfhood in the terms established by Freud
and Burckhardt has been taken up and developed further by prominent figures working within the broad field of textual studies. In his
groundbreaking work *Renaissance Self-Fashioning*, Stephen Greenblatt
makes a series of comments about the shaping forces behind an
emerging Renaissance sense of selfhood, and the ways in which that
sense of self is connected to our own, which draw directly on this
Burckhardt/Freud version of civility. These remarks occur as preparation for Greenblatt's discussion of a literary work for which, he
argues, such a peculiarly Renaissance civility is critical – Edmund
Spenser's epic poem of the 1590s, *The Faerie Queene*:

> If all civilization rests, as Freud argues, upon repression, nevertheless the
> particular civilization we produce and inhabit rests upon a complex technology
> of control whose origins we trace back to the Renaissance . . . We continue
> to see in the Renaissance the shaping of crucial aspects of our sense of self
> and society and the natural world, but we have become uneasy about our whole
> way of constituting reality. Above all, perhaps, we sense that the culture to
> which we are as profoundly attached as our face is to our skull is nonetheless
> a construct, a thing made, as temporary, time-conditioned, and contingent as
> those vast European empires from whose power Freud drew his image of
> repression . . . In the midst of the anxieties and contradictions attendant
> upon the threatened collapse of this phase of our civilization, we respond
> with passionate curiosity and poignancy to the anxieties and contradictions
> attendant upon its rise. To experience Renaissance culture is to feel what it
> was like to form our own identity, and we are at once more rooted and more
> estranged by the experience.[6]

'If it is true that we are highly sensitive to those aspects of the
Renaissance that mark the early, tentative, conflict-ridden fashioning
of modern consciousness', Greenblatt goes on,

> then *The Faerie Queene* is of quite exceptional significance . . . This mirror-
> ing – the conscious purpose of the work seeming to enact the larger cultural
> movement – may help to account for the reader's sense of encountering in
> Spenser's poem the process of self-fashioning itself.[7]

'To experience Renaissance culture is to feel what it was like to
form our own identity'; in Spenser's poem, the reader has a sense
of encountering 'the process of self-fashioning itself', as it comes
bracketed together with that emerging 'complex technology of
control' which continues to set the bounds of possibility on that
selfhood. Greenblatt's suggestion is that if we can give an account

of the way in which tensions and anxieties around identity function in *The Faerie Queene*, then we will have gone some considerable way towards understanding our contemporary predicament as thinking subjects.

What we point out here is the way in which Greenblatt's Renaissance self-fashioning, adroitly constructed as it is by overlaying the theoretical frameworks of psychoanalysis and social anthropology on that of a more traditional Renaissance text criticism, is already bedrocked upon a Burckhardtian version of civilization. This version is itself already refracted through the lens of late Freud. So as historicist criticism continues Greenblatt's project, the long shadow of Freud's Burckhardtianism continues to fall across our revised and re-historicized version of the Renaissance.

Suppose, then, that we stay for a moment with *The Faerie Queene*, which Greenblatt singles out as a telling example of a cultural artefact that manifests significant features of a lastingly influential contest between civilization and barbarism. Anticipating the detailed analysis that forms the substance of the present work, our own argument can be summarized as follows.

Within Spenser's text, a varied collection of pre-existing elements in what Spenser himself defined as a 'continued Allegory'[8] is mobilized and revivified, so as to animate crucial conflicts of identity surrounding ideas of nationhood and empire. These take the form of a cultural currency coined and circulating within and between the domains of what we refer to here as East and West established a full century earlier.[9] Detached from their originating context, these elements nevertheless retain a powerful capacity to connote imperial aspiration and territorial and doctrinal contestation.

When we detect multiple, competing textual strategies in a work like *The Faerie Queene*, we find, as they resolve into a pattern of cultural tensions and strains and a layered sequence of overlapping and interlocking East/West frames of reference, that they are in fact residual traces of a developed set of cultural referents whose origins lie in the 1450s. As we will argue, this was a period in which competing imperial challenges in the political arena were actively matched, in a newly entrepreneurial world of marketable cultural commodities (not unlike our own), by struggles for ownership of cultural meaning in the domain of what we today call art.

Spenser tells Sir Walter Raleigh in his prefatory letter that the overall hero of *The Faerie Queene* is the 'historical' Prince Arthur, future King of England, 'before he was king':

I labour to pourtraict in Arthure, before he was king, the image of a braue knight, perfected in the twelue priuate morall vertues, as Aristotle hath deuised, the which is the purpose of these first twelue bookes: which if I finde to be well accepted, I may be perhaps encoraged, to frame the other part of polliticke vertues in his person, after that hee came to be king.[10]

In fact, however, as the author goes on to explain, the questing protagonist who inhabits the narrative topography of Book I is not Arthur (who does not make his entrance in the poem until more than halfway through that first book), but another knight, whose allegorical function is the representation of Holiness and Truth, and whose 'Englishness' is less robustly assured:

In the person of Prince Arthure I sette forth magnificence in particular, which vertue for that (according to Aristotle and the rest) it is the perfection of all the rest, and conteineth in it them all, therefore in the whole course I mention the deedes of Arthure applyable to that vertue, which I write of in that booke. But of the xii. other vertues, I make xii. other knights the patrones, for the more variety of the history: Of which these [first] three bookes contayne three, The first of the knight of the Redcrosse, in which I expresse Holynes.[11]

It is Redcrosse who first enters, championing the 'louely Ladie' Una, in true questing knight style: 'A Gentle Knight was pricking on the plaine, / Y cladd in mightie armes and siluer shielde.' Halfway through Book I, when Redcrosse is near-fatally weakened and imprisoned by the Giant Orgoglio, Arthur steps in and takes over as Una's champion (even so, he is not identified by name until the ninth canto).[12] Arthur substitutes for Redcrosse in the story of the knightly quest to slay a monster and thereby win the love of the rescued lady. After he has slain the Giant, the grateful Una, apparently forgetting herself for a moment, offers herself to Arthur in recompense: 'Accept therefore / My simple selfe, and seruice euermore.'[13] Arthur, however, is spoken for, having given his allegiance unreservedly to the 'Queene of Faeries' herself.[14]

Arthur is England's fixed and unshakeable champion. Not so Redcrosse, whose identity and allegiance shift as the plot of Book I unfolds, in spite (we would argue) of the author's efforts to hold him firm as 'faire ymp, sprong out of English race'.[15] Some of the difficulties for the reader, associated with exactly who Redcrosse is, can be traced to one crucial choice of alias, as identity-giver for the mysterious champion. At key moments in the poem, the knight without a name, designated by his insignia as 'Redcrosse', is brought sharply into focus by being explicitly identified with St George. Critics have, on the whole, accepted this as unproblematic (a picking up and honing into contemporary relevance of a figure associated with English chivalry since Edward III chose George as the Crusader-protecting saint to preside over the Order of the Garter). However, the identification is oddly oblique, and wherever it occurs it creates, as a consequence, significant textual awkwardness.[16]

We suggest that, textually, a kind of evasion is consistently associated with the figure of St George. This evasion skirts a potential narrative problem centred upon Redcrosse/George's relationship with Una (a figure with whom the critical tradition is a good deal more comfortable, in her doubled representation of Elizabeth I and the True Faith). That problem is avoided when Arthur is temporarily substituted for Redcrosse as Una's champion. Whether or not Spenser was aware of the problem (a question on which we reserve judgement at this stage), a fracture opens up between the heroic 'Englishness' of Book I (the imperial dream) and the resolutely dynamic, multicultural internationalism of the imperial symbols deployed (which resist appropriation by a single 'nation'). As Spenser tries for textual imperialism, we suggest, his materials splinter to reveal a local parochialism.

St George is a soldier-saint associated with a particularly varied and colourful collection of legends and miracles culminating in his martyrdom. In the Greek and Coptic traditions, George was born in Cappadocia (in modern Turkey) to Christian parents. His father died for his faith while George was still a child, and he and his mother fled to Palestine. George served with distinction in the Roman army and on his mother's death used his inheritance to establish himself at the court of the Emperor Diocletian (284–305) in Constantinople. After publicly declaring himself a Christian, George was put to seven tortures; he was crushed with stones, bound to a wheel set with sharp blades, cast into a pit of quicklime, made to run in red-hot iron shoes, boiled in molten lead, scourged and made to drink poison. Each time, he was restored to life and health. Meanwhile, he encountered an angel, raised a man from the dead and instructed his servant that after his death his body was to be taken to Lydda for burial. Finally, by making the sign of the cross, he caused all the statues of the gods to fall before him. This miracle converted the Empress Alexandra to Christianity. Diocletian sentenced Alexandra to death and had George successfully executed by decapitation on 23 April 303.[17]

It was Jacobus of Voragine's *Legenda Aurea* (Golden Legend) (1265) that created in its established form the centrepiece tableau of the slaying of a dragon and rescue of a distressed princess, as an intrinsic part of the St George legend. 'George, a native of Cappadocia' happened to travel to the city of Silene in Libya, where 'a plague-bearing dragon lurked'; having exhausted their livestock, the townspeople began feeding the monster their children to appease it, until the lot fell to the King's daughter. Happening upon her on the point of being devoured by the dragon, George subdued it with a 'grievous wound' from his lance, then instructed the princess to throw her girdle round the dragon's neck and lead it 'like a little dog on a leash' into the city. At this astonishing sight, the entire population converted to Christianity. George then embraced the King and set off to confront the Emperor Diocletian.[18]

In the fifteenth century, the cult of St George was shared by the Eastern and Western Christian churches, while the autonomous Coptic and Syrian churches gave him particular prominence and he also figured as a soldier-saint in Islam. As a consequence, during the period of greatest religious upheaval in the territories sandwiched between Islam to the East and Western Christendom, his iconography turned up repeatedly, all over the globe, as part of the bravura 'show of force' that occurred in graphic imagery along the cartographic lines of doctrinal and territorial contestation wherever Christians and Muslims confronted one another.

During the critical years in the mid-fifteenth century between the Council of Florence and the fall of Constantinople, followed by that of Trebizond, the final bastion of the Eastern Christian Orthodox Church, the figure of St George was repeatedly used by artists to articulate the crisis accompanying the suppression of 'true religion' in Eastern territories.[19] The Italian artist Pisanello's curious Verona fresco *St George and the Princess of Trebizond* (1437), for instance, allegorizes the defence of Trebizond in the familiar terms of the red-cross knight slaying the dragon.[20] As a result, we can detect a graphic tactic that becomes increasingly familiar as the period goes on. At the moment when Islam was overwhelming the Christian church, the artist recalled, in an ideologically defensive gesture, the originating moment when the heroic deed of a Christian soldier engineered a mass conversion from Islam to Christianity. In a piece of anxious public-relations bravado, the rescue becomes that of the 'princess of Trebizond'. It is thus a statement of determination to withstand the pressure of contemporary military reality (Trebizond fell to the Ottomans shortly thereafter). The story of the saint's slaying of the dragon becomes a site for resistance to the historically inevitable, a defiant gesture towards the victor on the part of the vanquished; it is negotiated eastwards and westwards simultaneously, the aesthetic dimension modulating the distinctive viewpoints.

In the generation following Pisanello's, we argue, the possibilities for manipulating the iconography of St George to dramatize adversarial relations between East and West became even stronger. We pick up our general argument in a single series of St George images executed in Venice around 1500, a little less than a century before Spenser's epic poem. Our contention is that these images show the saint pivotally placed on the permeable boundary between East and West. George can be read as interpellating both cultural communities with equivalent vigour, thereby transmitting their querulously triumphalist message in both directions. The tautology here is intended; as we will show, the triumphalism is in the possession of the Venetians, and the triumph is accorded to the Ottomans.

Around 1500, Venice rewarded the Knights of St John from Dalmatia with a sumptuous chapel attached to the Chapel of St John. This chapel was a thanks-offering – funded by grateful private donors – to the Knights who had resisted to the bitter end the Ottomans' westward drive, with the obvious threat it posed to the Venetian economy, until they were finally forced to retreat to safety. The chapel's dazzling decorative paintings (canvases crowded onto every inch of its walls), painted by Vittore Carpaccio, represented key episodes in the life of saints Jerome (a native of Dalmatia), Triphimus (patron saint of the region) and George (illus. 2). Once again, the iconographic emphasis is on the Christian soldier's heroic capacity to compel the infidel to convert to Christianity. Pictured on horseback, St George slays the monstrous dragon with his lance and is then portrayed using his individual act of courage as the inspirational means to bring his faith to non-believers without the use of force; they lay their turbans to one side as they are baptised (illus. 3, 4). Here again, the silent subtext is the failure to hold the line against the military might of

2 Vittore Carpaccio, *St George and the Dragon*, *c.* 1504–7, oil on canvas. Scuola di San Giorgio degli Schiavoni, Venice.

3 Vittore Carpaccio, *The Triumph of St George*, *c.* 1504–7, oil on canvas. Scuola di San Giorgio degli Schiavoni, Venice.
4 Vittore Carpaccio, *The Baptism of the Selenites*, *c.* 1504–7, oil on canvas. Scuola di San Giorgio degli Schiavoni, Venice.

all-engulfing Islam, the event that immediately preceded, and provided the occasion for, the execution of the paintings. Carpaccio's extraordinarily vivid portrayal of North African life, his loving simulation of the texture and sheen of fabric and turban, exotic buildings and unfamiliar landscapes, take us to the heart of the territorial and spiritual loss of the refugees from Dalmatia for whom he was painting. Surrounded by authentic representations of Mamluk religion and culture, Carpaccio's St George recognizably commands the attention and respect of the Libyan community. The paintings vividly recapitulate the moment when the two great Religions of the Book inhabited the scene, strenuously and openly competing as familiar neighbours for the belief of the faithful.

We take Carpaccio's St George here as the talismanic hero of our present exploration. Poised between East and West, he announces the power of European Christendom with luminous aesthetic intensity. Yet, troublingly, the exquisiteness of the story's rendering conceals Venice's articulated sense of territorial powerlessness around 1500, faced with the infidel on its very doorstep. Perhaps this is discreetly conveyed in the fact that George himself – once he has slain the dragon in conventionally mythologized fashion – descends from his horse and moves among recognizably 'real' oriental figures. His conversion is a delicately fragile gesture in a landscape laden with a sense of the wealth, power and beauty of the Orient.

Given the proliferation of only partially compatible exploits associated with the saint, it is not surprising that in Spenser's *Faerie Queene* it is Redcrosse's appearance rather than his deeds that marks him out as 'St George' (illus. 5). What is more curious is that when Redcrosse is so identified for the first time, it is by negation. The villainous magician Archimago, having separated Una and Redcrosse in Book I, canto ii, stanza 10, disguises himself as a counterfeit Redcrosse. It is this interloper, this symbolic inversion of the true knight, who is 'deemed to be' St George on the basis of his insignia:

> But now seemde best, the person to put on
> Of that good knight, his late beguiled guest:
> In mighty armes he was yclad anon,
> And siluer shield vpon his coward brest
> A bloudy crosse, and on his crauen crest
> A bounch of haires discolourd diuersly:
> Full iolly knight he seemde, and well addrest,
> And when he sate vpon his courser free,
> Saint George himself ye would haue deemed him to be.
>
> But he the knight, whose semblaunt he did beare,
> The true Saint George was wandred far away.[21]

Meanwhile, the real Redcrosse – the true St George – has wandered 'far away' and is fighting the faithless Saracen, a type of encounter with the infidel whose graphic and violent details are repeated at regular intervals throughout the course of Book I:[22]

> Still flying from his thoughts and gealous feare;
> Will was his guide, and griefe led him astray.
> At last him chaunst to meete vpon the way
> A faithlesse Sarazin all arm'd to point,
> In whose great shield was writ with letters gay
> Sans foy: full large of limbe and euery ioint
> He was, and cared not for God or man a point.[23]

While Una negotiates an allegorical world of obstacles to true devotion – despair, envy, error – Redcrosse (either the real Redcrosse or his wickedly concocted oppositional double, already identified with St George as we have shown) embarks on his own journey of self-discovery. This involves travelling through a topographically altogether more real and recognizable world, in which he takes on the infidel in single combat and is drawn unerringly eastwards. Like the St George of tradition, he takes his identity as a Westerner from his capacity to convert the infidel by his soldierly prowess and martial fortitude. Scarcely grounded at all in a geographical 'England', his exploits are referred back to the central locus of *The Faerie Queene* only by association.[24]

The moment of greatest role-confusion for Una's champion occurs at the end of Book I, canto x, when Redcrosse, rescued by Arthur and succoured by Una, is shown his future by the virtuous 'aged holy man' Contemplation. Contemplation prophesizes that Redcrosse will win a famous victory (over the dragon), but that he will then discard his armour and weapons to embark upon a 'painefull pilgrimage'. Throughout this segment of Book I, St George is simultaneously English and oriental, patron saint of 'Britane' and proud champion of Silene, and martyr of Lydda. Contemplation's final instruction to Redcrosse that he should now fulfil his destiny is, as a result, almost perversely oblique. He advises Redcrosse to set off to the Holy Land, to complete his 'ordained' history (one which in the legend of the saint does not, as it happens, end with his marrying the princess and living happily ever after):

> Then seeke this path, that I to thee presage,
> Which after all to heauen shall thee send;
> Then peaceably thy painefull pilgrimage
> To yonder same Hierusalem do bend,
> Where is for thee ordaind a blessed end:
> For thou emongst those Saints, whom thou doest see,
> Shalt be a Saint, and thine owne nations frend
> And Patrone: thou Saint George shalt called bee,
> Saint George of mery England, the signe of victoree.[25]

In the end, we are told, St George's destiny is to be patron both of East and West: 'thine own nations frend and Patron', and 'Saint George of mery England, the signe of victoree'. He is a pivotal, Janus-faced saint, whose cult is shared by Eastern and Western churches (and indeed by Islam). It is Arthur who decisively will be Gloriana's knight, the champion and partner of England's true religion; we have had a premonition of this outcome in Una's curious response following

Arthur's rescue of her. The claim upon St George/Redcrosse as the standard-bearer for 'mery England' is too weak, too contested elsewhere, to hold. The failed literary attempt at that claim, we are suggesting, if carefully scrutinized, can unpack the strong element of wishful thinking in English epic and imperial aspiration in the 1590s, as Elizabeth I's reign drew to its waning close.

Our contention is that these highly charged St Georges, strenuously negotiated between Byzantium and Italy, established the cultural signi-fications on which later generations could draw effortlessly. George, according to his legend, would suffer intolerably for his faith. His figurative rescue of a 'princess' from a 'dragon' is bound up with a particular moment of persecution of the early Church by the Romans which is contested by its heirs east and west of Constantinople. That contestation is, we suggest, central but unrecognized among all those 'saracens' and 'pagans' in Book I of *The Faerie Queene*. George cannot be England's champion securely, just as he cannot wed the princess he rescues, since his destiny is to be mutilated many times and finally martyred for his faith – it is the far more parochial Arthur (for whom

5 'St George and the Dragon', engraved illustration from Edmund Spenser, *The Faerie Queene* (1596 edn).

there is no comparable competition on the international stage) who must finally step into the breach and steer the narrative's 'Englishness' to the book's conclusion.

Such an argument can, of course, be presented here only in outline, and by way of introduction to our larger themes. We believe, however, that, with its help, a coherent reading of Book I of the *Fairie Queene* can be established. Such a reading responds with appropriate subtlety and sensitivity to the dyad St George / Arthur and its play on residual two-way East / West imperial dreams and aspirations that resonate far beyond the stanzas of the epic poem.

III

Our own detailed explorations of cultural identity's early two-way traffic starts with a peculiarly Renaissance type of influential art object, the portrait medal, aptly termed the 'currency of fame'.[26] Designed to be produced in multiple copies, these images of the famous and influential formed the basis for lastingly recognizable identities of those they represented. Highly portable, hand-sized and deliberately created to resemble surviving antique coins, portrait medals were eminently exchangeable. The vogue for portrait medals followed on from a revived humanistic interest in antique Roman coins – the term *medaglia* was transferred from such non-circulating collectables to new commemorative items.[27] Given as gifts or purchased by those who accumulated gemstones and cameos with equivalent enthusiasm, these images of powerful individuals were transmitted around Europe and beyond with a vigour unmatched by other forms of portraiture. Like coins, they carried the stamp of dominion and authority.[28]

Ultimately, the desirability of portrait medals as luxury consumer objects can be traced back to surviving antique examples of coins, which were emulated by early Renaissance exponents of the form.[29] Crucially, however, for our present argument, the two prototypes on which fifteenth-century medals were directly modelled both claimed Eastern provenance. The exemplars were acquired on behalf of the Duke of Berry around 1402 and repeatedly copied and circulated inside Europe thereafter. First, a medal whose obverse shows Constantine the Great on horseback, with the discovery of the True Cross on the reverse (illus. 6). Second, a medal with a profile portrait of the Byzantine Emperor Heraclius I (illus. 7), triple-crowned, on its obverse and, on the reverse, an image of Heraclius seated in a chariot drawn by three horses, returning the True Cross to Jerusalem.[30] Since the Paleologus dynasty of Byzantine Emperors took considerable pride in their

6 Duke of Berry's medal showing Constantine the Great (obverse and reverse), *c.* 1402, silver. Bibliothèque Nationale de France, Paris.

ownership of a relic of the True Cross (which eventually passed to the Western Church via Cardinal Bessarion), we may surmise that these medals derived from the culture of Constantinople around 1400.[31]

The cultural value of Renaissance portrait medals, in other words, was, by virtue of their origins, equally recognizable by both Eastern and Western recipients. They therefore provide a useful means of conveying 'meanings' associated with the East-West contest for power, from East to West and vice versa. Finally, in spite of our sense that these cultural artefacts have a stable position as Western art objects, this is our retrospective illusion. In the fifteenth century, the portrait medal carried the visible marks of its Eastern origins; the passage of time has entirely 'europeanized' the portrait medal (re-assimilated

7 Duke of Berry's medal showing Heraclius (obverse and reverse), *c.* 1402, bronze. Bibliothèque Nationale de France, Paris.

it to European artistic traditions), overlaying its 'exoticism' and 'orientalism' with the mantle of cultural familiarity.[32]

The medal that particularly interests us here is the first important Renaissance commemorative one of this type, created by Antonio Pisanello in 1438.[33] In the history of portrait medals as a supposed revival of an ancient image-circulating practice, it is generally agreed that this medal, showing the Byzantine Emperor John VIII Paleologus (illus. 8), was the first such successful artistic memorial to an event of enormous European cultural significance.[34] This much-imitated art object was produced on the occasion of the Emperor's visit to Florence for the 1438 Council of the Eastern and Western Churches. We do not know whether the Emperor or his Florentine hosts commissioned it. Either way, it commemorates a negotiation of lasting importance between two widely separated cultural spheres – that of the late Byzantine world centred on Constantinople and that of the Western, European world centred on Rome. Already at the outset, the Emperor

8 Antonio Pisanello, Portrait medal showing Emperor John VIII Paleologus (obverse), 1438, lead. Staatliche Museen zu Berlin – Preußischer Kulturbesitz.

Paleologus medal is an East–West transaction – a cultural exchange between Europe and its putative Other.

On one side of the medal is a profile head of the penultimate Byzantine Emperor of Constantinople, John VIII Paleologus. He wears a distinctive sharply peaked hat with a high, domed crown – a hat that, subsequent to Pisanello's representation on this medal, became associated with rulers of Constantinople in general. (This means, confusingly, that after 1453, when Constantinople fell to Mehmet II, even Ottoman sultans were occasionally given such headgear for purposes of immediate recognition.)[35] The Greek inscription reads 'John, king and emperor of the Romans, the Paleologus'. A preparatory drawing for this portrait survives in the Louvre.

The reverse of the medal shows the Emperor on horseback, in the same hat and carrying a hunting bow and quiver of arrows, in a rocky landscape, with a cross on a stone pillar to his right (illus. 79). On his left, another horse with a diminutive page-rider is seen in almost complete rear view.[36] The inscription, in both Greek and Latin, reads 'the work of Pisano the painter'. A group of preparatory drawings, now in Paris and Chicago, can be associated with this reverse.[37] The sheets concerned contain various sketches of the Emperor, on foot and on horseback, together with detailed drawings of various types of Byzantine garment and headgear. There are two particularly fine drawings of a horse, seen from the front and rear, harnessed exactly as on the medal (illus. 9). They portray the distinctive slit nostrils of an oriental mount (the Ottomans believed that the enlarged nostrils allowed the horse to take in more air, thus making it faster).

The occasion for the Emperor's high-profile visit to Italy was the 1438 Council of Eastern and Western Churches, convened by Pope Eugenius IV. In the face of an increased threat from the East in the shape of the Ottoman sultan Murad II, whose forces were moving up through Hungary and Transylvania, the Pope proposed a doctrinal and military alliance of the two most powerful Christian churches.[38] On 8 February 1438, the Byzantine Emperor and the Patriarch Joseph II, head of the Church in Constantinople, arrived in Venice for the council. They brought with them a retinue of some twenty Byzantine bishops and a large advisory body of other Greek prelates, monks and learned laymen, about seven hundred Greeks in all. All the expenses of the visit, it had been agreed, would be paid by the Papacy.[39]

Originally, the council was to have been held at Ferrara, but an outbreak of plague there necessitated the transfer of the proceedings to Florence. In any case, the Pope and the Este family in Ferrara were already finding the cost of the enterprise a financial embarrassment.

9 Antonio Pisanello, 'Horse seen from front and back', 1438, pen and ink on paper. Musée du Louvre, Paris.

In Florence, the rising Medici merchant-banking family bore the burden of almost the entire enterprise. Although the early sessions at Ferrara were financed by the Papal Chamber, it was in fact Medici loans that provided the necessary ready money, and when the council moved to Florence, the Florentine Commune (heavily subsidised by the Medici) paid for the Byzantine delegation's accommodation and living expenses. The Medici family bank also underwrote the entire cost of the delegation's return journey to Constantinople.[40] The strict dependence on Medici financial support for the success of the entire expensive operation is strikingly illustrated in a begging letter sent to Cosimo de' Medici by Cardinal Giuliano Cesarini, who was in charge of arrangements to transfer the council from Ferrara to Florence. He had run out of money en route at Faenza and urgently needed two hundred horses and mules to complete the journey: 'For the honour of our Latin Church which is in question, and so that we can keep our promises firmly made to the Byzantines, I beseech you to take all possible steps to send the horses and mules.'[41]

Quality horses were not simply required by the council participants for purposes of transport. Before he even reached Ferrara, in May 1438, the Byzantine Emperor approached the Pope to supply him and his entourage with horses suitable for his personal passion, hunting.

The contemporary Greek chronicler Syropoulos recounts that 'at the end of three months, and after numerous requests, he was sent eleven small ponies that were useless and in no way horse-like.' Fortunately, another of the council participants, Gydeles, had recently arrived from Russia with a retinue matching his superior financial means:

The Basileus bought from Gydeles one of his mounts on which to go hunting. As for Gydeles's other horses, they were bought by the Despot Demetrius. The Emperor, having discovered a convent some six miles from Ferrara, set himself up there with a few archons, some soldiers, and janissaries, leaving the greater number in town. He spent all his time hunting without bothering in the slightest with ecclesiastical affairs.[42]

Such was the Emperor's addiction to the recreational slaughter of game of all kinds that on the way to Italy from Constantinople for the council, he travelled on horseback from Cenchrea while the Greek convoy rounded the Morea, rejoining his ship at Navarino.[43] Once he had established his residence in the Ferrara convent assigned to him by the council organizers, he hunted so enthusiastically that on two occasions the local ruler Niccolò d'Este had to ask him 'to restrain his enthusiasm for the chase owing to the damage he was causing to the property of the countryfolk and the decimation of the game that the Marquis had imported for his own pleasure'. According to Syropoulos, even after the council began its formal meetings, John Paleologus continued to absent himself from many of its sessions and go hunting instead.

As early as 1886, Weisäcker identified the horse on the reverse of Pisanello's Emperor Paleologus medal, with its curiously long body and powerful head, as originating 'in the Danube area or in the steppes of Russia'.[44] As the first step in our argument concerning the signification of art objects such as these, we suggest that we should treat the precision with which Pisanello recorded the horse on the reverse of this medal as providing a strong clue to its interpretation. The admiring individual who turns the medal over, cradled in the palm of his or her hand as a commemorative item, is being asked to recognize in it an enduring reminder of a specific period of strategic political importance, spent by the Byzantine Emperor in Italy.

What was 'officially' being commemorated was the Union of the two Churches (a union that turned out to be historically null, since on the Emperor's return to Constantinople, the Church there refused to ratify the agreement). For that public purpose, the figure in hunting garb, arrested in mid-chase by the sight of a cross, may, it has been argued, be related iconographically to St Eustachius,[45] whose similar vision was also the inspiration for Pisanello's *Vision of St Eustachius* (illus. 11). Venerated by, and the subject of, local cults in both the Eastern and Western Churches, Eustachius, patron saint of hunters, could plausibly have been chosen to represent the revelation of a single true faith to the two ancient Churches.[46] But by particularizing the reverse 'from life', so that it represents the Emperor himself, pursuing his favourite pastime, the medal could simultaneously be made to figure in both East and West as a lasting monument to John Paleologus, fashioned by and for himself. The portrait of his own favourite mount, acquired in Italy at considerable cost in terms of badgering, effort and funds, graces the reverse. The generalized occasion of the Council of Florence was personalized and particularized memorially so that it 'belonged to' the Emperor and became his own occasion.

We might want to go a little further in trying to describe the way in which the medal's imagery pivots between East and West, and doubles between the Emperor and his role. Scholars are undecided as to who the client was for the production of this important first European Renaissance portrait medal. Neither Niccolò d'Este nor his son and heir, Leonello, is likely to have commissioned it, it is argued, since the Este were already in financial difficulties arising from the Emperor's expensive stay in the Ferrara region. Perhaps, as with all other financial transactions involving the Council, the Medici merchant-bankers footed the bill.

It is not particularly important, in the case of a medal, to be sure who the client is, since (as was not the case with painted panel portraits) both Italian and Byzantine participants in the council could have been (and in this case probably were) presented with identical versions of the treasured art object. In any case, in the sense that each element of graphic representation involved in the medal was taken from life from a Byzantine model (the Emperor himself, his attire, his mount, the activity in which he is engaged), the medal crucially combines the Italian, humanist, revived classical tradition in which the Este family was distinctively involved (as indeed were the neighbouring Florentines) with the peculiarly Byzantine culture from which the Emperor came. The Pisanello medal is a landmark transaction between East and West.

IV

The Pisanello Paleologus medal is to be found discreetly reproduced in several art-historical analyses of Italian Renaissance works of art, as a source for the head of the Emperor John. Invariably, however, that acknowledgement represents it as a robustly Western artefact (by a distinguished Western artist), its influence circumscribed by Western

European preoccupations and agendas. Here, however, we pause for a moment to acknowledge one study of fifteenth-century Florentine art whose argument runs compellingly parallel to our own, but which scholars of mainstream art have incorporated into their interpretations of Renaissance painting with a degree of reluctance.

The Italian scholar Carlo Ginzburg was one of the earliest cultural historians to draw attention to the critical importance of the Florence Council for our understanding of the complex concealed 'meaning' of particular works of Italian high Renaissance art. In 1985, he published a book-length study of Piero della Francesca's iconography in which he set out to unravel the 'enigma' of some of Piero's most interpretation-resistant works.[47] Ginzburg's objective was to challenge the monopoly over late twentieth-century interpretations of great paintings and frescoes of Erwin Panofsky and the Warburg School's iconographic method of interpretation. This method broke graphic images up into constituent parts, each of which could be allocated a 'meaning' based on a full understanding of classical mythology or of some humanistic narrative grounded in antiquity.[48] As Peter Burke explains in the intro-duction to the English edition, Ginzburg modelled his alternative method on that of his classical archaeologist-friend Salvatore Settis:

Ginzburg wants to replace iconographic laxity with a more rigorous method. They both [Ginzburg and Settis] believe in the possibility of successful detective work in this field, provided that the detective follows strict rules. 'The first rule', writes Settis, 'is that all the pieces should fit together without leaving blank spaces between them. The second is that the whole should make sense'. Ginzburg adds a third rule . . . to the effect that 'other things being equal, the interpretation requiring fewest hypotheses should generally be taken as the most probable'.[49]

The Pisanello portrait medal of the Emperor John Paleologus, and the council it celebrated, were crucial components in an interpretation of Piero della Francesca's mid-fifteenth-century *Flagellation of Christ* (illus. 12), which Ginzburg maintained fulfilled his three rules and was thus the 'most likely' version of the painting's programme or agenda.

There is a clear relationship between the seated figure on the left of the painting and the profile portrait of the Emperor John on Pisanello's medal. On the basis of an essay-length argument, Ginzburg's proposal is that this figure is indeed John VIII. He presides in the place of Pilate at the scourging of Christ, a scourging occurring under the direction of the turbaned Turk who stands with his back to us. In other words, here is a representation of the tribulations of the Eastern Christian Church at the hands of Islam, with its secular leader powerless to intervene.[50]

The painting's dramatic architectural perspective, Ginzburg argues, separates two areas with what he calls 'different ontological status'. The scene just described is a political and theological allegory, located in an imaginary space, whose details recall Greco-Roman antiquity and the shared intellectual tradition of the Eastern and Western Churches. The figures to the right in Piero's painting, by contrast, are 'real' figures recalled from that critical late 1430s moment in attempted East-West reconciliation (the painting, according to Ginzburg, was executed in late 1459). The figure on the far right is shown, on compelling evidence, to be Giovanni Bacci, the Medici representative in Arezzo who commissioned the work. The figure on the left, whose clothing, hat and beard identify him as Byzantine and who gestures welcomingly to Bacci, is, Ginzburg maintains, Cardinal Bessarion, one of the prime movers in the Eastern Church delegation to the Florentine Council. In 1440, in the wake of the collapse of the agreement signed in Florence, Bacci travelled to Constantinople as Papal emissary, to bestow the title of Cardinal upon Bessarion on behalf of the Western Church. By the 1450s, Bessarion had returned to the West and was permanently resident in Florence.[51] According to Ginzburg, the *Flagellation of Christ* is designed as a direct figurative appeal to the parties meeting at the Ecumenical Council in Mantua in 1459, as part of a campaign urging the Italians to send a crusade eastwards to recapture Constantinople for Christendom.

It was Bessarion, according to Ginzburg, who owned a copy of the Pisanello portrait medal showing John VIII and who devised the programme for the *Flagellation of Christ*. Whether the Byzantine figure is Bessarion himself (it is a good deal more dashing than any other surviving image of the Cardinal) or an idealized representation of the Eastern Church, the overall interpretation of the painting as a politically charged recollection of a critical moment in recent international Church politics is a plausible one. It complies with Ginzburg's own explanatory rules by achieving maximum explanatory force on the basis of a single historical event.

Ginzburg's 'detective work' uncovers another Florentine Council-centred image, whose symbolic content is equipoised between East and West, legible to both Eastern and Western Churches (though not, it seems, to us). Carefully crafted out of precisely those doctrinal and hagiographic elements which belong to a shared heritage, they enable either Eastern or Western adherents to meditate on the predicament of the Christian Church, with its second spiritual home in Constantinople in the possession of Islam, and the Ottoman forces at its door.[52]

The reciprocating East–West and West–East cultural exchanges to which we have drawn particular figurative attention are vividly developed in two commemorative items which postdate the Fall of Constantinople (the event the Council of Florence was intended to prevent) and in which the original unificatory occasion pivots across the East–West divide, developing locally and specifically in its Eastern and Western locations. One is Costanzo da Ferrara's portrait medal of Mehmet II (illus. 10, 78), the other Benozzo Gozzoli's *Adoration of the Magi* frescoes in the Medici Chapel in Florence.

In spite of the high anxiety of the Eastern and Western Churches and the political standoff between Western Europe and Mehmet II following the latter's conquest of Constantinople, cultural exchange between West and East flourished in the 1460s and '70s.[53] One of those Europeans who spent 'many years' at the Ottoman court was Costanzo da Ferrara. According to the practice whereby Gentile Bellini was loaned to Mehmet for a period by the Venetian Doge, Costanzo may have been sent in response to a direct request to Ferrante I of Naples for a suitable artist to assist in the decorations of Mehmet's new palace, then under construction.[54] A number of early drawings of Ottoman subjects once attributed to Bellini have recently been assigned to Costanzo, including a standing figure (illus. 20) which Bernardino Pinturicchio later borrowed for his fresco in the Sala dei Santi at the Vatican, the *Disputation of St Catherine* (illus. 13).[55]

Executed sometime circa 1481, Costanzo's portrait medal of Mehmet II is a resolutely Ottoman artefact, yet in a strenuously

10 Costanzo da Ferrara, Portrait medal showing Mehmet II (obverse and reverse), *c.* 1481, bronze. National Gallery of Art, Washington, DC.

11 Antonio Pisanello, *Vision of St Eustachius*, *c.* 1436–8, tempera on wood.
National Gallery, London.

12 Piero della Francesca, *Flagellation of Christ*, 1445–9?, oil on panel. Palazzo Ducale, Urbino.

13 Bernardino Pinturicchio, *Disputation of St Catherine*, *c.* 1492–4, fresco. Sala dei Santi, Appartamento Borgia, Vatican.

14 Benozzo Gozzoli, *Journey of the Magi*, 1459, fresco. Chapel of the Palazzo Medici-Riccardi, Florence.

15 Benozzo Gozzoli, *Journey of the Magi*, 1459, fresco. Chapel of the Palazzo Medici-Riccardi, Florence.

16, 17 Benvenuto Cellini,
Portrait medal of Francis I
(obverse and reverse, the
latter inscribed *Fortunam
virtute devicit*), 1537,
bronze. Museo Nazionale
del Bargello, Florence.

18 Titian, *Portrait of Francis I*, 1538, oil on canvas. Musée du Louvre, Paris.

19 Costanzo da Ferrara, 'Seated Scribe', *c.* 1470–80, pen and gouache on parchment. Isabella Stewart Gardner Museum, Boston.

20 Costanzo da Ferrara,
Standing Ottoman,
c. 1470–80, ink on
paper. Musée du
Louvre, Paris.

Western European artistic tradition. Mehmet's profile, encircled in
Latin with the formidable title 'The Ottoman Sultan Muhammed,
Emperor of the Turks', became, like Pisanello's portrait profile of
John Paleologus, the lasting likeness of the Conqueror, transposed to
generations of representations of Ottoman rulers.[56]

The reverse of Costanzo's medal, however, was even more influential,
its figuration of the Sultan on horseback exerting an uncanny hold
eastwards and westwards (illus. 10, 78). In 1495, visiting Italy for
the first time, Albrecht Dürer copied a wide range of Italian drawings
to add to his figural repertoire. Among these, as has been well
documented by Raby, are a number of oriental figures, copied from
'from life' drawings made in Venice and Florence during the 1470s
and '80s, including a number that Dürer subsequently included in

large-scale works. Because of Dürer's own artistic prestige, copies were also widely disseminated and found their way into orientalist works by other artists.[57]

One of these drawings, Dürer's 'Ottoman rider' (illus. 21), however, is based not on a drawing by Bellini or Costanzo da Ferrara, but on the reverse of the Mehmet medal. This goes some way to explaining the curiously awkward pose of both horse and rider in the drawing. The image became a standard, immediately recognizable representation of Eastern power. Thus, for example, a 1529 German woodcut of Süleyman the Magnificent's influential grand vizier Ibrahim Pasha clearly recalls the image, in spite of modifications to the figure of the rider (particularly his headgear).[58]

Here we have a portrait medal from Constantinople, commissioned by or on behalf of the Sultan, in direct emulation of a Western artistic practice. An imported Western artist is employed to produce a coveted art object whose cultural and political worth will be equally recognizable to both East and West. The images it incorporates (carefully chosen to conform to visual idioms of imperial might in the West) then re-circulate westwards, to provide an archetype of the oriental power-figure that is at once a Western stereotype and authentically Eastern in its origins. We argue that this is a typical movement of cultural currency, creating an undivided, seamless cultural sphere within which each distinct power centre recognized and responded appropriately to the items circulating.[59]

Although it goes somewhat beyond the scope of the present study, we should also point out that the sort of circulation of images we are tracking here in fact went beyond the Ottoman Empire, producing percolations that enabled recognition and disseminated signifying art objects yet further afield. One of the 'from life' oriental drawings recently convincingly attributed to Costanzo da Ferrara is an exquisitely observed 'seated scribe' (illus. 19).[60] There is a remarkably faithful late fifteenth-century copy of this drawing by the Persian artist Bihzad (illus. 22), who has his seated Turkish figure at work on a portrait of a figure in Persian dress.[61] Later drawings in this genre (which became extremely fashionable in Persia) show the artist at work on a painting of a European.[62] A further example of this absorption of a Western image into an oriental tradition can be seen in Abu'l-Hasan's copy of Dürer's St John the Evangelist (illus. 23), taken from the German artist's engraving of Christ on the cross in the 1511 *Passion* series.

Our second example derives directly from the East-West encounter at the 1438–9 Council of Florence, which circulates its vivid images

eastwards and westwards: the frescoes in the Medici Chapel, executed by Benozzo Gozzoli in 1459 (illus. 14, 15).

The most compellingly economical explanatory programme for the Gozzoli frescoes of the Adoration of the Magi that densely fill the chapel walls identifies the allegorical occasion as the Florence Council.[63] In Ginzburg's terms, a collection of 'real' historical figures from the 1430s and '50s inhabit the biblical moment, in a work that affirms the centrality of the Medici family to the grand project of East-West Christian consolidation against the infidel Turk. Leading the Magi is a young, blond, male figure identified by the Medici insignia on his gelding's harness and by the laurel bush that frames his angelic crowned head. He is a symbolic 'Lorenzo de' Medici', heir to the burgeoning Medici commercial empire, whose train includes senior figures of his family as they appeared at the time of painting. Behind him rides a figure representing the Patriarch Joseph, side-saddle on a white mule as befits an elderly man of the Church. Behind him is the Emperor John Paleologus, astride a massive (and rather explicitly male) white stallion – a mount worthy of the Emperor of Byzantium, who also considered himself something of an expert in pedigree horses.

Between and around the three Magi are arrayed huntsmen in various stages of preparation for the hunt, with bows and arrows and lances, accompanied by an exotic collection of hunting animals (several

22 Bihzad, 'Portrait of a painter in Turkish costume', late 15th century, colour and gold.
Freer Gallery of Art, Smithsonian Institution, Washington, DC.

23 Abu'l–Hasan (after Dürer, 1511), *Figure of John the Evangelist*, *c.* 1600, drawing with gold tint. Ashmolean Museum, Oxford.

cheetahs, hawks and hounds). In the distance, the chase is actually taking place in all its varied forms. There could hardly be a more appropriate reminder that a passionate interest in blood sports united the European and Byzantine aristocracies and provided lasting memories of shared pleasures during the long, often tedious months of the council. The Gozzoli frescoes are, indeed, animated by the hunting scenes, which bind the individual entourages together.

Lorenzo de' Medici is followed by his family, on horseback and on foot, while behind them are ranged a collection of exotic portrait heads, around the portrait head (conveniently labelled) of the artist himself. Some of these are strongly reminiscent of figures in Pisanello's paintings as, indeed, are many of the animals and birds.[64] Processions of exotic travellers snake through the background landscape, accompanied by mules heavily laden with boxes and including camels, two of them with African riders.

In 1459, Pius II (elected Pope in 1458) summoned the Italian States and Christian princes to another council, in the hope of raising the money and troops to launch a crusade against the Ottomans and recapture Constantinople. This time, the council was held in Mantua, and the power broker who lavishly hosted the gathering of dignitaries was Ludovico Gonzaga, Marquis of Mantua. Ludovico exploited his connections with the Holy Roman Emperor to persuade the Pope to hold the council in Mantua by promising that he could get Emperor Frederick III to attend. Although the Emperor never arrived, the Papal court spent nine months in the city.[65] Bessarion once again led those pleading passionately for intervention to retrieve his native Constantinople for Christendom.[66]

The Council of Mantua was a political failure. In spite of his own considerable gifts as a scholar and orator, Pius II failed to rally the European princes to his and Bessarion's cause; two years later, Christianity's last bastion in Byzantium, Trebizond, fell to the Turks. But however reluctantly the leaders of the Italian city-states responded to the Pope's call to arms, they were vigorous and enthusiastic in their efforts to provide a lasting cultural version of their importance in the unfolding events. In particular, the Medici, whose high-profile participation in the Council of Florence as financial backers had raised them from prominent merchant bankers to power-brokers on the international political scene, took the opportunity to fix in symbolic form the union of devotion to Christendom and financial acumen that had gained them dynastic prestige. Artistic production under princely patronage, affirming past help given and symbolic success achieved, was substituted for more material help for Pius II's present, politically precarious cause.

In April 1459, Pius II was received ceremonially by Cosimo de' Medici in his recently completed family chapel. The occasion was a meeting between the Pope and Galeazzo Maria Sforza, son of the Duke of Milan, who had gone to Florence to collect the Pope and escort him across the Apennines to Mantua.[67] The choice of escort was not fortuitous; the young Galeazzo had in all likelihood been summoned by Cosimo to provide an appropriately distinguished train to accompany the Pope on important international business. The Medici accounts for the year 1459–60 show that 42 per cent of the bank's profits had come from the sale of silks, brocades and jewels for Sforza's court. The interest on Sforza loans of 53,000 ducats amounted to 35 per cent of the profits (by 1467, the Sforza were in debt to the Medici to the tune of 179,000 ducats).[68] The fifteen-year-old Galeazzo wrote home describing the scale and luxury of the Palazzo Medici, the costliness of Cosimo's tapestries, his priceless silver and the workmanship of his carved wooden chests. Imaginative and flattering arrangements of Medici and Sforza coats of arms had been planted in grass in the palace gardens in honour of the occasion.[69] But if Cosimo was the behind-the-scenes backer as usual, on this occasion the Marquis of Mantua had beaten him to the prestige position of council host.[70]

Structurally, the Medici Chapel was complete when Pius II admired its splendour (the architect was Michelozzo di Bartolommeo). Decoratively, it was close to being finished, except for the cycle of paintings on the walls. In any event, it had already become the focal location in the Palazzo Medici. Two months after the Pope's departure, Gozzoli began his wall paintings as the crowning glory of the sumptuous centrepiece to the Medici family home; they were completed by the end of the same year.

By then, the East–West political arena had moved elsewhere. As the Pope set off for the Gonzaga Palazzo Ducale, where he would be able to admire virtuoso frescoes depicting figures from Arthurian legend which Pisanello had painted on the walls of the main reception hall, Gozzoli commenced a Pisanello-inspired series of paintings for the Medici Chapel.[71] In their programme, princely magnificence and ostentatious splendour are coupled with serious international political content. A religious moment that combines lavish gift-bearing with the spiritual quest for the Saviour elevates the financier into a prince. Gozzoli's frescoes dignified past Medici investment with a doctrinal and political importance recognizable by both Byzantines and Europeans, and ensured that the Medici would remain permanently centre-stage in the cultural representation of Christendom's confrontation with Islam.

VI

We are arguing that each of the art objects we have discussed constitutes a transaction, by means of which those who commissioned them negotiated their positions in a network of power relations which stretched from Western Europe to Constantinople and beyond in shared iconographic terms. However 'universal' or 'timeless' these representations now appear to us, they were once full of contestational meaning. Circulating, crucially, in multiple copies, the portrait medal is superficially about likeness, but in reality expresses its status as likeness with the addition of power and authority. By the early sixteenth century, we suggest, those in a position to commission and acquire medals had become aware of the propaganda possibilities they offered. In a period when the major imperial powers were the Ottoman Empire of Süleyman the Magnificent and the Hapsburg one of Charles V, we turn to a portrait medal commissioned by a 'minor player' on the international stage, the Valois King of France, Francis I.

Francis I's manipulation of received iconography in the medals he commissioned deserves Greenblatt's description of 'self-fashioning'. We may take as an example the reverse of a portrait medal by an unknown artist executed in 1515, the year Francis ascended the French throne (illus. 24). It depicts a celestial and a terrestrial globe side by side on stands, with the French crown above them. The inscription, taken from Juvenal's tenth satire, reads *unus non sufficit orbis* (one globe is not enough).[72] The imperial ambitions of the new king are explicit in this composition; in Juvenal, the full line runs 'One globe is not enough for the youth of Pella [Alexander the Great].' The poet continues: 'he chafes uneasily within the narrow confines of the world.'[73] Alexander and Constantine the Great were the two key figures whose iconographic personae Charles V and Süleyman competed to inhabit during precisely the same period. Here, then, is an announcement of global aspiration, concisely conveyed in emblematic form.[74]

By the 1530s, a sequence of diplomatic and military failures had not apparently deterred Francis from his pursuit of aspirational iconography. One might even suspect that (like Cosimo de' Medici in 1459) his enthusiasm for triumphalist iconography increased as his international political fortunes waned. Benvenuto Cellini executed his finely engraved portrait medal of Francis I during his first visit to France in 1537 (illus. 16, 17). The obverse of Cellini's medal shows Francis *à l'antique*, with laurel wreath and fleur-de-lis sceptre. The inscription reads 'Francis I King of the French'. The reverse shows a muscular,

24 Portrait medal of Francis I (reverse), inscribed *unus non sufficit orbis*, 1515, silver. Bibliothèque Nationale de France, Paris.

semi-nude rider seated on a rearing horse and swinging a club. A naked woman lies under the horse's hooves. The inscription reads *Fortunam virtute devicit* (Victory of Virtue over Fortune). Fortune's insignia – her rudder and globe – lie on the ground behind the horse.[75] Here, once again, we have the aspiration to heroic Roman status on the face of the medal and a classically inspired moral victory on the reverse.

In spite of what we might consider to be the self-consciously contrived quality of the Cellini medal, its circulation followed the pattern we have been exploring in this chapter. Titian used the profile portrait on the obverse as the model for the portrait of Francis he executed in 1538 (illus. 18), a lavish personal gift from Pietro Aretino to the French King. Titian never visited France, and could not have worked directly from life in 1538. The medal provides an acceptable and recognizable 'type' of the King's likeness and power. To enhance this power imagery still further, Titian added Francis's personal order – the Order of St Michael – around his neck.[76]

Perhaps Aretino owned a copy of the Cellini Francis medal, or perhaps he simply borrowed it for Titian's use. But as Titian held the medal in the palm of his hand, he could turn it over and admire Cellini's exquisite rearing horse and rider, with the rider's enemy beneath his feet. Ten years later, when he came to paint Charles V's equestrian portrait after the King's victory at the Battle of Mühlberg, Titian would return to that image, as indeed would his friend and advisor Aretino.[77]

VII

To bring this exploration, finally, closer to home, we turn to the civilized values of beauty, cleanliness and order in the artefact with which Stephen Greenblatt, in 1980, began his groundbreaking exploration of the historically fashioned self. This is itself an artefact much interpreted both before and since as quintessentially Renaissance in spirit.[78]

Hans Holbein's *The Ambassadors* (illus. 25) was painted for Francis I's ambassador, Jean de Dinteville, in London in the spring of 1533. Dinteville had taken up the post of resident French ambassador at the court of Henry VIII in early February of that year, shortly after Henry's secret marriage to Anne Boleyn.[79] The new ambassador's residency was politically significant, since it constituted low-key acceptance of the King's divorce and thus aligned the Valois King with English, rather than Hapsburg, interests.

Although *The Ambassadors* hangs in the National Gallery in London and was executed by a German artist in the employ of the English

25 Hans Holbein, *The Ambassadors*, 1533, oil on canvas. National Gallery, London.

King, it is a thoroughly French composition. Commissioned by the French ambassador as an affirmation of his international standing (in terms to which we will come shortly), the painting left England when Dinteville returned to France in November 1533, there to hang in his chateau at Polisy.[80] The double portrait shows him with a friend, the visiting emissary Georges de Selve, who was in England briefly, on secret ambassadorial business from the French King, in April/May. Georges de Selve arrived shortly before the public announcement of Henry's marriage and left before the pageantry of Anne's coronation in May/June.[81]

Holbein, a German from Basle, was retained as a technician and all-purpose designer and painter by the King. Most of the artist's portrait commissions in London (outside the Court) had been of German merchants resident in the city. The setting for this particular painting (identified by the pavement on which the two men stand) is the chapel in Westminster Abbey. It was here that Anne Boleyn was crowned with great pomp and ceremony.[82]

The period of the painting's execution was one of fraught Anglo-French diplomatic activity. Anne was pregnant, and Henry VIII would not risk a son being born a bastard by delaying her recognition as his legitimate wife. Francis I was meanwhile trying to persuade Henry not to go public until he had smoothed the path of divorce and remarriage with the Medici Pope, Clement VII.[83] Jean de Dinteville's brother, Francis, Bishop of Auxerre, was Francis I's ambassador to Rome. A week before the coronation, Jean wrote to his brother (in a letter whose evasive phrasing clearly shows he expected that it would be intercepted) with a veiled warning that it might be necessary for the French to intervene with the Pope. Things in London were coming to a head.[84] He added a comment on his own frame of mind:

This country is beginning to displease me, as I wait for the expiry of my six months term (which expires on July 22). I was promised by the Grand Master that I would not have to stay longer than that. I pray to God that he will keep his promise. I have had a tertian fever which it took a long time to get rid of. Please put in a word for me with M. de Paris about my recall. I must tell you that I am the most melancholy vexed and tiresome ambassador that ever was.[85]

The two skulls in Holbein's painting are apparently a fair reflection of the commissioner's and sitters' gloomy emotional states.[86]

Some of the issues associated with the French envoy's mission in England are figured, apparently programmatically, in the conjunctions of objects painted on the lower (mundane) shelf on which he leans (illus. 26). The foreshortened lute (its discarded case lies under the table on Dinteville's side), with its prominently broken string, even now is recognizably an emblem of broken harmony or discord. Beneath

26 Detail of illus. 25 showing the objects on the table.

its neck lies an open hymn-book, in which we can still read the opening verse in German of Luther's 'Kom Heiliger Geyst' (Come Holy Ghost) on the left, and 'Mensch wiltu leben seliglich' (Man wilt thou live blessedly) (with the music for tenor voice). The discord here specified is thus apparently that within the Church. It seems an appropriate symbolic reference; Jean de Dinteville and his brother were actively engaged in brokering a political agreement between the Pope and Henry, in spite of Anne Boleyn's known Reformed sympathies. By remarrying in advance of Papal consent to his divorce from Katherine of Aragon, Henry also risked excommunication. A collection of harmonizing flutes under the hymn-book lie alongside the lute, ready for use (should the mission prove successful) though still in their case.

On the left of this lower shelf is a terrestrial globe and a German merchant-accounting book, held open by a surveyor's square. A pair of compasses spans the table between globe and lute. The markings on this globe continue the theme of terrestrial discord – this time territorial.[87] The globe is tipped away from the viewer, so that the names on it (for instance, *AFFRICA*) are upside-down. However, significant names have been written so that the viewer can read them right way up. All names within Europe are legible, and a number of further names have been added (including that of Jean de Dinteville's hometown of Polisy). Strikingly, in the New World, Brazil's name (*Brisilici R.*) is written legibly for the viewer, complementing the clearly drawn *Linea Divisionis Castellanorum et Portugallenum* – the line agreed under the 1494 Treaty of Tordesillas, whereby all New World territory to the east was to belong to Portugal, all that to the west to Spain. In 1529, another such line had been agreed between Spain and Portugal under the Treaty of Saragossa, which divided the map equivalently on the other side of the globe, this time allocating the Moluccas (the Spice Islands) to the Portuguese after a long period of competitive venturing on the part of the two nations' merchants and explorers, and a number of violent and bloodthirsty contests for mastery over the new regions.[88] Holbein's meticulously rendered globe (to which we shall return) figures the contemporary contest for territorial possessions between competing national commercial interests.

In front of the globe lies the German astronomer Peter Apian's arithmetic book, *Eyn Newe unnd wolgegründte underweysung aller Kauffmannss Rechnung* (A New and Well-grounded Instruction in All Merchants' Arithmetic). Books for reckoning up profit and loss and maps recording routes and trading rights belonged together in the expanding markets of the first half of the sixteenth century. The mercantile mathematics book alongside the globe, with its clear partitioning of ownership between Spain and Portugal, summarizes the financial power-brokering around the flourishing East-West commercial opportunities of the early sixteenth century.[89]

On the upper shelf between Dinteville and Selve is a celestial globe, a collection of scientific, astronomical instruments and a closed book. This globe, too, can be identified. The most up-to-date celestial globe available at the time, it was made by Johann Schöner in 1532/3. The scientific instruments appear in an earlier Holbein portrait of Nicolaus Kratzer and were probably borrowed from him for *The Ambassadors*.[90] The objects on the upper shelf figure a vigorously exploratory and expansionist version of the pursuit of knowledge (astronomy, calendars and calculations of time and space were vital components of navigation and travel).[91] In contrast with the local and particular contests of the lower shelf, the concerns implied by the upper shelf can be seen as more global.

On this upper shelf, at the visual centre of *The Ambassadors*, an array of instruments and apparatus for mastering the heavens and gaining precise knowledge of time and place, for navigating the globe and mapping and recording geographical findings, claim the viewer's attention.[92] Influential work in social anthropology has drawn attention to the way in which there is in many cultures a tendency to link esoteric knowledge – and the control it gives to élites within a society – with travel, distance and experience of the geographically remote:

To the extent . . . that geographically distant places, peoples and experiences are perceived (either at first hand or by some manner of extrapolation) within essentially supernatural or cosmological contexts, then knowledge of, or acquaintance with, geographically distant places, peoples, and things rightfully falls within the domain of political-religious specialists whose job it is to deal with mysteries. Knowledge of geographically distant phenomena, whether acquired directly or indirectly, may be expected to form part of the corpus of esoteric knowledge controlled by these traditional specialists, even as esoteric knowledge of vertical or other dimensions of the sacred falls within their domain. Stated somewhat differently, the select few who are either able or expected to become familiar with geographically distant phenomena may be accorded an aura of prestige and awe approaching the same order, if not always the same magnitude, as that accorded political-religious specialists or elites in general. In fact, those whose direct experience of such distant matters are themselves likely either to be political-religious specialists or elites (or their agents) or, if derived from other sectors of society, may be accorded comparable honors, though to be sure these rewards may vary in accordance with the nature and context of their foreign experience.[93]

Ambassadors are above all élite travellers. Jean de Dinteville's status as a traveller-scholar, a man possessed of esoteric knowledge that gave him power over more mundane matters, is succinctly symbolized in the Order of St Michael he wears round his neck.[94] Once this singular honour had been awarded, the recipient was obliged always to wear it. Under specified circumstances, however, he might dispense with the elaborate and heavy Great Collar, an elaborate chain of linked cockleshells, from which the image of Michael the Archangel was suspended:

He shall not be obliged to wear the Great Collar when bearing arms, when the image of Saint Michael may simply be worn suspended from a thin gold chain or a silk lace, however he prefers to wear it. And similarly when the King or one of his Knights of the Order is travelling, or is in his private home, or hunting, or in other places where there is no gathering or assembly of men of distinction, then he only needs to wear the emblem of the Order, as indicated.[95]

Jean de Dinteville is represented fully in public, in the company of another person of distinction. He wears his order as permitted, on a thin gold chain, because he is in transit – a traveller in a foreign land. In Holbein's programme for the painting, the equipment of astronomical inquiry, navigation and travel encodes Dinteville's knowledge status, and thus his ambassadorial prestige and power.[96]

At the same time, the Order of St Michael also alerts us to something parochial about the international community to which Dinteville advertises himself as belonging. This Order was Francis I's own personal mark of favour, the one in which he chose to have himself depicted in Titian's great portrait. Much as Francis might have liked to think of it as equivalent to the Order of the Golden Fleece prominently worn by Charles V (for instance, in Titian's standing portrait), it could hardly compete for power significance with the Hapsburg Emperor's personal mark of favour. So this is an image heavily freighted with specifically French imaginings of glory, in a period when France and England were comparatively minor players.

VIII

We are arguing that some of the difficulty we face in 'reading' Holbein's *Ambassadors* stems from the fact that Dinteville's programme for the picture included elements of diplomatic wishful thinking regarding French imperial power in the period of its painting. To illustrate this point further, we return to the objects represented on the lower shelf, in particular to the terrestrial globe.

27 The 'Ambassadors' Globe', *c.* 1526. Beinecke Rare Book and Manuscript Library, Yale University, New Haven, CT.

Holbein's precisely delineated globe replicates a surviving printed one (illus. 27) executed around 1526 in southern Germany, most probably Nuremberg, the home of the printed globe industry in the 1520s and '30s.[97] This globe, referred to as the 'Ambassadors' Globe', contains the earliest known cartographic representation of the route taken by Magellan in his circumnavigation in 1522.[98] The diplomatic and commercial impact of this voyage was considerable, not least on the field of cartography. Whereas earlier conceptions of the overseas voyages of the Spanish and Portuguese Crowns had been traced across the surface of flat maps (as in the case of the agreement between them at Tordesillas in 1494), Magellan's circumnavigation led rapidly to the political predominance of terrestrial globes as the objects with which to display political power and negotiate territorial disputes.[99]

As a consequence, the 1520s witnessed the development of a recognizably global geopolitics in the struggle for territorial possession, however nominal and fanciful, in the wake of Magellan's voyage. The French court, however, remained on the periphery of events surrounding Magellan's voyage. The expedition had been financed primarily by Charles V and his backers the Fuggers, keen to wrestle the long-distance commercial initiative away from Portugal. Magellan had anticipated reaching the Moluccas by sailing westwards, via southern America, and thereby claiming the islands as lying within the Spanish half of the known world as stipulated under the terms of the Treaty of Tordesillas. Before setting out, he had outlined his audacious plan in 1519 in an audience with Charles V, with the help of a terrestrial globe. Within months of the return of the remnants of Magellan's crew, Charles was presented with a terrestrial globe to mark this voyage.[100]

In 1535, just two years after Holbein painted *The Ambassadors*, Charles sponsored the production of Gemma Frisius' terrestrial globe on which the Hapsburg ensign, the imperial eagle, flies ostentatiously over the city of Tunis, which had fallen to the Emperor that summer.[101] As the early sixteenth-century globe took shape, the Hapsburg empire competed successfully with the Portuguese and Ottoman ones to leave its imperial mark, in the shape of territories explicitly claimed and labelled, on this three-dimensional representation of the world. The globe in Holbein's painting offers an account – muffled for us by the familiarity of globes and their markings – of Hapsburg pre-eminence in matters of overseas adventuring and global cartography.

Significantly, on the globe in the painting, the line of demarcation established by the Treaty of Tordesillas does not extend right around the globe, as had been agreed between Charles V and John III of Portugal under the terms of the 1529 Treaty of Saragossa. As a servant of the French Crown, Dinteville was presumably reluctant to confirm (however passively) the self-proclaimed global authority of two of France's closest rivals for imperial power. For similar reasons, Holbein's globe fails to trace the route of Magellan's voyage, despite the fact that its source, the 'Ambassadors' Globe', includes on its surface a vivid representation of the Hapsburg-sponsored expedition. Instead, Holbein's terrestrial globe parochially marks Dinteville's home town of Polisy.

The globe is turned so that the viewer also sees, carefully marked, the location of Brazil. Franco-Portuguese intercontinental commercial conflict emerged as early as the 1450s, when French interlopers intruded into established and officially recognized Portuguese trading activities in Africa. By the 1520s, this conflict had intensified as a result of the voyages of Giovanni da Verrazzano.[102] In 1522, following the return of the Magellan expedition, Verrazzano, sanctioned by the French Crown, sailed southwards down the North American coastline and claimed to have discovered a route into the Pacific. In 1528, he returned to the region, trading along the coast of Brazil until his disappearance in March 1529. For the beleaguered Portuguese court, the implications of these claims were potentially disastrous. Already on the defensive from Hapsburg claims to the Moluccas in the wake of Magellan's voyage, they now found themselves answering French territorial claims in the New World, specifically Brazil. Repeated attempts by the French to establish trading posts in the region led to the massacre of a group of Breton merchants in Bahia in 1527, to which the French Crown responded by blockading French (and by implication Flemish) ports from Portuguese trading vessels.[103]

While Holbein was painting *The Ambassadors*, Franco-Portuguese rivalry entered a particularly sensitive phase, as Francis persuaded Pope Clement VII to reinterpret the original Papal bull of 1493, which had simply divided the world in two between Castile and Portugal. In October 1533, Clement announced that the bull referred to 'known continents, not to territories subsequently discovered by others'.[104] This allowed Francis to lay claim to territories in the New World with the Pope's blessing. The prominence that Holbein's globe gives to Brazil is therefore not accidental. It announces optimistic French claims to imminent imperial expansion in the New World, desperately counterpointed against the far more successful and authoritative claims of the Portuguese and Hapsburgs. The appearance of the globe registers the global aspirations of the painting and the scope of the imperial powers that frame it.

IX

The centre of *The Ambassadors* is recognizable, for us, as a recurrent, fictional representation of an equivalence between élite status, esoteric knowledge and power. But if the painting meticulously figures the kind of diplomatic negotiations in which Jean de Dinteville was engaged between the French and English kings, designed piecemeal to counter a build-up of imperial power elsewhere, are we justified in labelling the aesthetic culture he inhabited as itself imperialist? We propose that for Holbein and his sitters, Empire was indeed a key issue, but that it figures in the painting (and thus in Anglo-French culture) as the *problem* around whose absence the entire composition is structured. In other words, far from this painting being itself imperialistic, it is the counterpoint of an imperialism elsewhere.[105]

In late 1532 and early 1533, the problem around which Francis I and his ambassadors were negotiating was the growing consolidated power of the Hapsburg Emperor, Charles V. Francis's involvement with Henry's divorce and his participation in Anne's coronation were bound up with the French desire to secure the solid support of the English as part of an anti-Hapsburg power bloc. Charles had inherited the Austrian empire and Burgundian territories of his paternal grandfather Maximilian, and the Spanish territories (including Naples, Sicily and Sardinia) of his maternal grandparents, Ferdinand of Aragon and Isabella of Castile. In June 1519, the German electoral princes chose Charles as Holy Roman Emperor (an election facilitated by substantial bribes on his part, for which the Fugger bankers provided the funds). The result was an unprecedented concentration of territory in the hands of a single prince.[106] Between 1519 and 1559, Francis I manoeuvred continuously to try to produce by negotiation and diplomacy an international alliance that could resist the expansionist tendencies of Charles's empire. This meant courting the Northern Reformers of the Church (since Charles was pledged to support Catholicism to the utmost of his ability), notably the non-aligned German principalities and England. It also meant fostering friendly relations with the two other powers outside Charles's domains – the Papal States and the Ottoman Empire of Süleyman the Magnificent.[107]

The Ottoman carpet that covers the upper shelf of the table in *The Ambassadors* and links the resting arms (and perhaps the political intrigues) of Dinteville and Selve reminds us that the only other empire to be reckoned with in the 1530s was that of the Turks.[108] By 1529, the Ottoman Empire extended around the Mediterranean from Tunis to Bosnia, and Süleyman's army looked poised to invade Austria.[109] It was not just a military force to be reckoned with, however. Under Süleyman, it was also a cultural and intellectual power on a par with any in Western Europe, as well as the main source of high-quality luxury goods from locally manufactured silks, gems, carpets and metalwork to the porcelains, dyes and spices imported from China and India via Istanbul. In spite of a public rhetoric of hostility to the Turks and infidels in general, most of Europe was on trading terms with the Ottomans, with the Genoese and Venetians (and ultimately the French) enjoying special privileges in exchange for annual payments into Süleyman's exchequer. Strategically, alliance with the one contender for imperial power throughout the Mediterranean offered the only possible hope of resistance to Charles V. Francis I confided in the Venetian ambassador:

I cannot deny that I keenly desire the Turk powerful and ready for war, not for himself, because he is an infidel and we are Christians, but to undermine the Emperor's [Charles V's] power, to force heavy expenses upon him and to reassure all other governments against so powerful an enemy.[110]

Under these circumstances, public hostility regularly covered for something approaching diplomatic cordiality behind the scenes.[111] When Francis and Henry were on the point of signing their treaty of alliance at Calais in October 1532, Francis wrote to Dinteville's brother:

To anyone who asks you about the preparations which might be taking place with a view to an understanding between the King of England and myself, you can tell them that seeing the major preparations for an invasion of the Christian territories, which the Turks are currently involved in, we want to be prepared to combine to initiate whatever is necessary as much for the good of those Christian territories, of which we are by God's will the principal leaders, as in order not to be at the mercy of the Turkish troops.[112]

In fact, the treaty signed between Henry and Francis was intended to be the first stage in the assembling of an alliance that would include Süleyman.[113] While the Dinteville brothers were negotiating in Rome and London with the Pope and Henry VIII respectively, Francis's special envoy Rincón was negotiating in Venice with Süleyman's most trusted interpreter, Yunus Beg.[114] As an early seventeenth-century treatise on ambassadors points out, it was entirely acceptable for those of differing religious persuasion to sustain cordial diplomatic and commercial relations: 'Christian Princes and Estates make no difficulties to hold their Agents and Factors with the Turkes when they haue occasion.'[115]

The second sitter in *The Ambassadors*, Georges de Selve, moved, during 1532 and 1533, between Venice (whose relations with the Ottomans were traditionally close), Rome, France and England, carrying intelligence between Francis I's various potential allies as part of the anti-Charles faction and alliance-forming exercise. His presence registers the *absence* of Empire. The intimate Dinteville/Selve exchanges of information during the latter's brief visit (a visit the pro-Charles faction in France was not to know about) are recorded in the painting as a liaison whose purpose is occluded, marked by the residual presence of the Ottoman carpet and German artefacts.[116] At the centre of *The Ambassadors* is a visual space that is *empty* of all signs of imperial power. Where the Emperor might stand flanked by his envoys (or a Madonna might stand flanked by donors or saints),[117] we have a collection of symbolic objects, whose possible meanings have none of the stability or certainty of such a figure. And hanging over Dinteville, barely concealed behind the sumptuous curtains that set off the ambassadors' portraits, is an exquisitely crafted silver crucifix, a reminder that the political and doctrinal might of the Catholic Church and its protector, the Holy Roman Emperor, wait just beyond the bounds of the painting.[118]

At the heart of *The Ambassadors*, the lovingly simulated globes are a reminder that one of the functions of high art objects in the period was to recall the transactions and exchanges that gave them value. Holbein's painting presents the conjunction of the globe and the associated instruments of commercial transaction (the merchant arithmetic, the square) as devices whose technological sophistication disguised the more dubious implications of plundering voyages and long-distance commercial speculation. The Renaissance art world is strewn with examples of objects thus confidently celebrating the marks of their travel – works whose circulation is simultaneously a confirmation of the objects' function as signifiers of affluence and testimony to the territorial influence of their commissioners.

X

When we trace the cultural encounters and commercial transactions that underpinned the circulation of prized material objects such as Holbein's Turkish rugs, it emerges that official state rhetoric turned a discursive blind eye (or rather, deaf ear) to the cultural transactions that structured the commercial relations with the Ottomans as well as those among a range of other competing European powers. The shared acquisitive (mercantile) drives of Ottomans, Italians and Portuguese brought these territories together in light of a shared political and commercial goal which the official state narratives were happy to allow, but not to sanction publicly.[119] What these exchanges emphasize is that there was a centre of commercial interest which we need to imagine as inhabiting a space to the *east* of our contemporary notions of Europe. Within this account, the Ottoman Empire becomes a politically sensitive, problematic point of mediation between Europe and the markets to the east, rather than the shadowy limit at the bounds of Europe.[120]

The drive towards commercial expansion in the sixteenth century saw ambitious alliances forged and knowledge exchanged whose geographical horizons extended well into what Edward Said has referred to as the East. These exchanges took place on terrain unrecognizable to Renaissance specialists who set out to analyze the textual traces of what has been taken to constitute the period in terms derived from neo-Burckhardtian Renaissance studies, inflected, more recently, by an iconographical tradition derived from Panofsky.[121] Furthermore, the nature of these exchanges suggests a critical problem with the account of Europe's construction of the East as offered by Said in his important critique of post-nineteenth-century East-West discourse, *Orientalism*; a problem to which Said himself has recently begun to draw attention. In his reconsideration of *Orientalism*, entitled appropriately 'East Isn't East', Said stresses his commitment to what he refers to as '[t]he idea of rethinking and reformulating historical experiences which had once been based on the geographical separation of peoples and cultures'.[122] On the basis of our early sixteenth-century investigations, we would endorse this shift in Said's position from that expressed in *Orientalism*. We would also stress that this sort of project involves an enlarged analysis of the circulation of art objects, on which we have been focusing within the field of Renaissance studies.[123]

What we have tried to indicate is that within the context of the historical material we have been analyzing, such arguments enable us to circumvent an account of the marginalized, exoticized, dangerous East within Renaissance studies as not only politically unhelpful but also historically inaccurate. Paris, Lisbon, London, Mantua and Venice (for instance) were connected with Istanbul through shared political and commercial interests whose transactional power bases problematize the cultural binaries originally developed by Said in his account of the discourse of Orientalism.[124]

Our exploration of portrait medals, alongside our re-readings of Spenser's *Faerie Queene*, Carpaccio's paintings of St George, Gozzoli's *Adoration of the Magi* and Holbein's *Ambassadors*, set out to problematize the Burckhardtian (and with it the new historicist) view of emerging Western European selfhood in the Renaissance. We are now in a position to reject the appropriateness to this period of Said's version of Western Europe's construction of the Orient as an alien, displaced other, positioned in opposition to a confident, imperialist Eurocentrism.[125]

We undertook to dismantle Renaissance Man as constructed by Burckhardt and Freud. In the process, we lost the antithetical, dark, dirty, exotic, Eastern Other as the negative to which that humane individualism has been opposed – the other ostensibly held at bay by its constructed version of civilization.[126] Sixteenth-century art-based transactions reveal a pragmatic engagement between East and West in which each fully acknowledged the participation of the other and negotiated workable relationships.

This surely means that the critique of a Western cultural representation of the East that assumes an origin in the Renaissance, a supposed point in time at which the East was fantasized as the dark, demonized opposition to the brightly illuminated integrity of the emerging early modern civilized self, also fails (or falls). Just as Renaissance Man turns out to be a retrospective construction of nineteenth-century ideology, so does its alien Other.

In Holbein's *Ambassadors*, as in Gozzoli's *Adoration of the Magi*, the aspiration towards imperial power figures as an absence or as a space between and beyond the participants portrayed. In Holbein's painting, the array of objects codes (or symbolically represents) a transactive commercial and territorial relationship between England and the major imperial powers with which it was negotiating – the Valois, Hapsburg and Ottoman empires – brokered by French diplomacy. The possibility of filling the void at the centre of the composition depended on the outcomes of events imminent at the time it was painted, for instance the birth of a male heir to Henry VIII; an ensuing binding alliance with the French, who had supported the marriage to Anne Boleyn; a successful treaty with the Ottomans; a possible appeasement of the Pope. All of these outcomes were political failures; neither Dinteville's nor Selve's career prospered as a consequence. In *The Ambassadors*, finally, as in the portrait medals and the Gozzoli frescoes, the East is neither a fantasy nor an omission. It is the location for the entire set of transactions represented (for example) in the objects between Dinteville and Selve – a representation that was neither mysterious nor obscure at the time when the painting was produced, but that has become so during the intervening period.[127]

We began with Ciriac of Ancona because his reputation also survives in a curiously fractured form, two incompatible halves that the present exploration enables us to reunite. The roving scholar of antiquity moved, in his own day, across a map without intellectual impediments or ideological boundaries. In the East, his scholarly reputation rested on the classical heritage he revived as personal advisor to Mehmet II, tailoring the Sultan's image and actions to the imperial forebears – Alexander the Great, Constantine, Charlemagne – he hoped to emulate. This enabled Mehmet to lay claim to the unifying imperial power that would unite Christianity, Judaism and Islam under one rule.

Meanwhile, Ciriac took back to the West descriptions of ancient Greek and Roman monuments and their inscriptions, which encouraged Western Europe to bond culturally with its Eastern neighbours, as participating in a shared classical heritage, recognized and inhabited by both. Once again, his scholarly activities encouraged a generation of Byzantine exiles to dream of a Christian Church – the fragments of Greece, Asia and Trebizond – reunited under a great European imperial power. The fact that we now have such difficulty in recognizing these projects as mirror reflections of one inclusive imperial ambition is surely our loss.

2 Telling Tapestries: Fabricating Narratives of Conquest

In chapter 1, we suggested that a range of fifteenth-century portrait medals and their circulation contrived to mediate a particularly fraught attempt to bring together the Eastern and Western Churches in permanent union in the face of the apparently unstoppable westward expansion of the Ottoman Empire. That attempt, which pivoted crucially around the councils of Florence and Mantua in 1438 and 1459, ended in dramatic failure, a failure whose direct result was the swallowing up by Islam of the two key eastern centres of Christianity – first Constantinople and then Trebizond.[1]

In this chapter, we argue that this particularly highly charged but also artistically rich moment in which East and West fixed each other with an equal, reciprocal gaze was intensified and revised in the subsequent contests for power and legitimation that defined the escalation in inter-imperial confrontation in the course of the sixteenth century. The artistic product with which we have chosen to illustrate this point is one that, in spite of its contemporary status as an expensive prestige object, has tended to be overlooked in artistic accounts of the period. We argue here that in the early sixteenth century, the large-scale tapestry series became a symbolically over-determined artefact upon which the political hopes and aspirations of the imperial courts of the period were repeatedly projected. We explore the ways in which a range of narrative tapestries mediated imperial tensions at the courts of Europe, from Burgundy in the fifteenth century through to the escalation of religious conflict in the Low Countries in the final decades of the sixteenth century. In the process, we argue that, from the start of their open and easy circulation with the East in the late fourteenth century, such tapestries were increasingly appropriated to support a far more exclusive and aggressive vision of European 'civility'. This process culminated in the aesthetically magnificent but, we would argue, politically coercive series of tapestries designed to adorn the Spanish and French courts of the Hapsburgs and the Valois.

I

In 1519, one of the most prestigious tapestry weavers based in Brussels, Pieter van Aelst, completed a series of ten tapestries entitled *Acts of the Apostles* (illus. 33). Commissioned between 1513 and 1514 by Pope Leo X, the *Apostles* series, based on cartoons by Raphael, was one of the most ambitious tapestry cycles of their day.[2] Unveiled in Rome in December 1519, they caused a sensation, being celebrated for their size (most were over twelve metres long and four metres high), lavishness and artistic verisimilitude. Drawing on Raphael's skills as a draughtsman, the tapestries achieved a depth and richness in tone and modelling beyond anything that had been accomplished in previous fifteenth-century tapestries woven in the workshops of the Low Countries. In his life of Raphael, Vasari gives a vivid account of the transfer of cartoon to tapestry, and of the reception of the finished product:

Raphael drew and coloured in his own hand all the cartoons in the exact form and size needed and these were sent to be woven in Flanders. After they had been finished, the tapestries were sent back to Rome. The completed work was of such wonderful beauty that it astonished anyone who saw it to think that it could have been possible to weave the hair and the beards so finely and to have given such softness to the flesh merely by the use of the threads.[3]

On the triumphant completion of the *Apostles*, van Aelst immediately began another incredibly ambitious series of tapestries, to celebrate the coronation of his patron, the future Holy Roman Emperor Charles V, in Aix-la-Chapelle (Aachen) on 23 October 1520. The weaver entitled this ambitious nine-piece set *Los Honores*.[4] These new art objects consisted of a series of monumental images, drawing on the increasing vogue for narrative tapestries, designed to instruct the young Emperor in the attainment of princely virtue. The tapestries were designed to offer him models of personal behaviour, military valour and imperial authority in line with the responsibilities that came with his control over his new dominions.[5]

The first tapestry in the series, entitled *Fortune* (illus. 34), ostentatiously bears the explicit imprint of Hapsburg imperial power: the date of Charles's coronation is woven into the fabric. At the top, the tapestry depicts the blindfolded goddess Fortune riding across the heavens astride a rearing mount. She scatters roses upon those she favours among the figures depicted on the left, and with her left hand drops stones upon the unfortunates on the right. From the upper left corner of the tapestry, Phoebus Apollo watches over the fortunate, whilst in the upper right corner, Vulcan showers the unfortunate with fiery thunderbolts struck from his forge.[6]

Schematically, the tapestry depicts the definably 'Eastern' or 'Asian' figures of Cleopatra, Hecuba, and Priam, King of Troy, among the ranks of the unfortunate.[7] Watched over by Phoebus Apollo, the fortunate include figures from the Greco-Roman world who were subsequently incorporated into a tradition of liberal humanism within the pantheon of Western European 'civilizing' influences.[8] These include, most prominently, Romulus and Remus, Julius Caesar, Servius Tullus and the particularly striking figures of Europa (the personification of Europe) and the Bull. Blindfolded Fortune is personified here as a figure whose intentions are fundamentally arbitrary. Sitting atop the Palace of Fortune, she entrusts humanity's destiny to a young woman aimlessly spinning the Wheel of Life.

The sheer cost and time required to manufacture such an extraordinarily ambitious series of tapestries meant that they were not in fact completed until 1523, a good three years after Charles's coronation. Their financing proved so costly that in 1522 van Aelst had to take out a loan with the Fuggers' Antwerp agents, partly in cash and partly in materials. Upon his failure to repay the loan in 1525, the Fuggers took possession of the tapestries and negotiated their sale to Charles, in whose honour they had originally been designed.[9] The Fuggers' involvement in the sale of the tapestries was particularly appropriate and in many ways unsurprising. Charles had borrowed the enormous sum of over 850,000 florins from them to offer inducements to the German Electors, who were crucial to his election to the imperial title and thus to the defeat of his main rival, Francis I.

Charles took possession of the complete cycle of *Los Honores* in 1526, and the tapestries were put on display in Seville to coincide with the festivities that commemorated his marriage to Princess Isabella of Portugal – an event representing another increment added to his growing dynastic authority. The overpowering presence of all nine tapestries at the union underlines the fact that from the beginning of Charles's reign, tapestries were the visual focus of his self-presentation as a supremely powerful, virtuous and legitimate imperial sovereign.

Today, any attempt to unravel the 'meaning' of such an iconographically ambitious series of tapestries as *Los Honores* inevitably involves the critical tradition of iconography and iconology established in the work of art historians of the first half of the twentieth century, most notably Erwin Panofsky, Jean Seznec and Ernst Gombrich.[10] According to these influential authors, Renaissance artists reworked classical themes and subjects so as to combine the recognizable story lines and moralized arguments of their sources with an emotional and intellectual vigour that infused new meaning into the old forms. According to this approach, where the Middle Ages had Christianized the Greek and Roman stories and used them to contrive equivalencies between pagan and Christian morals, the Renaissance generated powerful new relationships with what was defined as the 'typical'.

Here, for example, is Panofsky's account of how a well-known drawing by Dürer, representing the Rape of Europa (illus. 28), is fundamentally 'modern' compared with the flat, naive versions of the Middle Ages:

A drawing by Dürer, copied from an Italian prototype probably during his first stay in Venice, emphasizes the emotional vitality which was absent in the mediaeval representation. The literary source of Dürer's *Rape of Europa* is no longer a prosy text where the bull was compared to Christ, and Europa to the human soul, but the pagan verses of Ovid himself as revived in two delightful stanzas by Angelo Poliziano: You can admire Jupiter transformed into a beautiful bull by the power of love. He dashes away with his sweet, terrified load, her beautiful golden hair fluttering in the wind which blows back her gown. With one hand she grasps the horn of the bull, while the other clings to his back. She draws up her feet as if she were afraid of the sea, and thus crouching down with pain and fear, she cries for help in vain. For her sweet companions remain on the flowery shore, each of them crying Europa, come back. The whole seashore resounds with Europa, come back, and the bull looks round and kisses her feet.

Panofsky's conclusions emphasize Dürer's artistic treatment of Europa as constitutive of the emergence of the very notion of what it means to be humane:

Dürer's drawing actually gives life to this sensual description. The crouching position of Europa, her fluttering hair, her clothes blown back by the wind and thus revealing her graceful body, the gestures of her hands, the furtive movement of the bull's head, the seashore scattered with lamenting companions: all this is faithfully and vividly depicted; and, even more, the beach itself rustles with the life of *aquatici monstriculi*, to speak in the terms of another quattrocento writer, while satyrs hail the abductor.

This comparison illustrates the fact that the reintegration of classical *themes* with classical *motifs* which seems to be characteristic of the Italian Renaissance as opposed to the numerous sporadic revivals of classical tendencies during the Middle Ages, is not only a humanistic but also a human occurrence. It is a most important element of what Burckhardt and Michelet called the discovery both of the world and of man.[11]

Our own view is that Dürer's drawing looks most like a sketch based on a tapestry like the section containing Europa on her bull from

28 Albrecht Dürer, *The Rape of Europa*, *c.* 1495, ink on paper. Graphische Sammlung Albertina, Vienna.

the *Fortune* panel in *Los Honores* (illus. 29). Panofsky, however, identifies precisely these tapestry-like features as the innovative elements of acutely observed and felt psychological realism – not only humanistic but humane – overlaid on the originating classical tale, which are the typical contribution to Western art of the Italian Renaissance – of civilization.

The text critic readily recognizes and responds to the art historian's strategy. He or she reinserts the visual description into a graphic history of genres and themes and reads the figural representation with the confident expectation that the poet or dramatist will have located in it a taut relationship with the narrative or plot, and that exegesis will yield interpretative clues in the form of moral comment and emotional colour. To the art historian following in Burckhardt's footsteps, the resulting interpretation will be historical in the broad sense that it is grounded in that founding moment of modern consciousness for which the transition from Medieval to Renaissance stands. Our aim in this chapter is to historicize more precisely the reading that accompanies our experience of the tapestry.

The text critic who invokes art-historical iconology and iconography as a strategy for reading Renaissance images does so unreflectingly. But we would argue that iconographic interpretative techniques are not agenda-free. Returning for a moment to Panofsky's discussion of Dürer's *Europa*, we might detect that the account of Renaissance iconology that licenses this kind of literary reading carries a recognizable freight of assumption about the humaneness of Renaissance creativity that goes beyond the merely interpretative:

Dürer's drawing actually gives life to this sensual description. The crouching position of Europa, her fluttering hair, her clothes blown back by the wind and thus revealing her graceful body, the gestures of her hands, the furtive movement of the bulls head, the seashore scattered with lamenting companions: all this is faithfully and vividly depicted.

Faithfulness and vividness here carry connotations of emotional sensitivity and a deftness of touch with psychological realism that we could trace back to Burckhardt's version of what constitutes the civilized. So it is not altogether a surprise to find a more traditional European historian like John Hale using this very graphic representation of Europa to ground an argument about the Renaissance as precisely the period when Europe as we know it became civilized (as we understand the term):

To an age that liked to have pictorial images of abstractions, whether it was Architecture, or Commerce, or Theology, or a Continent, how would Europe have looked to the mind's eye?

It was the only continent whose name was linked to a Greek myth. Europa was the daughter of Agenor, King of the Levantine city of Tyre. One day Jupiter, who from Olympus had noted her charms, swam ashore in the form of a white bull when she was whiling away the time with the young women of her entourage. The attraction was immediate (though the encounter was later sensationalized as a rape). The story was paraphrased in the late 1470s by the Florentine scholar-poet Angelo Poliziano . . . [Hale then quotes the same verses as Panofsky].

Jove carries her from Asia to Crete. Here he turns into a man, impregnates her, and her progeny, thus divinely sired, become the Europeans and she the tutelary deity of their continent.[12]

Sure enough, the visual representation of this myth of origin, which Hale goes on to gloss in detail, is Dürer's, selected because it caught the Italian habit of revitalising myth and assuming a familiarity with its subject matter:

Leaving her wailing maidens, Europa, wondering but unfrightened rides on while one hand grasps [the bull's] back, the other his horn, across a sea peppered with reedy islets and those creatures, satyrs and sea-nymphs, through whom the Greeks had expressed their feelings about natural phenomena.[13]

As in Panofsky's account, Dürer's *Europa* is used here to capture that essential humaneness that is Hale's version of an emerging Renaissance European consciousness. It is important at this point to remember that the Renaissance was the first age in which the words *Europe* and *European* acquired widely understood significance.[14] It saw the emergence of a new and pervasive attitude to what were considered the more valued aspects of civilized life and, according to Burckhardt (as we saw in the previous chapter), witnessed the most concentrated wave of intellectual and cultural energy that had yet passed over the continent. We find, predictably, the following in Hale's preface:

I hope it will not be thought presumptuous that my title adapts that of a book of really seminal importance, Jacob Burckhardt's *The Civilization of the Renaissance in Italy* of 1860. I have carried it for so long in my mental baggage as a talisman at once protective and provocative that this was not a journey I could undertake without it.[15]

Finally, Hale's Europa herself offers us a clue as to why the Burckhardtian version of civilization does damage to the story of the relationship between art and history in the Renaissance. According to Hale, the culmination of the process of transition from uncouthness to civilization in Europe occurred when the continent came to be represented as a white, well-clad, stolid and commanding Europa, and the image of the original Europa, the ravished Asian princess on her yearning mount, quietly faded. As we shall see, the image of Asia as the location through which Europe's civilization was transacted certainly did not fade. Rather, in crucial ways it provided the parameters for Europe's definition of her own cultural pre-eminence – the origin of luxuriousness and exoticism against which those in the West who aspired to magnificence measured the extent to which that aspiration was successful.

We also propose a different relationship between the representational function of the art object and the culture within which its meaning is transacted. We choose the medium of tapestry for our exploration because its unfamiliarity, as an art form that has largely been disparaged or neglected by traditional art history, leaves our minds clear of preconceptions as we attempt to locate its cultural meaning. This chapter therefore also addresses the extent to which tapestries have been put to one side in Renaissance studies, hidden in plain view within the visual and literary landscape of the period. We argue that this is primarily due to the extent to which, throughout the sixteenth century, the relationship between claims to imperial legitimacy and tapestry production became so intimate that it became impossible to ascribe any artistic autonomy to tapestries' aesthetic dimension.

We suggest that, rather than producing an uncomfortable and aberrant sense of the relations between artistic production and political authority, sixteenth-century tapestry production offers a new way of conceptualizing our perceptions of relations between art and power. Imperial authority was increasingly measured through the conspicuous purchasing power required to commission, transport and repeatedly display massive, visually overpowering tapestry cycles. The progressively politicized transactions that we trace throughout the early sixteenth century culminated in the effective destruction of the tapestry industry in the Low Countries in the aftermath of the Spanish Fury of the 1570s. One decisive chapter in this history came to an end with the destruction of the weaving industry around Brussels and Antwerp. The flowering of this industry had itself been the result of intensive investments made by the imperial courts, whose desire to control the means of production required to produce these lavish objects ultimately led to the industry's collapse.

II

We begin by offering a brief contextualization of tapestry production within the culture of Renaissance Europe.

When Hamlet stabs Polonius hiding 'Behind the arras' at the beginning of the closet scene in *Hamlet* (III.iv), the critic's eye tends to slide over the significance of that 'arras', or tapestry, seen as part of the mundane fabric of an Elizabethan domestic interior. Tapestries had been central to the domestic economy of élite European house-holds for centuries.[16] From the fourteenth century onwards, the craft grew in demand, providing immense made-to-measure wall hangings for castles, palaces and churches. Such commissions often involved highly specific pieces to hang over doorways (*portières*) or between windows (*entre-fenêtres*), as well as canopies to suspend over thrones (*baldachins*).[17] Patrons would often order a 'chamber' or set of pieces to insulate and decorate particular domestic spaces. However, as Candace Adelson has pointed out, tapestries were not simply orna-mental insulation:

In an age when tapestries were an integral part of European decoration, they were a luxury item only the wealthy could afford. In terms of workmanship, tapestries, along with finely chased armour, were the most costly form of movable art that could be bought . . . Tapestry was considered a more luxuri-ous, movable form of monumental painting, and appraisals in inventories of the time indicate that tapestries were much more highly valued than paintings . . . They were also the most practical of furnishings for the mobile courts of feudal and early modern Europe. As lords and rulers inspected their dominions, they could carry tapestries with them from castle to castle, where they not only impressed subjects with their master's grandeur but also provided warmth and aesthetic pleasure.[18]

As well as being conveniently portable, decorative interior insulation, tapestries were invested with a more intangible splendour and awe due to the intensive nature of the skill, labour and materials expended on their creation.

Tapestry weavers wove from cartoons, usually commissioned by either the master weaver or the patron from a painter or draughtsman. Cartoons usually become part of the capital assets of the master weaver's business and were used for subsequent reproduction if the initial set was a success. The subjects of cartoons became more ambitious and complex as weavers became increasingly sophisticated in their ability to represent shape, texture, shade and colour. Techniques included hatching, whereby alternate colours of weft are used to create intense, comb-like colouring, and tweeding, where each weft thread is composed of several strands of different shades woven as one.[19] Technical developments were also tied to the growing range of available materials. Yarn was invariably composed of linen or wool (often from England), increasingly supplemented with silk from the East and yarns composed of silver or gold imported from Africa or the Americas. Natural dyes were extracted from plants or insects, including saffron, lac and alum, along with other dyes imported from the East, which increased the vividness and intensity of the weaver's palette. The increasingly sophisticated use of mordants – metal salts in which yarn was boiled to increase its ability to absorb colour – added to the range and intensity of colours available to the sixteenth-century weaver.[20]

From the fourteenth century onwards, tapestry production was almost exclusively focused on the Low Countries. In 1302, the so-called 'Tapissiers de la haulte lisse' were admitted into the corporation of tapestry weavers in Paris.[21] However, the distinction between tapestry weaving and other forms of textile production remained ambiguous and porous. Reference is made in 1405 to Janne van Paris, termed a *sarasinoyswerker*, a term derived from the French for Saracen (*sarasinois*).[22] As Guy Delmarcel has pointed out, this clearly refers to the influence and cross-fertilization of textile traditions between East and West from as early as the fourteenth century, and probably even earlier. Documentation of the development of high-loom tapestry manufacture in Arras survives from 1313. Until its fall to Louis XI of France in 1477, Arras remained the centre of the tapestry-weaving industry, finally eclipsed by Bruges, Brussels, Middleburg and, most importantly, Tournai from the end of the fifteenth century.[23] So complete was Northern Europe's hold on the industry by the early sixteenth century that Paolo Giovio could refer to tapestries as 'Belgarum ars suprema', the highest art of the Low Countries.[24]

As the scale and technique of tapestry production throughout Flanders and Brabant expanded and developed, so design and style diversified, often according to the context and cost of a particular commission. Many tapestries were predominantly ornamental. One particularly popular genre was the *verdure* tapestry, based primarily on gardens or landscapes and portraying dense fields of vegetation to the exclusion of virtually anything else. *Verdure* tapestries were also closely connected to so-called *millefleurs* designs, highly stylized renderings of flowering plants, usually on red or blue grounds. *Millefleurs* designs bear close affinities with Persian and Ottoman motifs and are also found in the geometric designs of carpets and textiles from the East depicted in paintings of the period.[25] Such designs were often built into emblematic or symbolic tapestries, such as those portraying heraldic devices or significant animals. However, the highest form of design remained monumental cycles of narrative tapestries. Compositions were often based on moralized stories from the Bible, as well as narratives from the ancient world. Some of the most popular ones included the Return of the Prodigal Son, the history of Alexander the Great, the Trojan War (illus. 30) and the Labours of Hercules.[26]

Growing courtly demand for tapesty cycles throughout the fifteenth century led to the establishment of workshops all over the Low Countries which employed up to 40 weavers working on any one

30 Workshop of Pasquier Grenier, *Hector and Andromache* from the *Trojan War* tapestry series, *c.* 1472–4, silk and wool. Metropolitan Museum of Art, New York.

tapestry series at a given time. By the middle of the sixteenth century, this scenario had reached epic proportions. In 1545, whilst negotiating with tapestry weavers in Brussels, an agent of the Medici estimated that some fifteen thousand people were involved in the manufacture of tapestries – nearly a quarter of the city's population.[27] However, it was under the early fifteenth-century Burgundian dukes of Flanders that Arras became the centre of tapestry production. Between 1423 and 1467, the register of craftsmen for the town lists the names of 59 high-loom tapestry weavers, most of whom were patronized by one of the House of Burgundy's most zealous promoters of tapestries, Philip the Good (1418–1467), whose collection became so extensive that by 1440 he had erected a vaulted building adjacent to his residence for the sole purpose of housing it. Philip had learned the significance of tapestries from his forebears, including Philip of Burgundy (*d.* 1404), who had commissioned the largest one ever woven in fourteenth-century Arras, representing the Battle of Roosebecke, which had been completed in 1386, four years after the battle. Measuring 238 square metres, it was both magnificent and cumbersome, and in 1402 it was cut up into three separate hangings. Philip quickly mastered the more subtle dimensions of tapestry display. In 1440, he presented the new Pope, Eugenius IV, with a specially commissioned series woven in Arras and entitled *Three Moral Histories of the Pope, the Emperor and the Nobility.*[28]

In 1468, Philip's son Charles the Bold married Margaret of York in a diplomatically delicate marriage. The House of Burgundy ensured that its most dazzling tapestries were prominently displayed at the ceremony.[29] These included *The History of Gideon and the Golden Fleece*, *The History of the Great Battle of Liège*, *Coronation of King Clovis*, *The First Christian King of France* and *The Marriage of King Clovis with the Daughter of Gondebaut*. The chapel in which the marriage took place was itself hung with a tapestry depicting Christ's Passion, an example of the knowingly strategic ways in which the House of Burgundy deployed its classical, biblical and contemporary tapestries to maximum political effect. Contemporary witnesses recorded their wonder at the sight of these works:

. . . the costers of the said hall of rich arras; marvelous in my mynd the curyous makyng that is in the forsaid arras and is of auncien ystory of the Bible, of famous Gideoñ . . . and att the [subsequent] banquett iii ystoriez of Erculez countenaunceing and no speche; the ystory of the Duckes grett chambre was of the marriage of the doughtr. of Kyng Clotte of Fraunce and the Kynge of Burgoyne, and what issue they hadde: right riche arras; and aftr that other chambrez hanged wt arras silke and tapstre to the noumbre of xxxii chambre.[30]

Combining astute political iconography with an overbearing (even oppressive) ceremonial presence, Philip's tapestries were to become a model for the ways in which narrative textiles would be displayed to maximum effect by heads of the House of Burgundy over subsequent years. Towards the end of the fifteenth century, they took on an even more intensely political role, being utilized as part of a self-conscious fashioning of a pan-European political identity in favour of the growing authority of the House of Hapsburg. Charles V's fascination with and commissioning of tapestries from the early years of his reign continued the Burgundian tradition of vividly establishing princely magnificence, displayed on the walls of the highly mobile Hapsburg court as it moved across his growing dominions throughout the Iberian peninsula and the Low Countries. However, we would also suggest that tapestries such as van Aelst's magnificent *Los Honores* were also accomplishing something more politically specific, as both material objects and 'icons', than a strictly iconographic interpretation would suggest.

As our analysis of Panofsky and Hale indicated, we should be wary of simply reading the depiction of Europa and the bull within the pantheon of the fortunate in the *Los Honores* cycle as part of the 'natural' cultural inheritance passed down to such a quintessentially 'European' sovereign as Charles. His election as Holy Roman Emperor in 1519 provided the conditions around which a range of politically resonant images clustered, both lending legitimacy to an emergent political power and consolidating their own symbolic effectiveness in the process. This, we will argue, is a very different scenario through which the creation of aesthetically compelling objects are produced than that proposed by Panofsky and, implicitly, Hale, a scenario we can recognize more clearly if we look again at the *Fortune* tapestry.

In *Los Honores*, Fortune literally hangs in the balance as the Wheel of Life spins round. Yet what the tapestry records is Charles V's explicit tilting of the Wheel of Life in his own favour, an image already adopted in his coronation entry into Bruges in 1515.[31] This is itself a highly self-conscious, backward-looking reference, more in keeping with an earlier medieval tradition of tapestry composition than with the more politically freighted nature of the spaces mapped out across the surfaces of these tapestries. What *is* at stake within this tapestry is the Hapsburg appropriation of the figure of Europa and Charles's reclamation of her iconography as part of his own cultural inheritance. As we have seen, Europa transformed from Asian princess into Hapsburg imperial icon in the *Fortune* tapestry does not represent a natural, inevitable movement of her figure from the Graeco-Roman world to Renaissance Europe. Indeed, it is more appropriate to register this juxtaposition of

East and West (which, as we shall see, is a recurrent motif in tapestries associated with Charles V) as part of a strategy for enhancing the power and magnificence of the Emperor and his Empire, set both over and against the only other contemporary empire of comparable extent and military and economic might, that of the Ottomans.

It seems appropriate at this point in our argument to recall that Charles's Burgundian antecedents had shared a range of cultural trans- actions with the Ottoman Empire, most vividly encapsulated in the circulation of carpets and tapestries. In 1396, Philip the Bold had led a military expedition against the Ottoman Sultan Beyazit. Philip's army was routed at Nicopolis, and his son, the future John the Fearless, was taken prisoner. The Sultan agreed to release John in exchange for tapestries made in Arras, on condition that they represented good old stories. Subsequently, John was exchanged for two packhorses laden with the finest Arras hangings available.

The 'good old story' Philip felt to be the most appropriate in the circumstances was that of Alexander the Great.[32] By now, we hope that the significance of such an exchange becomes clear. A figure like Alexander was strenuously contested, claimed by Burgundian and Ottoman courts alike. In providing Beyazit with tapestries representing Alexander's triumphs, carefully crafted by Low Countries weavers, Philip tellingly conceded a figure of potentially global imperial power in favour of his Ottoman counterpart, to whom the concession would have been gratifyingly recognizable. Beyazit's prized tapestries came to adorn the walls of the Topkapi Saray in Istanbul upon its completion by that other self-styled Alexander, Mehmet the Conqueror, in 1478. This circumstance vividly represents the retention of a prototypical imperial icon in keeping with the global aspirations of Mehmet, whose military power and territorial possessions gave him a much more legitimate reason to claim such an inheritance well before Charles V.

Tapestries such as *Los Honores* therefore return us to the ongoing struggles over political identity and imperial authority between East and West, which stretch right back to the 1438 Council of Florence. As with portrait medals, whose legibility circulated freely between East and West, tapestries such as *Los Honores* were designed to be equally comprehensible to the courts of London, Paris, Lisbon and Constantinople. What we can also see emerging is a highly specific, deliberately fashioned imperial identity, a Hapsburg-controlled vision of European identity, as Europa is enlisted in the process of wrapping Charles in the mantle of both Roman emperor *and* European prince. Whereas earlier tapestries depicting Alexander the Great could easily and openly be appropriated by either the Ottoman or the Burgundian court to their mutual political advantage, the Hapsburg tapestries of the early sixteenth century weave an image of Charles's imperial (and ultimately global) aspirations through the highly selective appropriation of the myth of Europa. This is a highly partial and selective process, representative of the House of Hapsburg's wider aspirations.

III

The political investments we have outlined were not confined to the Burgundian and, subsequently, the Hapsburg courts. The courts of the houses of Valois, Tudor and Avis also became intimately involved in the increasingly competitive and aggressive pursuit of narrative tapestries throughout the early decades of the sixteenth century, although their ability to credibly challenge the cultural and imperial pre-eminence of the Ottoman and Hapsburg courts was seriously compromised by their lack of financial and military muscle. Both Henry VIII and Francis I subsequently drew on the model of Hapsburg magnificence mediated through the medium of the tapestry. However, their transparent 'quotation' of Burgundian and Hapsburg works was itself indicative of French and English political weakness; their own ready-made tapestries were either too derivative of Hapsburg models or too confusingly overdetermined in their range of iconographic allusions to be politically convincing.

An example that illustrates this point is from one of the other great collections of early sixteenth-century tapestries, that of Francis I. In August 1532, Francis took possession of the first batch of tapestries from one of the most ambitious narrative cycles to be produced in the sixteenth century. Entitled *The History of Scipio Africanus* (illus. 35), they were commissioned on behalf of Francis by the Italian entrepreneur Marchio Baldi and produced by the Brussels workshop of Marc Crétif.

The surviving documentation detailing the specific nature of the commission is typical in terms of the time, effort, planning and expense that went into the execution of monumental cycles of this kind. The initial contract agreed between Baldi (acting on Francis's orders) and Crétif stipulated that 'l'histoire de Scipion l'Africain' be woven in gold and silk, 400 *aunes* in size (equivalent to approximately 560 square metres). Crétif would be paid 50 *écus d'or soleil* for each *aune*, evidence of the lucrative nature of such a prestigious commission. After receiving three completed tapestries, Francis drew up a final contract with Crétif, ordering him to

. . . execute, furnish, and deliver the amount of roughly 400 aunes, by Parisian measurement, of rich gold and silk tapestry representing the history of Scipio Africanus, of the same quantity, quality, type, and style as the three works of tapestry which were shown to the said agent [Baldi], and the present transaction to be done for the price and sum of fifty *écus d'or soleil* per aune.[33]

Designed from a series of cartoons by Giulio Romano, who had recently completed work on the Palazzo del Te in Mantua, the final series consisted of a massive 22 tapestries, with a total surface area of approximately 680 square metres, at a staggering cost of 23,448 *écus d'or soleil* (more than 50,000 *livres*).

The *History of Scipio* series was broken down into two parts, the first thirteen tapestries consisting of representations of the deeds of Scipio, the rest portraying his triumphs. The scenes shown were from the Second Punic War between Rome and Carthage. Scipio had been instrumental in destroying the Carthaginian threat against Rome, having landed in North Africa in 204 BC with a force of 30,000 soldiers, and defeated Hannibal at the battle of Zama 120 kilometres outside Carthage in 202 BC. Scipio's subsequent triumphs, celebrating his victory and return to Rome, became a template for displays of imperial power and authority, qualities that Francis was particularly anxious to establish in his rivalry with Charles V throughout their respective reigns. Having lost out to Charles in his bid for the title of Holy Roman Emperor in 1519, Francis's choice of Scipio Africanus as a prototypical imperial figure with which to adorn the walls of his court was clearly not arbitrary, nor were the carefully calculated diplomatic points at which the tapestries were displayed.

As soon as Francis began to receive the tapestries, he deployed them in an attempt to extract maximum political impact. For example, he displayed them as part of his lavish *faste* with Henry VIII, held at Boulogne in October 1532. Recording the event in his memoirs, Martin Du Bellay noted:

And there is . . . a room which is the monks' refectory, which is draped; the ceiling is of flesh-colored taffeta, with taffeta flags in the king's colors, and hung with four main tapestries depicting the victories of Scipio Africanus, executed in high-warp, all in gold and silk thread. These characters are well executed and as natural as one could do, and no painter on earth could possibly do better on panel. They say that each *aune* cost 50 *ecus*.[34]

Just four months later, in February 1533, the Venetian ambassador to the court of Francis I, Marino Giustiniani, also found himself admiring Francis's new tapestries, this time at a carnival banquet held at the Louvre in Paris:

There were many pieces [of tapestry] hung around a large room, the larger one, as big as our library. At the end of this room was a tribunal as large as ours in Venice, which was half decorated with gold fabric and half with purple velvet, on which were embroidered rich branches in relief. Around the rest of the room there were some tapestries which His Majesty had had made recently, representing the deeds of Scipio Africanus, very rich in gold, silver and silk, which I observed to be very beautiful . . . The most Christian king came to see me, praising the quality of the series [*historia*] that he knew to have been woven, after paintings by Raphael of Urbino, before those hangings above [us]; but, comparing these tapestries with those done for the Pope by the said Raphael of Urbino, His Majesty affirmed that the former were much richer.[35]

Both Du Bellay and Giustiniani stressed the visual splendour of Francis's new tapestries, their vivid opulence bearing down on and dominating the ceremonial interiors over which they cast an intimidating atmosphere, evoking Francis's imperial authority as well as his purchasing power. What is conspicuous about both Du Bellay's and Giustiniani's observations is the extent to which the display of tapestries was more striking than that of paintings: '. . . no painter on earth could possibly do better on panel.' Francis's reported comments to Giustiniani only served to underline this point. The sheer scale and obvious expense of the tapestries inevitably invited comparisons with Leo X's *Apostles* set completed in 1519, and Giustiniani's comments emphasize the extent to which the French King's commission was a highly self-conscious attempt to both appropriate the imperial mantle of Scipio Africanus and outdo the Pope in his commissioning of technically innovative and visually arresting tapestries. This point is strengthened by the fact that at the same time as Francis received the first consignment of *Scipio* tapestries, he was also in the process of ordering an exact copy of Leo's *Apostles*. Nor was he alone in his desire for one; Henry VIII, Margaret of Austria and Cardinal Ercole Gonzaga all possessed copies woven from Raphael's cartoons.[36]

Francis's lavish and daring commissioning of the *History of Scipio* was symptomatic of the ongoing but increasingly competitive ways in which the imperial courts of Renaissance Europe defined their political pre-eminence through their possession and display of narrative tapestry cycles. As a direct response to Leo's *Apostles*, and as an oblique riposte to Charles V's *Los Honores*, the *History of Scipio* suggested that Francis could match his imperial rivals in the commissioning and display of costly, technically innovative works, which coincidentally offered him a model for his own pretensions to imperial power. It also provided a devastating response to the attempts of his rival, Henry VIII, to emphasize his own claims to imperial magnificence in his display of a set of *History of David* tapestries in 1527, when the French ambassador went to London to arrange the marriage between Francis I's son and Princess Mary. On this occasion, the halls of the banqueting house at Greenwich were 'hung with the most costly tapestry in England, representing the history of David'.[37] The English court under Henry possessed over two thousand tapestries, held mainly at Hampton Court, but most of these were ready-made cycles purchased by diplomatic go-betweens and entrepreneurs for the English King and Cardinal Wolsey.[38]

However, recent evidence suggests that Henry was also acutely aware of the political usefulness of tapestries; in the 1520s, he purchased a series showing the story of David and Bathsheba (illus. 36) which sought to strengthen his perception of himself as the anointed ruler of God's chosen people.[39] Guy Delmarcel has argued that the explicitly moral themes of these tapestries – the personal ethics of rulers and their public achievements – reworked in more artful form the issues presented by van Aelst in *Los Honores*.[40] The *David* set was a standard reworking of what had become a carefully disseminated convention artistically and politically inhabited by the Hapsburgs. Henry remained keen to insert his own personal and political identity into the ready-made personae which the tapestry provided. This response was already politically and artistically derivative in comparison with the abiding power of the Hapsburg-sponsored tapestries, with their taut relationship between contemporary political event and fluently responsive art object. Nevertheless, in the face of such an artistically innovative series as Francis's *History of Scipio*, Henry can have been left in no doubt as to the French King's far stronger claims to imperial grandeur as he viewed the series at Boulogne in 1532.

Francis's commissioning of the *Scipio* tapestries was even more daring as a bold appropriation of a prototypical Roman figure of Empire, a model presumably more readily suited to the inheritor of the imperial mantle of Rome, Charles V (indeed, Charles's earlier series of tapestries celebrating his elevation to the title of Holy Roman Emperor, *Los Honores*, drew extensively on the image of Scipio Africanus to make their point). However, Charles was to reclaim the initiative, and the role of Scipio Africanus, in an even more audacious response, through his subsequent exploits on the battlefield and negotiations with the tapestry workshops of Brussels.

Conflict between Charles and Francis had been intensifying since the Hapsburg prince's triumphant defeat of his French rival in his bid to become Holy Roman Emperor in 1519. The increasing factionalism this caused throughout subsequent years, as the various states of Europe lined up on one side or the other of the Hapsburg-Valois divide, came to a head at Pavia in February 1525. Attempting to advance into northern Italy, the French army engaged Charles's forces with disastrous consequences (estimates of the French dead range between ten and fourteen thousand). In the course of the battle, the French King had his horse shot from underneath him, and suffered the humiliation of being captured by his great Hapsburg rival and forced to submit to Charles's terms under the Treaty of Madrid. As both monarchs had already deployed tapestries in the service of their rising imperial power, it comes as no surprise that in this highly charged atmosphere Charles's court rapidly commissioned a series commemorating the Hapsburg victory. Entitled *The Battle of Pavia* (illus. 31), it was produced in Brussels in the immediate aftermath of the battle. Apparently following a series of cartoons by Bernard van Orley, the tapestries were presented to Charles by the States General of the Lowlands in Brussels in 1531.[41] Whilst this seven-piece set drew extensively on the classical models employed in earlier fifteenth-century tapestries depicting the Trojan War and the exploits of Alexander, the *Pavia* tapestries were particularly novel and distinctive in their graphic delineation of the battle, as well as its precise topography and the portrayal of its participants.[42] This series marked a significant departure in the ways in which the Hapsburg court utilized its tapestries. Superseding the traces of medieval allegory discernible in *Los Honores*, the aggressive statements of military supremacy and imperial might expressed in the *Pavia* tapestries were in fact a logical

31 Bernard van Orley, *The Surrender of Francis I* from the *Battle of Pavia* tapestry series, *c.* 1531, wool and silk. Museo Nazionale di Capodimonte, Naples.

development of the earlier works' intimidating political power rather than their iconographic antithesis.

Despite his humiliating defeat at Pavia, as well as a rout at Landriano in 1529, Francis continued his attempts to form a military axis in opposition to the Hapsburg Emperor. By 1534, Charles was becoming increasingly uneasy about the diplomatic and military alliance between Francis and Süleyman the Magnificent. This alliance, established in direct response to the growing military and commercial power of the Hapsburg Empire, was aimed at isolating Charles from unrestricted movement throughout the Mediterranean. Towards the end of 1534, he decided to take military action against this Franco-Ottoman axis, fixing on Tunis on the North African coast as a suitable point at which to fragment the alliance.

Even as Charles made preparations for war, he also made plans for commemorating his actions. In June 1535, he hired Pieter Coecke van Aelst and the artist Jan Cornelisz Vermeyen from Haarlem in the Netherlands to travel with his military retinue and make drawings recording the progress of the campaign, to be turned into tapestries celebrating what he hoped would be a resounding victory. Charles's fleet sailed for Tunis from Cagliari on 14 June led by the imperial admiral Andrea Doria, with four hundred ships and thirty thousand fighting men. By late July, Tunis had fallen to Charles, who ordered its sacking – a deliberately brutal punishment for the fact that the town had refused to surrender. Symbolically, the campaign was a triumph for him, a decisive victory over the increasingly invulnerable Muslim forces and a blow to the international prestige of Francis I (who declined to be drawn into a North African war). Ultimately, however, the expedition achieved very little, as Francis retained his close association with Istanbul, and Süleyman retained close association with North Africa.

For Charles, however, the propaganda value of a victory at Tunis was clear from the moment the expedition was planned; he represented it as a direct attack on the infidel, thereby taking upon himself the role of crusading Holy Roman Emperor. Vermeyen's job making detailed sketches of battle locations and troops was clearly defined – he was, in effect, Charles's personal reporter in the war zone. The technology of the printing press meant that on return from the field, such on-the-spot visual material could be turned into woodcut blocks and marketed throughout Europe, broadcasting the might of the victor and the humiliation of the defeated party. Plans were drawn up for a series of tapestries that would commemorate the capture of Tunis, using Vermeyen's eye-witness drawings, and a room in the imperial palace at Toledo was constructed specially to house its twelve panels. The organization that went into the commissioning of these tapestries was even more exacting than that for Francis's *History of Scipio*. On 15 June 1546, Mary of Austria, Queen of Hungary and sister to Charles, signed a contract with Jan Vermeyen in Brussels for full-scale cartoons from his *Conquest of Tunis* drawings. The amount agreed for these full-sized patterns was 1,900 Flemish pounds – an enormous sum.[43]

Mary also approached Willem de Pannemaker, the leading tapestry maker in Brussels, to manufacture twelve tapestries from Vermeyen's cartoons. The final contract with Pannemaker, drawn up in February 1548, stipulated that only the very best materials were to be used – gold and silver thread and the finest silk thread obtainable from Granada (nothing but Granada silk, either for the crimsons or for any other colour):

The warp of each of the said tapestries is to be made from the best and finest Lyons thread that is manufactured there, and if possible to make a finer selection still, whatever the cost . . . Not to economise on the said Granada silks for the said tapestries, of any colour whatsoever, which is needed. For the borders, when the pattern specifies that gold or silver thread should be used, the said gold or silver thread should be used together with a silk thread, then two other layers of silk should be applied, before getting to the fine sayette. And as for the figures, landscapes, trees and greenery, here also in the same way, after the gold or silver thread, two, three, four or five different silks should be used before getting to the said fine sayette.

   To account carefully for the silver and gold thread which her Majesty will provide, and to use that and no other in the said tapestry, and not to economise on silver and gold thread in any way unless absolutely necessary.[44]

The *Tunis* tapestries were a grandiose project planned as meticulously as the military operation they depicted. Under the terms of his contract, Pannemaker was to subcontract the work to seven fellow master tapestry makers. At least 42 weavers were employed, and the cost of labour and materials was vast. Pannemaker himself was guaranteed an annual pension for life upon satisfactory completion of the series. He was paid a total of around 15,000 Flemish pounds, which included an advance of 6,637 pounds for the silk threads.

   Lavishness was a key element in the *Tunis* commission, reiterated throughout the contract in the quality of the materials and the way they were to be used. Mary's agents authorized the shipment of 559 pounds of Granadan silk threads in 63 different shades. Mary also ordered seven types of gold thread and three types of silver from the Antwerp financier and merchant Jacob Welser. The amounts, types of thread and precise quality were specified in detail. When all the payments are included, the *Tunis* tapestries cost, quite literally, a fortune.

The resulting works are remarkably detailed images that depict every stage of Charles's campaign, from the departure from Barcelona to the disembarkation from Carthage, including precise depictions of the logistics of the whole operation, as well as recognizable portraits of Charles himself and his retinue (illus. 32). The first tapestry (illus. 37) offers an elaborately detailed map of the theatre of operations. At the bottom right of this extraordinary image, the figure of the cartographer holds a cartouche containing the following inscription:

The conquest of Africa in 1535 of Charles the Fifth Holy Roman Emperor and the first king of Spain of that name . . . As it is necessary for a clear understanding to know the country in which the events took place and what preparations had been made, the action is treated in this tapestry according to nature, all that concerns cartography/cosmography, leaving nothing to be desired. In the distance the coasts of Africa, like those of Europe and its boundaries, are seen with their chief ports, their broad gulfs, their islands, their winds, at exactly the same distances at which they really lie, the author having taken more care over their precise situation than over the requirements of painting. All has been done, for the countries as well, in strict accordance with cartography/cosmography, and the painter has observed the canons of his art, considering that the spectator's viewpoint is from Barcelona, where the embarkation for Tunis took place. This town lies between the spectator and the south, with the north behind, over the right shoulder. With accuracy thus established, the peculiarities of the other tapestries can be better understood.[45]

What is so compelling about this use of a cartographic image within such iconographically powerful tapestries is the extent to which cartographic accuracy was combined with aesthetic magnificence to produce an imperial art object that could be both admired and read critically.

The *Tunis* tapestries were particularly remarkable for their radical use of pictorial and geographical space. Whereas previous cycles such as *Los Honores* adopted a static, low-level visual perspective, the *Tunis* tapestries adopted a mobile, high-angled perspective on the events depicted. In this respect, they drew on Macrobius' *Dream of Scipio*,[46] with its similar invocation of a global, god-like perspective. The first tapestry is typical of the ways in which the series adopted this bird's-eye view, a divine perspective intended to bring Charles V's imperial aspirations to mind. This work functioned as both figuration and substance of the ability of Charles and his imperial forces to move through distant space, conquer such space and recover information which could then be transformed into images. The tapestry map therefore depicts imperial triumphalism whilst also manifesting itself as a material embodiment, the substance that emerges from such geographically distant activity. By the time the *Tunis* series had been

84

completed, the victory itself could no longer be regarded as anything other than a symbolic landmark in Charles's imperial fortunes. As art objects, however, the tapestries were sensational masterpieces, whose lavishness and beautiful execution were appropriate monuments to the magnificence of the Hapsburgs. Huge but conveniently portable, they could (and did) travel with the Hapsburg retinue (which was constantly on the move because of the sheer size of the Hapsburg dominions). Those who visited the imperial quarters could be dazzled by the tapestries' splendour whilst at the same time registering, panel by panel, depicted with awesome visual realism, the Emperor's formidable power.

Pannemaker completed the *Tunis* series in April 1554, nearly twenty years after the campaign it depicted so meticulously. The set's completion and delivery were nonetheless events of considerable significance, both culturally and politically. The *Conquest of Tunis* stood (as it had been commissioned to do) for a key moment in the political struggles of the Holy Roman Emperor with the infidel, as well as for the sheer breathtaking wealth and power of the German Imperial line.

In the summer of 1554, the tapestries were packed up in Brussels under the supervision of Simon de Parenty, and their maker Pannemaker accompanied them to London, where they arrived on 3 July. The entire series made its first public appearance at the wedding of Charles V's son Philip II of Spain to Mary Tudor, which took place in Winchester Cathedral on 25 July of the same year.[47]

In England, Philip was a deeply unpopular choice as consort for the Queen regnant. Astutely brokered marriages had consistently been one of the Hapsburgs' most successful means of consolidating their territorial holdings. Philip's first marriage to his first cousin, Maria of Portugal, had already secured him rights to that country (to which he finally laid claim in 1580); no less was to be expected from his marriage to the English Queen. Charles V's personal ambitions to triumph over the Ottoman infidel and to stamp out the heresy of Protestantism in Europe in the name of a Holy Roman Church did not bode well for the country that had lately had two Protestant kings and that now stood to be ruled by Charles's son. The twelve panels of the *Tunis* series narrated, episode by episode, the symbolic enactment of the Hapsburgs' power and their commitment to scourging the infidel (illus. 38). Proudly displayed, its message must have been clearly read by those admitted into the presence of the royal bridegroom. Within the context of this particularly tense political union, Turk was conflated with Protestant, the former symbolically crushed under the hooves of Hapsburg military power, the latter threatened with the same fate if it continued on its path of 'heresy'. The tapestries can have done nothing to allay Protestant English fears concerning the royal union's implications.

The *Tunis* tapestries were a remarkably compelling series, which turned a relatively insignificant military victory into a culturally significant moment in the development of sixteenth-century notions of imperial power. Their abiding power and status as art objects lies in their fusion of a contemporary imperial event with its carefully identified classical analogue. We would argue that their perennial fascination lies in this politically resonant juxtaposition, an oscillation between past and present which remains far more suggestive for us today than either the highly dubious identification of Francis I with Scipio Africanus or the aggressively contemporary imperial ideology displayed in the *Battle of Pavia* tapestries. What was particularly significant about the *Tunis* tapestries was their ability to combine both elements in their vivid endorsement of Charles's imperial power, as well as his ability to wrest the iconographic initiative from Francis.

We have already offered a striking example of Francis's involvement in the competitive acquisition and calculated display of tapestries in the commissioning and exhibition of his *Scipio* tapestries, which were displayed at the *faste* with Henry VIII in 1532. However, if we place those works against Charles's *Tunis* series produced more than twenty years later, we can see that the Hapsburg tapestries were in fact a politically devastating response to the *Scipio* set, which acted as their direct inspiration. Fusing contemporary event with classical analogy, the *Tunis* tapestries take pride of place in the history of sixteenth-century tapestry as the most skillful and terrifying series to emerge from the Low Countries in this period.

Francis's iconographic connection with Scipio Africanus had always been particularly tenuous and potentially rather uncomfortable. The last French commander to lead troops into North Africa, St Louis (in 1370), had met a chaotic end, dying of dysentery with the remnants of his army bought off by the Tunisians.[48] The designs for the first series of *Scipio* tapestries had in fact initially been offered to the more obvious imperial candidate, Charles V.[49] Even in the aftermath of Francis's commission, the Hapsburg court was keen to establish iconographic affinity with Scipio. Whilst the French King possessed the 22-piece *editio princeps*, once they had been completed (as with all such cycles), the master weaver took possession of the cartoons and profited from their reproduction. In 1544, Charles's sister Mary purchased a seven-piece set entitled *The Story of Scipio* from the Fugger agent based in Antwerp, the merchant Erasmus Schatz;[50] this was a reduced set based on Giulio Romano's original cartoons. Mary made this purchase as a direct challenge to Francis, with whom she came into conflict as much around artistic patronage and collecting as around political difference.

Comparing Francis's commissioned tapestries depicting Scipio's much-celebrated victory over an African army at Carthage (illus. 39) with those portraying Charles's own conquest of sixteenth-century Tunis, it is evident that it was the narrative of Scipio upon which the commissioning of the *Tunis* series drew for much of its inspiration. Scipio Africanus' victory in North Africa was all the more poignant for Charles V because it involved careful attention to technical innovations in soldiering and military logistics.[51] Such issues were central to Charles's own imperial adventures not only throughout Europe and Africa but also in the Americas. As we have seen, the *Tunis* tapestries are packed with precise delineations of troop formations and military paraphernalia. The third tapestry in the series (illus. 43) also implicitly compares Charles's military activities to those of Scipio. Depicting the disembarkation before La Goleta, its cartouche reads:

Here they enter the port of Utica; old Carthage receives them in her ruins. The fleet [goes] along the shore. From there the Emperor marches with a small [group] to explore la Goleta, [to] see what fortresses and conditions those spots have. On ordering to disembark they joyfully attack the enemy who retire. He establishes his camp alongside the walls of what in other times was the illustrious Carthage.[52]

Mary was aware that her brother Charles valued models of military initiative and imperial decorum as defining principles of his reign. As a result, she appears to have been anxious to deny Francis any claim to Scipio and his triumphs (illus. 41) and to ensure that his military exploits were seen as more in line with those of Charles. It was Charles of course who could more legitimately claim some relation to Scipio, possessing as he did the title of Holy Roman Emperor.

Upon his return to Italy in August 1535 following his successful campaign in Tunis, Charles embarked on a triumphal progress of the type depicted in the second half of the *Scipio* tapestries. His entry into Messina in Sicily emphasized the global aspirations he encouraged in the wake of his victory. Two triumphal chariots led the way to the cathedral:

On one six Moors were bound prisoner at the foot of an alter laden with trophies, on the second, larger car stood the four cardinal Virtues, while angels revolved two hemispheres bearing the constellations. Above, a globe of the world turned, on which there stood the emperor crowned and bearing a Victory in his hand . . . These visions of a crusading emperor were elaborated at a solemn mass the next day. Suspended above the nave of the cathedral was a model of Constantinople with the Turkish arms over it. After the Gospel had been read an amazed congregation saw an imperial eagle soar through the air and lead an attack on the city in the middle of which, when the Turkish arms had been vanquished, a cross suddenly appeared.[53]

In the subsequent entry into Naples in November 1535, a series of canvases decorating a triumphal arch offered historical analogies which, Roy Strong has argued, were part of a specifically Hapsburg fashioning of a definably new perception of imperial authority: 'The historical parallels which the taking of Goletta and Tunis and the flight of Barbarossa evoked were humanist ones of Scipio Africanus, Hannibal, Alexander the Great and Julius Caesar, and not those of medieval crusading rulers.'[54] Following in Scipio's footsteps upon his entry into Rome in 1536, Charles passed the refurbished Arch of Constantine, where he stopped (it is recorded) to study some temporary arches designed by Battista Franco. These were draped with canvases depicting the triumphs of Scipio Major and Minor, celebrating Charles as the 'Tertio Africano',[55] an analogy echoed in the

33 Pieter van Aelst, *The Calling of the Apostles* from the *Acts of the Apostles* tapestry series, *c.* 1519, wool, silk, gold and silver. Vatican.

34 Pieter van Aelst, *Fortune* from the *Los Honores* tapestry series, *c.* 1519, wool and silk. Patrimonio Nacional, Madrid.

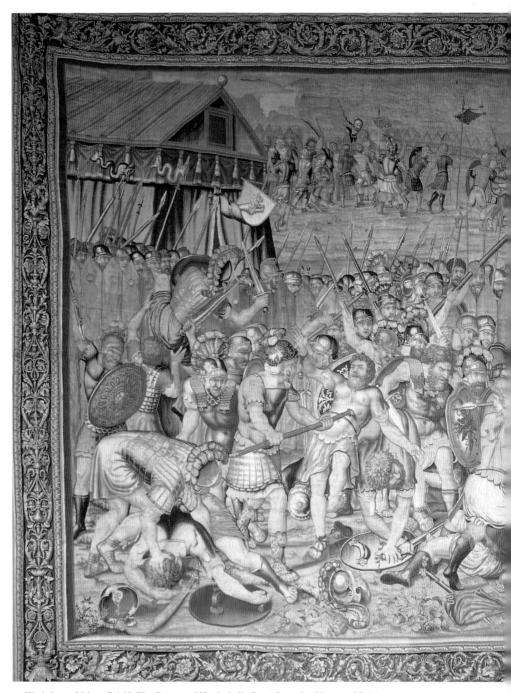

35 Workshop of Marc Crétif, *The Capture of Hasdrubal's Camp* from the *History of Scipio Africanus* tapestry series, *c.* 1532, wool, silk, gold and silver. Patrimonio Nacional, Madrid.

36 *The Assembly of the Troops* from the *David and Bathsheba* tapestry series, *c.* 1528, wool, silk, gold and silver. Musée de la Renaissance, Ecouen.

Hauiendo basteadin Barbarosa Capitan general de mar de Solymanno principe de los Turcos con vna armada de ciento y de otra gran parte de Aphrica con tan graue y euidente peligro de lo mas de la Christandad que fue necessario que el minado en la prosecucion della ordeno que el armada que el Rey de portugal su cuñado mando hazer en lisbona de carauelas o tiempo al Marqs de Mondejar cõ el armada hecha en Malaga en que venia nueue mill Españoles y las galeras de España El prin hecho en Italia y el Marqs del gasto cõ cargo que tenya de su M. de recoger las tenyedo en ellas seys mill alemães quatro mill e

Map labels:
MAR DE
MAR DE AOFFRICA
MAR DE ITALIA
SICILIA
MAR DE FRANCIA

Bottom cartouche (Latin):
IMPIA TVRCARVM CVPIENS CONTVNDERE C[...]
ARMA VIRVMQ. SIMVL SOLYMANI IVSSA SEQV[...]
ET PROCVL HESPERIAE REGNIS FERA BELLA M[...]

37 Willem de Pannemaker, *The Mediterranean* from the *Conquest of Tunis* tapestry series, 1548–54, wool, silk, gold and silver. Patrimonio Nacional, Madrid.

…echo mucho daño en algunas costas de Christianos: occupo el reyno de Tunes hasiendo se pacifico yabsoluto señor del
…arlo v. Rey de Espanna se opusiesse a estas nueuas fuercas y por su persona dixesse orden atan gran expedicio. y deter
…consu Capitan antonjo de saldaña vinicse en Barcelona. como a lugar mas apto a esta enbarcacion. Mando venyr ally al mesmo
…rtiendo de genoua co diez y seis galeras suyas llega a Barcelona despues de hauer ordenado las otras armadas que se hauia
…ados viejos cinco mill Italianos tocado en Napoles y sicilia llego en la Jsla de cerdeña cerca del cabo pola dode espero la llegada del emp

MAR ATHLANTICO

MAR DE BERVERIA

MAR OCCIDENTALE

Etne cho... de gebel...

Cuera de legua.
Cuera de millas

38 Willem de Pannemaker, *The Sack of Tunis* from the *Conquest of Tunis* tapestry series, 1548–54, wool, silk, gold and silver. Patrimonio Nacional, Madrid.

39 Workshop of Marc Crétif, *The Battle of Zama* from the *History of Scipio Africanus* series *c.* 1532, wool, silk, gold and silver. Patrimonio Nacional, Madrid.

40 Jehan Baudouyn, *The Triumphal Cortège* from the *Fructus Belli* tapestry series, *c.* 1545, wool and silk. Musées Royaux d'Art et d'Histoire, Brussels.

41 Workshop of Marc Crétif, *The Triumph of Scipio* from the *History of Scipio Africanus* tapestry series, *c.* 1532, wool, silk, gold and silver. Patrimonio Nacional, Madrid.

42 Pasquier
Grenier, Detail of
The Siege of Asilah
from the *Feats of
Arms of Alfonso V
of Portugal* tapestry
series, *c.* 1475, wool
and silk. Sacristy,
Collegiate Church,
Pastrana, Spain.

43 Willem de Pannemaker, *Landing Off the Cape of Carthage* from the *Conquest of Tunis*
tapestry series, 1548–54, wool, silk, gold and silver. Patrimonio Nacional, Madrid.

44 Workshop of Jean Grenier, *The Giraffe Caravan* from the *Voyage to Calicut* tapestry series, *c.* 1502, wool and silk. Banco Nacional Ultramarino, Lisbon.

HIC EST ILLVSTR
13·DE·EPO·VODEGO
SEXAGINTA·MILIE

45 Attributed to
Bartholomaeus
Adriaensz., *The
Triumph of João
de Castro* from the
*Acts of João de
Castro* tapestry
series, *c.* 1550,
wool and silk.
Kunsthistorisches
Museum, Vienna.

DANIS·DE·CASTRO·INDIE·PARTIS·GUBER·NATORIS
ATE·TRIVPHVS·SVBSTRATIS·REGIS·CABAIE
TIBVS·CV·QVIBVSDA·NOBILIBVS·ACT·V·1538·

46 *Elephant* from the *Valois Tapestries*, *c.* 1581, wool and silk. Galleria degli Uffizi, Florence.

47 *Fontainebleau* from the *Valois Tapestries*, *c.* 1581, wool and silk.
Galleria degli Uffizi, Florence.

reference to Charles as 'Caesar Africano' by Garcilaso de la Vega, the Inca/Spanish *mestizo* poet who accompanied the Tunis expedition.[56] Five years later, this renewed image of Charles as the conquering emperor reached its apogee in sketches for his triumphal entry into Milan. Giulio Romano's design for a triumphal arch portrayed Charles on a rearing mount (illus. 48), combining classical equestrian iconography (identified via Scipio Africanus) with contemporary conquest, as a Moor, a Native American and a Turk were trampled under the horse's hoofs. This is an image to which we will return in chapter 3.

Charles's triumphal tour through Italy in the wake of his victory at Tunis represents a deliberate reappropriation of the figure of Scipio, whose mantle had been temporarily and tenuously claimed by Francis with his commissioning of the *Scipio* tapestries. The delay between the completion of the Tunis campaign and the initial stages of the commissioning of the *Tunis* tapestries in 1544 suggests that the earlier set provided the Hapsburg court with the model for the later one. It is clearly no coincidence that in the same year in which Mary of Hungary successfully completed the purchase of a set of *Scipio* tapestries based on Francis's *editio princeps*, she also began to plan the commissioning of the *Tunis* tapestries.

Francis's attempt to appropriate Scipio was in many ways a piece of allegory executed in bad faith. At least Charles had the real-life basis for creating tapestries whose contemporary political significance

48 Giulio Romano, Woodcut showing the triumphal arch for Charles V's entry into Milan, 1541.

was based on direct political analogy to events, not the elaborate allegorical and iconographic readings that have been applied to them by later interpreters.

Nor did the impact of the *Scipio* tapestries end there. In the winter of 1544–5, Ferrante Gonzaga, Duke of Ariano and son of Francesco II Gonzaga, commissioned a series of eight tapestries entitled *Fructus Belli* (illus. 40) from the Brussels workshop of Jehan Baudouyn. Ferrante had established himself as one of Charles V's most trusted lieutenants on the battlefield, in 1527 leading the imperial forces during the sack of Rome (where he took possession of several Papal tapestries). Named to the Order of the Golden Fleece in 1531, he fought alongside Charles at the conquest of Tunis in 1535 (for which he was rewarded with the exclusive rights to alum mining in Sicily). As Clifford Brown and Guy Delmarcel have pointed out, the cartoons for Ferrante's tapestries can be attributed to Giulio Romano and bear a close resemblance to his *Scipio* designs for Francis I, created nearly two decades earlier.[57] The eighth tapestry in Ferrante's series, *Reward and Punishment* (illus. 49), showing Charles dispensing crowns to his generals, reproduces the image of Scipio distributing crowns after the siege of Carthage in the fourth tapestry of the *Scipio* series. The *Fructus Belli* tapestries also bear striking similarities to reliefs designed

49 Jehan Baudouyn, *Reward and Punishment* from the *Fructus Belli* tapestry series, *c.* 1545, wool and silk. West Dean College, Chichester.

by Giulio for Federico II's Palazzo del Te in Mantua in the late 1520s.[58]

The first recorded mention of the *Fructus Belli* tapestries comes from the description of a banquet held by Ferrante on New Year's Day 1549, at the Villa Gualtiera on the outskirts of Milan, in honour of Charles's son, Philip II. The cycle is described as 'rich pieces of tapestry on which, with subtle art and great skill, were represented all the facets of military life and the art of war and what usually happens to a warrior prince and a great captain'.[59] As *The Triumphal Cortège* panel illustrates, the *Fructus Belli* series appears to consist of a heavily moralized, transhistorical portrayal of politics and warfare. However, as with the artistic creations of Gozzoli and Holbein, the *Fructus Belli* tapestries are artful designs which counterpoint the development of empire elsewhere. They capture a particularly poignant moment as the Gonzaga dynasty literally hitched its colours to the mast of Hapsburg magnificence and conquest. This is reflected in the self-conscious display of the Order of the Golden Fleece, hanging as it does from the coat of arms woven into the apex of the tapestry, with its central portrayal of Ferrante as triumphal commander.

IV

As with the *Tunis* series, the *Fructus Belli* tapestries emerged from detailed and painstaking negotiations between their aspirant imperial clients and the workshops of Brussels. The production of both sets – the former series fusing contemporary event to artistic design, the latter series derivatively 'quoting' from the former set – illustrate the ways in which the Hapsburgs utilized the workshops of the Low Countries as a way of placing their imperial imprint upon tapestry production itself. As Brussels and especially Antwerp functioned as the brokers of imperial and financial power (commercial locations where Charles bankrolled his entire imperial operation), it is hardly surprising that the tapestries emerged from these locations, graphically displaying the scope of Hapsburg power and authority.

In effect, the imperial courts of Europe defined a dimension of their authority through the ability to control not only the designs that emerged from the tapestry workshops of the Low Countries but also the means of production themselves. In the same way that the ability to vividly represent geographically distant phenomena provided an index of imperial authority and purchasing power (as in the case of Charles's *Tunis* series), the ability to fashion such images through control and manipulation of workshops in distant Brussels proved even more compelling. As the *entrepôt* of early modern Europe, the Low

Countries provided the raw materials and workmanship required to fashion images of imperial power and authority, although such power lay unevenly distributed elsewhere, in Lisbon, Seville, Milan and Constantinople.

Charles V's financial power and military authority ensured that his control over the means of tapestry production exceeded all competing imperial attempts to manipulate the industry. As his grip became stronger, the courts of Henry VIII, John III and Francis I put even greater store by their Low Countries tapestries, as it remained possible to commission works that offered some challenge, however nominal, to Hapsburg imperial hegemony. In 1544, two years before his sister Mary of Hungary commissioned the *Tunis* series, Charles formulated a series of prescriptive laws to regulate the weaving industry throughout the Low Countries. The first article forbad the production of works woven without the prior approval of an appointed corporation of tapestry weavers. Subsequent weavings were subject to the regulations of the corporation, which specified the quality of material and workmanship, down to insisting upon the use of woollen thread for the warp from Lyons, Spain or Aragon, and the weaving of the master's mark into the base. The regulations also insisted that each tapestry must be woven in a single piece. As W. G. Thomson has pointed out, whilst such initiatives were undoubtedly designed to stamp out abuses in the industry, they also contributed to its ultimate decline:

> . . . the weavers had been able to get through more work, and could contract with their clients at a cheaper rate, than when working under the rules of the ordinance. The effects of these restrictions must have been paralysing to workshops of the cheaper sort . . . The low or '*basse*' loom made its appearance felt at this time, giving quicker results and yet in accordance with the ordinance. This haste was the ruin of the finer work of Brussels.[60]

As the Hapsburg authorities sought to leave their imperial stamp upon the means by which tapestries were produced, a decline in weaving set in as a result of the crushing of entrepreneurial diversity amongst smaller workshops. As we shall see, this decline became terminal with the increase in religious persecution through the 1560s.

What this account of imperial contestation over tapestries emphasizes is the extent to which they need to be read as politically and visually overdetermined material objects. We have argued that they openly display the marks of their commercial value and skilful construction as objects whose preciousness made them suitable candidates through which figures like Charles and Francis could give voice to their competing claims to political supremacy.[61] Tapestries such as the *Story of Scipio* were not mysteriously imbued with some classically derived iconographic value, as Panofsky would seem to suggest. Instead, their encoded meanings were appropriated and fought over by competing political figures. The transactions that gave meaning and value to such objects were in turn utilized by tapestry firms in an attempt to secure wider and more lucrative markets, markets which, we argue, extended beyond the boundaries of Renaissance Europe as defined by Hale and, implicitly, Panofsky. To illustrate our point, we offer two particularly telling examples of both the global reach of tapestries and the extent to which their transactions give a compelling account of international communities in both East and West utilizing each other's artistic production.

Our first example is taken from tapestries commissioned for the Portuguese court in Lisbon. The strategic deployment of Low Countries tapestries by the Hapsburgs had already been anticipated in the ways in which the House of Avis had used such works as part of its own increasingly global pretensions. As early as the 1470s, the Portuguese king Alfonso V had commissioned huge cycles of narrative tapestries from the workshops of Tournai. By 1475, the Tournai weaver Pasquier Grenier had completed a series known as the *Feats of Arms of Alfonso V of Portugal* (illus. 42), which depicted Alfonso's military expedition against Muslims in Morocco in 1471.[62] Known as 'The African', Alfonso's victory at the strategically crucial port of Asilah was particularly significant for the seaborne expansion of the Portuguese empire and resulted in his styling himself 'King of Portugal and of Algarve on this and on the other side of the sea in Africa'.[63] Whilst the topography and military paraphernalia of the tapestries is self-consciously contemporary, their design and iconography are almost identical to those of contemporary tapestries depicting the Trojan War, which emerged from the same workshops and which by the end of the fifteenth century were adorning virtually every significant court in Renaissance Europe.[64] The *Feats of Arms of Alfonso V* seems designed to invoke a classical model interwoven with the striking modernity of Portugal's imperial exploits in Africa, prelude to even greater accomplishments.

In 1504, King Manuel of Portugal commissioned a series entitled *The Voyage to Calicut* from the Tournai tapestry maker Gilles le Castre. These tapestries were intended to celebrate Portugal's eagerly anticipated breaching of the boundaries of the classical *ecumene*, its establishment of a sea route to India via the Cape of Good Hope in the aftermath of Vasco da Gama's first voyage in 1498 and Cabral's 'discovery' of Brazil in 1500. Le Castre's work, much in demand, was sold through the shop of Arnold Poissonier, who in 1510 also sold an

'Indian'-inspired tapestry, Gilles's *Gens et Bests Sauvages*, to Emperor Maximilian I. Poissonier was also responsible for selling a set entitled *Voyage de Caluce* to Robert Wytfel, Counsellor of Henry VIII, in 1513, as the English King laid claim to the town as part of his French dominions.[65] As with the *Feats of Arms of Alfonso V*, part of the appeal of the *Calicut* series lay in its invocation of the history of Alexander the Great and his encounters with the mysteries of the Orient.

As well as offering a strikingly contemporary gloss on the history of Alexander, however, the *Calicut* series also presents us with another graphic image of artistic exchange between East and West (as Phyllis Ackerman has pointed out), by drawing very specifically on Indian iconography. In one of the panels, *The Lion Hunt* (illus. 50), Ackerman noted of the representation of hunting, horsemanship and dress that

> . . . the turbans are gross distortions of the elegant Persian mode but they do show some knowledge of it, for the hunter . . . has a pointed *kulah* that is only a little wrong in form. Again, the hunter on the left has a short sleeved tunic of a type which was a fashion in Persia at the moment and the high soft boots that a number of them wear were a current Persian mode, too. The saddle blankets on Gilles' horses are ridiculously exaggerated but the Eastern horses did wear large saddle blankets . . . and the curb bits which are so conspicuous in the tapestry are typically Eastern. Even the conformation of the horses, with the heavy barrel, excessively long, thin neck and small head repeats that of contemporary Persian representations.[66]

As with Gozzoli's *Adoration of the Magi*, the focus on hunting, horsemanship and livestock suggests a profound fascination with the

50 Gilles le Castre, *The Lion Hunt* from the *Voyage to Calicut* tapestry series, *c.* 1502, wool and silk. Private collection.

objects and practices held in common between the Eastern and Western empires. If we read the *Calicut* tapestries as similarly porous images, they become less definably 'oriental' and more recognizably global currency in the transacting of cultural and imperial identity between East and West.[67] In this respect, the Portuguese court was as alert to such transactions as commissioners of tapestries in Florence, Paris or Seville. Our argument here is that this awareness was so pervasive that it extended well beyond Ottoman-Christian exchanges, also affecting Moghul and Persian encounters of a truly global nature (something we will see emerge again in Indo-Portuguese transactions over horses).

By 1525, the Portuguese court had commissioned a series of three tapestries to commemorate the Portuguese King John III's marriage to the Hapsburg Princess Catherine of Austria. Entitled *The Spheres*, this remarkable set showed the astrological, celestial and terrestrial worlds, with the final tapestry exhibiting the global pretensions of an increasingly powerful Portuguese maritime empire.[68] At the same time as the Portuguese set the terms for visual innovation in such designs, subsequent sets commissioned by the Avis court suggest that they were alive to the circulation of images at the Hapsburg, Valois and Tudor courts. Following the Portuguese commander Dom João de Castro's successful siege of the Indian coastal port of Diu in Gujarat in 1547, the Portuguese court commissioned a massive ten-piece tapestry set designed to celebrate this famous victory, based on cartoons attributed to Michiel Coxie, who also designed a now lost set of cartoons (dated *c.* 1550) depicting Charles V's victories in Saxony.[69] The magnificent *Acts of João de Castro* (illus. 45) were woven in the Brussels workshop of Bartholomaeus Adriaensz. The series clearly took its inspiration from Francis's *Scipio* and Charles's *Tunis* series, as well as anticipating Ferrante's *Fructus Belli* tapestries in their dramatic sweep and vivid attention to military detail.

These tapestries, all commissioned and woven in the Low Countries, are testimony to the power of the Portuguese seaborne empire to create a vision of its power and authority over geographically distant cultures through recourse to both a legitimating classical past and the relatively novel techniques of tapestry production. Yet as with the *Tunis* series, the *Acts* offer increasingly strident images of imperial authority which cash in their two-way legibility between East and West in favour of a more overtly aggressive image of military superiority and territorial possession over and against the East. This stance becomes dominant in graphic images of the latter half of the sixteenth century. Tapestries' transactive status nonetheless remained embedded in their very fabric. Themselves made up of raw materials extracted by the Portuguese from the East, they are also visually compelling *objects* of Portuguese encounters there, in particular in India.[70]

If these Portuguese tapestries offer a model of the ways in which the material and artistic practices of the East are woven into the fabric of their design, then our other example emphasizes the ways in which transactions could also flow in the other direction. In 1533, one of the draughtsmen for the *Tunis* series, Pieter Coecke van Aelst, was employed by the van der Moyen tapestry firm, makers of the *Scipio* tapestries subsequently purchased by Mary of Hungary, to undertake a speculative commercial journey to Istanbul. The firm's aim was to try and interest Süleyman the Magnificent in commissioning tapestries and hangings. According to the contemporary German chronicler Karel van Mander, van Aelst was to go to Istanbul and make drawings of the kinds of scene used as designs for tapestries: 'The Van den Moeyen firm intended to establish a trade and make rich carpets and hangings for the Great Turk, and to this end they employed Peter Coeck to paint divers things to be shewn to the Turkish Emperor.'[71] On a personal level, van Aelst did not do badly out of the venture, according to another contemporary account:

Peter of Aelst published some remarkable drawings of the life and manners of the Turks, which he had studied at Constantinople. There, for his rare skill in his art, he was so highly esteemed by the Emperor Suleiman, that that potentate, forgetting the law of his Koran, desired to have his portrait painted by him. By the royal bounty of Solyman's own hand, Peter was dismissed with honourable gifts, a ring, a jewel, horses, robes, gold, and servants, which at Bruxelles he converted into an annual pension.[72]

Having already profited from the imperial rivalry between Francis and Charles, van Aelst and the van der Moyen firm were clearly happy to establish a trade in luxury goods with Istanbul. As van Aelst's beautiful engraving of Süleyman riding through the Hippodrome in Istanbul with his entourage emphasizes (illus. 51), these were cartoons designed as studies for tapestries, powerfully broadcasting the military might and imperial grandeur of the Ottomans. Our analysis of the permeable nature of the political and artistic boundaries between East and West suggests that this was not simply an unprincipled attempt to sell sumptuous but iconographically incomprehensible tapestries to the Ottoman court. Rather, it showed an astute understanding of the shared imperial and iconographic preoccupations of the courts based in Paris, Brussels, Lisbon, London and Istanbul, skilfully (if ultimately unsuccessfully) manipulated by a firm, and designer, situated at the nexus of the European tapestry industry.

51 Pieter Coecke van Aelst, *Procession of Sultan Süleyman II through the Atmedan* (left-hand side), woodcut from *Ces Moeurs et fachons de faire de Turcz . . .*, 1533.

The tapestries we have analyzed so far shed sharp light on the investments made in production throughout the sixteenth century by all the aspirant imperial powers of Renaissance Europe. These cycles all announce urgent and aggressive claims to authority, whether imperial, religious or commercial dominion over those who viewed such overwhelming images at various crucial places and moments in the lives of the various courts with which they became associated. Despite their size, the portability of such tapestries allowed them to be packed up and exhibited in different locations at different times, thus permitting their imagery to take on a range of connotations at varying moments.

Thus the *Tunis* tapestries were a vivid image of Charles's imperial power and authority throughout Central and Southern Europe. But viewed by the English court at the dynastic alliance of the Hapsburg Philip's marriage to Mary Tudor, they took on an added religious significance. Whilst many of these tapestries share close iconographic similarities, as has been pointed out by several art historians,[73] our concern here is to emphasize the political distinctions that led to significant differences in the ways in which such items were commissioned and displayed, as a way of complicating standard iconographically based readings of such cycles. In this respect, the relationship between Francis I's *Scipio* series and Charles V's *Tunis* tapestries tells us that the superior military power of the Hapsburg empire allowed Charles to produce a series that effortlessly attracted iconographic associations (such as the identifications with Scipio Africanus). However, these tapestries were more specifically focused on disseminating a politically and militarily enhanced image of Charles, an image based upon a series of successful, if limited, military and political objectives. The Portuguese court was similarly focused upon its attempt to fashion a recognizably imperial image of its maritime power and overseas influence with tapestries of the stature of *The Spheres* and *Acts of João de Castro*.

The Portuguese series seemed as determined to offer an identifiably global currency legible to rival international communities (such as the Hapsburg, the Valois and the Ottomans) as they were to match Portugal's maritime expansion to that of the Roman Empire. However, the attempts by the Valois court, and Francis I in particular, to broadcast a similarly compelling image of imperial power was far more tenuous and disingenuous. Francis's imperial self-fashioning, in paintings and portrait medals as well as in tapestries, was a highly speculative attempt to inhabit iconographically compelling roles which bore little relation to his imperial stature in the face of the global power of his arch-rival Charles.

Francis's death in 1547 and Charles's abdication in favour of Philip II in 1555 left Europe riven by religious division and political conflict, one of the consequences of the contestation over political authority that had characterized the relations between the courts of early sixteenth-century Europe and that was given vivid expression in their carefully chosen tapestry collections. By the 1550s, tapestry production had been decisively expropriated for the announcement of political and dynastic power, a development that was to have significant consequences for the weaving industry itself. To elaborate and emphasize this point, we examine finally what is considered to be one of the last great series of tapestries produced in the Low Countries in the face of the 'Spanish Fury' unleashed on Antwerp in November 1576.

V

The *Valois Tapestries*, currently in the Uffizi Gallery in Florence, emerged from the workshops of the Low Countries as warfare and religious persecution effectively ended one of the most influential periods in the history of the medium. The series is composed of eight huge tapestries, most measuring approximately four metres in height and up to six metres in width. Their subjects are the elaborate court festivals, or 'magnificences', that punctuated Valois court life throughout the 1560s and '70s. Compositionally, all eight foreground the main members of the Valois dynasty against the backdrop of these court spectaculars. The designs have been attributed to a series of six drawings by the French artist Antoine Caron, undertaken between 1560 and 1570.

The innovative addition in the foreground of key figures in the Valois dynasty, presided over by Catherine de' Medici, widow of Henry II, son of Francis I, marks a significant difference between Caron's cartoons and the tapestries themselves; however Catherine appears in all eight tapestries, overseeing events from the margins in the same way that she influenced crucial aspects of French political life from her husband's death in 1559 until her own in 1589. The tapestries' subjects are drawn from particularly crucial festivals organized under her political auspices. The first of these, which took place at Fontainebleau in 1564, has been seen as Catherine's attempt to mediate in the open warfare that had broken out between Catholic and Huguenot factions, and that had only been uneasily quelled as a result of the Edict of Amboise (March 1563). The Fontainebleau Festival brought together both factions in apparent harmony, which is represented in the first tapestry of the series, entitled *Fontainebleau* (illus. 47). This work portrays the future King Henry III and his young wife, Louise de Lorraine, in the foreground, set against the elaborate tournaments and fêtes that characterized the festival. The Fontainebleau event was closely followed by the Bayonne Festivals held in the summer of 1565. Ostensibly designed to celebrate the christening of the son of Catherine's daughter Claude, married to Duke Charles III of Lorraine, Bayonne in fact provided the opportunity for Catherine to meet her daughter Elizabeth and the latter's husband, King Philip II of Spain. Catherine had hoped to extend the Valois' dynastic influence by arranging marriages between her own children and Philip's. The Hapsburg King had different ideas and sent his emissary the Duke of Alva to persuade Catherine to enforce the Council of Trent and scrap the religious toleration of the Edict of Amboise.

The backdrop for the tense political stalemate played out at Bayonne was the spectacular tournaments that make up the foreground of the second tapestry. Simply entitled *Tournament*, this work portrays Catherine with her daughter Marguerite de Valois and Marguerite's husband Henry of Navarre, with her daughter-in-law Louise. The crowning achievement of Catherine's festivals, and portrayed in the series, was the event held at the Tuileries in Paris in August 1563 to celebrate the arrival of Polish ambassadors on a diplomatic mission to offer her son Henry the crown of Poland. The fifth tapestry in the series, entitled *Polish Ambassadors*, offers this highpoint in Catherine's troubled reign as regent and then Queen Mother in the form of an elaborate spectacle.[74]

Despite the clearly intimate relationship between these tapestries and Caron's drawings of Catherine's magnificences, the series remains enigmatic. There is no firm evidence as to who commissioned or wove it. It nonetheless provided the foundation for one of the most remarkable pieces of scholarly detection in Renaissance studies: Frances Yates's remarkable *The Valois Tapestries*, first published by the Warburg Institute in 1959. Yates controversially dated the tapestries to 1582, arguing that the beleaguered William of Nassau, Prince of Orange, commissioned them as a diplomatic gift for Catherine de' Medici. Yates claimed that William presented the set in order to influence her and her son Henry to support his younger brother, François-Hercule, Duc d'Alençon-Anjou, in the struggle against the Spanish in the Low Countries.

Anjou's prominent position throughout the series, especially in the two final tapestries, *Barriers* and *Elephant* (illus. 46), in which he stands at the right holding the hand of his sister Marguerite, is, according to Yates, emblematic of his cultivation by William of Orange and Protestant factions in Antwerp. His elevation is as dramatic as the occlusion of the king who actually presided over the festivals at Fontainebleau, Bayonne and Paris for the entry of the Polish ambassadors – Charles IX, King of France from 1560 until his premature death through illness in 1574. Yates points out that whilst the background festivals emanated from Catherine's careful manipulation of magnificences which took place during Charles's reign, the foreground figures reflect the state of the Valois dynasty in 1582, the time of the tapestries' production.[75] According to Yates, Charles was virtually erased from the tapestries due to his decision to sanction the Massacre of St Bartholomew's Day, 24 August 1572, which horrified the Huguenots and set back William's plans for a pan-European Protestant alliance several years. This 'obliteration of the scapegoat for the massacre'[76] is, Yates argues, obvious if the tapestries are interpreted as a Protestant cry for help, aimed at a Valois court determined to resist the religious intolerance personified by the Catholic power of Philip II and the Duke of Alva. For Yates,

The world of the tapestries is a free world, or a would-be free world, in which festivals are preferred to the Inquisition and a wide outlook on the theatre of the world in all its variety is preferred to a narrow rigidity. It is also, in a sense, a world deliberately returning to a Burgundian type of chivalric magnificence as a counterpoise to the narrowness of persecuting orthodoxy. This was exactly the spirit which William of Orange tried to encourage when he placed the French Valois prince, François d'Anjou, in the position of ruler of the Southern Netherlands which his long campaigns had at last freed from Spanish tyranny.[77]

According to this interpretation, the tapestries become a series of enlightened, almost utopian visions of a European polity defined by religious toleration and political liberalism. They portray festivity and laughter, the mingling of Catholic and Protestant, and costumes and customs of many nations with the tolerant union of Poland and France lying at the harmonious centre.[78]

This vision of religious and political concord was made all the more poignant by the speed with which the projected world of the tapestries sketched by Yates dramatically unravelled. In February 1582, William of Orange achieved his long-cherished political objective as he witnessed Anjou enter Antwerp and accept the title of Duke of Brabant.[79] Faced with the Duke of Parma's advancing army, Anjou planned a reckless coup to take complete control of the town in January 1583.[80] Unfortunately, his poorly equipped and disorganized army was routed by local resistance, and Anjou fled the city, dying in dishonour in France just two years later. William of Orange never recovered the initiative from Anjou's disastrous actions and was assassinated at Delft in 1583. Antwerp yielded to the Spaniards in 1585, and as France descended into religious chaos, Catherine herself died in January 1589. Henry III was assassinated in August of the same year.

For Yates, the *Valois Tapestries* represented a beacon of benign cultural and religious diversity, prior to Europe's slide into religious fundamentalism, political intolerance and vicious ethnic cleansing. Sadly neglected by subsequent cultural historians, her study is a brilliant account of the extent to which, by the latter half of the sixteenth century, narrative tapestries were recognized as complex but powerful representations of political power and authority. However, the implications of our own analysis lead us to offer a radically different interpretation of the significance of the *Valois Tapestries* to that offered by Yates. Several scholars have already revised some of her basic assumptions. Roy Strong has questioned her crucial argument that the tapestries were produced in Antwerp under the supervision of Lucas de Heere, despite their Brussels markings.[81] R. J. Knecht has criticized Yates's heavily idealized portrayal of

Catherine de' Medici as an Erasmian, noting that the Valois were far more circumspect about being drawn into support for the Protestant Low Countries. He has also pointed out that evidence suggests that, following the Massacre of St Bartholomew's Day, both Catherine and Henry III were far more receptive to the political overtures of Philip II than those of William of Orange.[82]

In uniting this renewed historical perspective with our analysis of earlier tapestries, we would suggest that the *Valois Tapestries* are much more aggressive images of dynastic power than Yates would concede. What our analysis tells us is that the nature of such images is to broadcast the power of their owners, not provide 'politique' advice, as Yates suggests. Yates makes no reference to this earlier tradition, despite the extensive collection of Francis I's own tapestries, as well as the fact that the villain of her study, the Duke of Alva, also possessed an impressive collection of military tapestries. These included a smaller set of the *Tunis* series, ordered by Alva (a key figure in the Tunis victory) in the 1550s; a composite tapestry of the Tunis victory dated to 1568;[83] and an imposing series entitled *Victories of the Duke of Alba* woven in the Low Countries in the 1560s.[84] A line of descent can thus be drawn from Alva's threatening tapestries through Charles V's *Tunis* tapestries, right back to the aggressive assertions of Burgundian dynastic authority represented by the early fifteenth-century tapestries of Duke Philip the Good. In this respect, Yates's claim that the *Valois Tapestries* evoke 'a Burgundian type of chivalric magnificence as a counterpoise to the narrowness of persecuting orthodoxy' is particularly ironic. It betrays an idealized perception of the Burgundian court from which the Hapsburg empire of Charles V had learnt all it could about thepolitically calculated value of tapestries.

Nor was this deployment of tapestries as strategic imperial currency lost on the Valois court. As we have seen, Francis I was himself adroit (if ultimately unsuccessful) in his deployment of tapestries. However, this tradition did not end with him. The artist responsible for the cartoons upon which the *Valois Tapestries* were designed, Antoine Caron, had already executed several highly finished drawings specifically for their incorporation into tapestries prior to those he made of Catherine's festivities.[85] Perhaps most significant for our purposes is his series of 28 drawings done between 1560 and 1574, entitled *Histoire Françoyse de nostre temps*. Dedicated to Catherine, these drawings trace the exploits of the Valois from the reign of Francis I to that of Charles IX.[86] Ten refer to Francis's reign, and two deal with Catherine's marriage to Henry II, celebrated in October 1533. This union was brokered by Francis to form an alliance with Pope Clement VII, in the vain hope of fracturing the latter's alliance with Charles V and with the more optimistic hope of gaining territorial concessions from him regarding French claims to Brazil (encapsulated in the terrestrial globe that we analyzed in Holbein's *Ambassadors*).

Caron's second drawing of the marriage ceremony records the exchanges of gifts between the Pope and Francis (illus. 52). This remarkable composition shows Francis presenting Clement with an unfurled tapestry clearly modelled on Leonardo da Vinci's *Last Supper*. Here Caron provides a telling impression of Francis announcing his ability to commission lavish tapestries depicting religious subjects, which are then presented to the Pope himself at a moment when the cementing of dynastic alliances through marriage and the making of artistic claims to an aggressive imperialism come together in a single powerful image.

We would therefore argue that the coded meaning of the *Valois Tapestries* owes more to the tradition of the great court tapestries of the previous hundred years than to the enlightened and tolerant political outlook ascribed to William of Orange and Catherine de' Medici. Viewed from this perspective, they become deeply threatening. The carefree world of festivals identified by Yates starts to look much

52 Antoine Caron, *The Gifts*, drawing from *Histoire Françoyse de nostre temps*, 1560–74, ink on paper. Musée du Louvre, Paris.

more menacing in its elaborate scenes of combat, troop movements and rearing war-horses when these compositions are compared with the freely circulating images associated with the *Conquest of Tunis* and the *Victories of the Duke of Alba*. Yates surprisingly failed to identify the extent to which the designer of the *Valois Tapestries* borrowed extensively from Francis's celebration of ancient military might and imperial triumphalism, the *History of Scipio* tapestries. However, the *Scipio* tapestries remained part of the fabric of the Valois court; in his *Eloge de François Ier*, P. de Bourdeille, Abbé de Brantôme, records their strategic presence at the Bayonne meeting between Catherine and Alva. De Brantôme recalls seeing

> ... the *Triumph of Scipio*, which one often saw hung in large rooms for important holidays and assemblages [and which] cost 22,000 *écus* at that time – which was a lot. Today one could not get it for 50,000 *écus*, as I have heard said, because it is entirely made of gold and silk. It is the best illustrated, and the characters the best executed, ever known. At the Bayonne meeting, the Spanish lords and ladies greatly admired it, never having seen anything like it in the possession of their king.[87]

Here we have graphic evidence of the ways in which the Valois court utilized its finest tapestries, already marked with the recent history of imperial competition, as their best currency in combating the coercive expansionism of Philip and Alva.[88] Ironically, this display of Francis's *Scipio* series once again alluded to the humbling of the Valois monarchy, in the face of the imperial might of the Hapsburgs depicted in Alva's and Philip's *Tunis* tapestries.

The calculated display of the *Scipio* tapestries at Bayonne throws new light on the significance of the eighth tapestry in the *Valois* series. *Elephant*, as we have seen, portrays Anjou and Marguerite in the foreground, with their backs to the elaborate attack on an elephant by several groups of exotically attired horsemen, including Turks. The elephant's defenders hurl fire down on the attackers. Yates argued that the elephant was modelled on that depicted in the engravings of Anjou's entry into Antwerp in February 1582. The *Elephant* tapestry is also closely based on Caron's painting *Night Festival with an Elephant* (illus. 53),[89] which quite explicitly draws on the fifth tapestry in Francis's *Scipio* series, *The Battle of Zama* (illus. 39).[90]

As one of the most successful artists at the Valois court, Caron was undoubtedly familiar with the *Scipio* tapestries. His painting conflates the two elephants at the left centre in the *Scipio* tapestry, one raising its left leg (as in the Caron painting), the other carrying soldiers raining arrows down on its attackers (also closely reproduced by Caron). What is particularly striking about the painting is its substitution

53 Antoine Caron, *Night Festival with an Elephant*, *c.* 1573, oil on canvas. Private collection.

of Carthaginians on the back of the elephant in the *Scipio* tapestry for Turks, complete with turbans and crescent-shaped shields. As we have seen, the *Scipio* tapestries, like the subsequent *Tunis* ones, were graphic, violent images of imperial triumphalism depicting terrible military violence, utilized (with varying degrees of success) in the announcement and ratification of imperial power to present and potential subjects of that power. It is this overbearing atmosphere, we argue, that the *Valois Tapestries* inspire, drawing explicitly on earlier tapestries of imperial triumphalism rather than on a tradition of toleration and liberalism. In directly refuting Yates's conclusions, we argue that these works were intended to subdue and intimidate rather than pacify and conciliate. To determine *who* they were designed to intimidate, we have to reconsider Yates's claim that they deliberately erase the Massacre of St Bartholomew's Day.

According to Yates, all references to Charles IX and the massacre of Huguenots in Paris were expunged from the tapestries due to their Protestant sympathies. However, as Yates conceded, the imprint of the terrible events of August 1572 is present throughout the tapestries, despite her attempts to downplay their presence. Yates herself recorded one of the most extraordinary set pieces designed to commemorate the wedding of Marguerite de Valois and Henri of Navarre just prior to the massacre:

... the Louvre was prepared for the exercise of running at the ring ('courir la bague') with a stand for the watching ladies. Several troops presented themselves, amongst others the King [Charles IX] and his brother [Henri] attired as Amazons; the King of Navarre and his troop, dressed as Turks in long golden robes and with turbans on their heads; the Prince de Condé and others 'à l'estradiotte'; the [Catholic] Duc de Guise and his friends dressed, like the King, as Amazons. It was on the day following that on which this festival was held that the unsuccessful attempt was made on [the Protestant Admiral] Coligny . . . In that fatal August, 1572, Protestant Turks were taking part in such a show with Catholic-Amazons.[91]

This remarkable scene is reproduced explicitly in one of Caron's drawings of the Paris festivities.[92] Yates argued that the terrible shadow which the subsequent massacre cast over the wedding celebrations ensured that no such image was directly reproduced in the *Valois Tapestries*, but once we realize the importance of attending to the invariably intolerant conflation of Protestants and Turks as inter-changeable 'infidels', the whole atmosphere of the series changes.[93] *Fontainebleau* offers a fascinating gloss on the 'courir la bague' in its depiction of a boatload of soldiers in Turkish attire awaiting their turn to storm the island defended by Amazons. In *Tournament*, Turkish troops look on as French cavalry go through their paces in the centre of the composition. In *Elephant*, Turkish horsemen advance on the central figure of the elephant, only to be repulsed by a shower of flaming balls and explosions beneath their feet.

We have already seen the ways in which the Hapsburg court mobilized this conflation of Protestants and Turks in its devastating deployment of the *Tunis* tapestries at Philip II's wedding to Mary Tudor. In the religiously polarized climate of the period, such a conflation and its political consequences were clearly legible to both Protestant and Turkish communities. Bringing this insight to bear in our analysis of the *Valois Tapestries* leads us to stand Yates's argument on its head: the tapestries actually are deeply antithetical to the Protestant, and specifically Huguenot, cause. Probably designed and commissioned in France and woven in Brussels (like so many works commissioned by the Hapsburg court), they identify the Huguenot 'infidels' as an intolerable threat, undermining the future hopes of the Valois – unbelievers who, like the Turks, were to be chased out of the realm. The display of such a series in the aftermath of the Massacre of St Bartholomew's Day would only have added to the terror of the Huguenots.

No documentary evidence has survived to tell us how the French court used the *Valois Tapestries* in the aftermath of their production and prior to their removal to Florence in 1589.[94] We can, however, deduce from the ways in which they 'quote' from a range of earlier sixteenth-century tapestries that their political address was intimidating rather than benign. We would also suggest that these woven paraphrases of earlier tapestries of conquest are symptomatic of their ultimate failure as politically coercive images. As with Francis's *Scipio* tapestries, the Valois series is too busy deriving its own politically situated iconography from far more powerful rivals and patrons, such as Charles V and the Duke of Alva. The more politically compelling and visually arresting tapestries like *Los Honores* and the *Tunis* series wove a body of symbolic meanings at the moment of key political and military events, either Charles V's coronation or the conquest of Tunis. Subsequently, such images were appropriated by political rivals with the aim of producing recognizable 'meaning'. This appropriation failed in its transparent attempt to siphon off political authority, yet the symbolic effectiveness of such images contributes to our own sense that these narratives have become, over the intervening period, 'timeless'.

3 Managing the Infidel: Equestrian Art on Its Mettle

Both portrait medals and tapestries shared the capacity to circulate freely between courts and communities, and could be mobilized to produce mutually recognizable readings at different geographical locations. Fitting conveniently into the palm of a hand, the portrait medal was easily distributed, by virtue not only of its size but also of its replicability. Medals originally struck in precious metal, as items at the extreme luxury end of the market, could be reproduced over and over again in base metals and then circulated as required. The extent of this dissemination can be seen in the ways in which characteristic profiles, poses and settings were reproduced repeatedly across a range of medals from widely separated regimes and locations.

Despite their size, tapestries too were defined by their remarkably convenient portability, by the flexible ways in which they could be used and by the fact that multiple copies were produced by manufacturing workshops from the original cartoons as a matter of course. Tapestries formed an important aspect of the ostentatious occasions on which men and women of distinction visited one another. As we have seen, entire series would be packed up with due care and transported wherever their courtly owners travelled, to be unpacked and displayed prominently at crucial moments of diplomatic negotiation and dynastic alliance-formation.

This practice reached its peak in the sixteenth century as part of the triumphalist travelling show that was the constantly moving Hapsburg court. In his abdication speech of 1555, Charles V recalled that during his reign he had been ten times to the Low Countries, nine times to Germany, seven times to Italy, six times to Spain, four times through France, twice into England and twice to Africa. No wonder, then, that his triumphal entries and those of his son Philip were conceived in terms of portable artefacts like the *Conquest of Tunis* tapestry series.[1] Spreading a revived repertoire of classically derived imperial symbolism Europe-wide, such entries were also widely emulated. The *Tunis* tapestries were reproduced to order at least four times in the sixteenth century, at various levels of lavishness, for key members of the Hapsburg entourage (Mary, Alva, Perrenot).[2] Their transportation and relocation were themselves combinations of theatrical event and logistical feat. Alongside the calculated display of Charles's *editio princeps* of the *Tunis* series at the marriage of Philip II and Mary Tudor, the Duke of Alva spent a fortune on transporting his own set back to Spain, whilst evidence suggests that another of his tapestries based on the Tunis campaign remained in the Low Countries.[3] We have argued that this movement of luxury consumer objects went beyond the geographical and intellectual boundaries traditionally inscribed upon the early modern world. Its currency was the circulation of a repertoire of images recognizable to both Christendom and the Islamic world; indeed, it is this common identification which makes such images potentially so powerful and compelling.

In this final exploration of our theme, we move beyond the circulation of art objects as such, to focus our attention on another set of luxury objects with artistic potential that was equally highly regarded in both East and West. The horse has already reared its head a number of times during our exploration of the symbolic meanings of portrait medals and tapestries. Here we examine more closely the way in which an animal that was itself a recognized thing of beauty, an object of desire, an exchangeable item of great price, a customary gift between princes and a status symbol, was given figurative meaning.

I

Cultural identity in early modern Europe, we are arguing, was formed out of direct encounters between artefacts exchanged amongst international communities at distinct geographical locations. In the ensuing process of image-sharpening, representations recognizable by both partners in the cultural transaction tended to dominate. Ultimately, the 'meaning' or (in cultural historical terms) 'reading' tended towards the common interpretative ground between the two. Over time, further compromises and consolidation may take place, somewhat loosening the hold of the original strong sense of iconic meaning.

It is as an intrinsic part of that project that we turn our attention to pedigree horses as living, breathing luxury items, aware that the fact that they were sentient (and therefore required a more complex response from, and relationship with, the purchaser than an inanimate object, however treasured) meant that they created bridges, in some more specific and potentially instructive way, between geographical locations and peoples.[4]

Around 1465, Ludovico Maria Sforza, younger son of Francesco Sforza, Duke of Milan, then aged twelve, was sent to Cremona to act as his mother's representative (Cremona was her dower city). While he was there, his father sent him a horse. As an appropriately filial display of gratitude, Ludovico Maria commissioned a portrait of his mount, which he sent to his father with an accompanying letter:

The horse you sent me seemed, and seems still, for excellence and beauty, one fit for a king. I have taken such pleasure, both in the horse itself, but incomparably much more out of respect for the kindness you have shown in sending it to me, that I thought I would have its portrait taken, as your Excellency will see in the little panel which the bearer is carrying. I thought that I could combine two praiseworthy ideas by sending this portrait to your Excellency. One in showing you that I, despite having been unwell these days, have enjoyed discovering the talents and administration that operate in this city, so as to know where to go as necessary, and the conditions one will find. The other is to ensure that your Excellency understands in what great respect I hold your Highness's gift. I never tire of looking at and admiring this horse, nor only in the flesh, but also in this portrait.

Because of my illness, I was not able to have myself portrayed on the horse, as I would have wished. I therefore had one of my household shown, although for the excellence of the portrait I decided it was not necessary to place his name on it. I believe that in this I have done something that will find favour with your Lordship, and to this end I send it.[5]

'Had the unnamed servant been identified,' comments art historian Evelyn Welch, '[this] portrait would have become a portrait of a rider rather than an image of the horse itself.'[6] Here, then, is a portrait of a gift horse, commissioned by its recipient and regarded as a work of art which would double the aesthetic pleasure of the original gift. There was pleasure in the horse itself and pleasure in its painted representation, a point made repeatedly in other painterly images of the period (illus. 68).

If we unpack this incident a little further, we can identify two important strands in the scenario whereby our central theme of 'power on display' is played out. Milan to Cremona is a comparatively easy ride, the gesture of presentation of a fine horse to a son 'abroad' correspondingly modest.[7] Yet the arrival of such a splendid gift – a costly, specially reared animal and also an object of great beauty – with all pomp and circumstance enacted for Cremona the wealth and power of the Milanese ruling house. So the transaction across geographical distance involving the living horse was already performing a recognizable political function.

The painting with which Ludovico Maria presented his father invested the gift with further, explicitly symbolic meaning. Like the

Chinese porcelain in an *Annunciation* by Crivelli or the Iznik vase that holds the Virgin's lily in a painting by Van Eyck, the precious painted horse acquired an additional patina of desirability by virtue of its exquisitely executed beauty. The animal, in other words, became yet another exotic consumer item in the array of luxury objects assembled from the farthest points on the globe, which symbolically conferred status on the sitters in paintings in which they figured.[8]

Now, too, the horse takes on its representative function as a symbol of dominion (particularly in battle), and horse and rider enter a recognizable tradition of triumphant equestrian imagery. Registering that function, Ludovico gracefully underlined the fact that his painting was supposed to record his gratitude for the horse-gift by absenting himself as rider. Had he himself been portrayed on his new mount, the equestrian figure of the conquering hero would have run the risk of challenging the authority of the Duke of Milan himself. The withholding of identity from the rider returns the centre of attention in the painting to the horse itself – no mere omission, but an active representational gesture of deference to the giver on the part of the horse's new owner. Reverses of contemporary portrait medals regularly offer a second version of their subject, on horseback (illus. 54).

In the 1480s, by which time he had himself become regent to the dukedom of Milan following the assassination of his older brother, Ludovico Maria hired Leonardo da Vinci to work for him on a more grandiose equestrian statement of the conqueror's right to rule. On this occasion, the horse in question was designed as a monument to the power and authority of the Sforza family in Milan. Given the letter quoted above, we maintain that Ludovico understood the role of equestrian statues in representing contested claims to dominion.

54 Antonio Pisanello, Medal of Ludovico III Gonzaga on horseback (obverse and reverse), 1447/8, bronze. Museu Calouste Gulbenkian, Lisbon.

A large-scale horse and soldier rider reaffirmed and broadcasted, retrospectively, claims to power made on the basis of actual conquest on the battlefield.

This is indeed how Leonardo himself alluded to the over-sized bronze horse Ludovico wanted to create in the *curriculum vitae* he sent to his future employer:

In times of peace I believe I can give perfect satisfaction to the equal of any other in architecture and the construction of buildings both public and private, and in guiding water from one place to another. I can carry out sculpture in marble, bronze, or clay, and also I can do in painting whatever it is possible to do, as well as any other, whoever he may be. Again, the monumental bronze horse you wish for may be taken in hand, which is to be the immortal glory and eternal honour of the prince your father of happy memory, and of the illustrious house of Sforza.[9]

The purpose of the Sforza equestrian monument was to commemorate the dynasty's founder, the great *condottiere* Francesco Sforza, who had seized power in Milan from the Visconti family in 1450. Initially, designs featured a horse rearing above a fallen foe, including sketches also provided by Antonio del Pollaiuolo (illus. 55). This was a compelling image of dynastic power, but one that raised considerable technical difficulties as far as bronze casting was concerned.[10]

Under Leonardo's guidance, however, the project metamorphosed into a towering colossus of a horse – a triumph of design and engineering. The statue Leonardo planned – now to be riderless – was to be

55 Antonio del Pollaiuolo, *Design for an Equestrian Monument to Francesco Sforza*, c. 1489, pen and ink and wash. Staatliche Graphische Sammlung, Munich.

more than seven metres high and weigh approximately 72,000 kilograms. Its pose was modelled closely on that of the four horses on St Mark's in Venice (which Constantine, the first Emperor of Byzantium, had taken from Rome to Constantinople, and which had been brought as booty to Venice by Crusaders in the thirteenth century). Its other inspiration was the bronze equestrian statue just over four metres in height that stood in front of the Lateran in Rome at the time (illus. 56) and that had survived intact because it was believed to be a statue of Constantine himself.[11] The horse, then, was intended to recall the latter's imperial might on an equivalently impressive scale.[12]

In a move with which we will become increasingly familiar in the course of this chapter, however, Leonardo did not confine himself to copying antique prototypes, however well executed, but took many of his preparatory studies from life. He examined closely and took measurements from horses in the stables of prominent Milanese breeders and raisers.[13] His notebooks show keen observation of living horses in action. A sketch for the horse has marginal comments: 'Messer Galeazzo's big genet', 'Messer Galeazzo's Sicilian Horse', 'measurement of the Sicilian horse, the leg from behind, in front lifted and extended'. Notes made in 1493 show Leonardo's meticulous detailing of equine physical qualities: 'Messer Mariolo's morel (black) the Florentine is a big horse with a fine neck and a beautiful head';

56 *Marcus Aurelius on Horseback* (believed throughout the Renaissance to be Constantine the Great), bronze. Museo Capitolino, Rome.

'the white stallion belonging to the falconer has fine hindquarters.'[14] Despite Leonardo's painstaking drawings, including designs for a casting pit (illus. 57), the horse was never cast, though a full-sized model was created from clay before Milan fell to the French in 1499.[15]

We should be cautious, however, in believing too readily the story we have just outlined of the great bronze horse as an emblem of Ludovico Maria Sforza's *hubris*. Similarly, we should be careful in accepting his misplaced belief that a family of mercenaries who had seized power by brute force could aspire to a lasting monument to their dynastic right to rule. A curiously similar story is told about another wealthy and successful mercenary of the same period, Bartolommeo Colleoni, who had amassed his fortune providing distinguished military service to the Venetian Republic. At his death in 1476, Colleoni, who came originally from Bergamo, left a large bequest for a statue of himself on horseback to be erected in the Piazza San Marco. A competition was held in 1479, and the Florentine Andrea Verrocchio submitted a life-size model of a horse, which was sent to Venice in sections. When

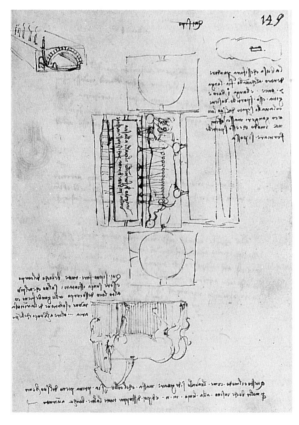

57 Leonardo da Vinci, *Design for a Casting Pit for the Sforza Horse*, *c.* 1493, ink on paper. Biblioteca Nacional, Madrid.

a Venetian sculptor was hired to design a rider for the horse, Verrocchio was so enraged, according to Vasari, that he smashed the head and legs of his model and returned to Florence. He was, however, persuaded back by a greatly increased salary, and at the time of his death in 1488 had completed a clay model of both horse and rider. The Venetian Alessandro Leopardi, who was an expert in bronze casting, eventually completed the monument, which was unveiled in 1496. In spite of Colleoni's insistence that it be located 'in front of St Mark's', however, the Venetian Council balked at a mere mercenary (and a foreigner to boot) being thus honoured, and placed the statue in front of the Scuola Grande di San Marco, in the Campo SS. Giovanni e Paolo, instead.[16]

The shape of this story mirrors that of the development of the Sforza horse. A great artist undertakes the superhuman feat of producing an oversized equestrian statue, as a grandiose memorial to the meteoric rise in prestige, power and wealth of a hired mercenary. In a protective narrative move which reserves the potent, recognizable symbol for those with a 'right' to such a representation of conquering imperial might, the problem of entitlement is transferred to the statue itself and to the difficulties of its construction. In the end, it is not completed, or it is completed in a form that registers the inferior status of the figure commemorated. The English mercenary Sir John Hawkwood prudently limited his ambitions to be remembered in the form of an imposing equestrian figure to a fine *trompe-l'oeil* painting of the monumental statue for which Medicean Florence would never have allowed a place (illus. 69).

II

A monument of a military man on a horse is not just any military man on any horse. The equestrian statue is at once a 'real representation' and a figure for the transposed power and glory of a dynastic or imperial personage. Actual horses and their artistic representations are tightly bound up with one another, to the point where it is difficult to separate carefully observed realism from contrived symbolic meaning. We suggest that the two have become so intimately related over time that the oscillating 'flicker-effect' we have noted between implied meaning (whose cultural currency is recognizable in both East and West) and carefully observed representation 'after nature' is particularly disorientating. The élite recreational activity of horse breeding and ownership (a shared passion down to the present day among the ruling houses of East and West) owes much of its energy and persistence to the fact that it participates, we suggest, in both 'real' and representational domains of power and prestige.

We take as our final example of the jostling for power that took place around entitlement to equestrian memorials in fifteenth-century Europe the Este family, rulers of Ferrara.[17] The dynastic reputation of the Este, like that of the Medici, was secured by their participation in the 1438 Council of Florence (whose early sessions took place in Ferrara). As we saw in chapter 1, that occasion was curiously bound up with a shared East-West passion for hunting, as well as some strenuous political manoeuvring around who had access to, and the right to ride, fine horses of eastern stock. In the case of the Este, too, subsequent scholarship concerned exclusively with the humanistic, Greco-Roman-based cultural foundation of Este art and literature patronized by them has tended to overlook the prominent role allocated to oriental allusions and influences in this key period of attempted collaboration between Christians from East and West.

Neither of the two great equestrian memorials planned by the Este survives. One, to the memory of Ercole I, was never actually built. The other, erected in memory of Niccolò III (illus. 58), host to the Byzantine delegation of 1438, was destroyed in 1796.[18] In 1443, two years after Niccolò's illegitimate son Leonello's succession, the city of Ferrara promoted a competition to design a bronze equestrian statue in his memory. The architect and humanist Leon Battista Alberti was involved with the judging. Antonio di Cristoforo won by a narrow margin on the basis of a model of the horse he had submitted.[19]

The documented details of this competition shed interesting light on a little-read treatise by Alberti, his De equo animante (On the living horse). In a fifteenth-century manuscript copy now in the Bodleian Library, Alberti, in his dedication to Leonello d'Este, states that it was in fact Leonello who requested Alberti's participation to find the artist for Niccolò's monument ('me Tuo iussu arbitrum cognitorem delegere'). It was, Alberti notes, his involvement with the Este monument project that led him to think long and hard about the form and nature of the horse, and hence to write De equo animante. Alberti may also have been involved in the design of the stone triumphal arch on which the completed statue eventually stood (some scholars, however, attribute a part in the arch's design to the medallist Matteo de' Pasti, who was also in Este employ at the time).[20]

What is perhaps more interesting for us about Alberti's involvement in the horse project is that his influential treatise on architecture, De re aedificatoria (which, he says elsewhere, he had been inspired to write by Leonello), contains no discussion of equestrian monuments at all.

58 Monument to Niccolò III d'Este, 17th century, drawing. Biblioteca Apostolica Vaticana.

The *De equo animante*, on the other hand, associates the well-trained horse directly with the glory of its rider:

And therefore, for these reasons, horses which are thus provided with a generous disposition, are said to be born to defend the country from the enemy, to increase the empire and make peace for the rulers; and so much do they merit glory by means of the art and skill of the trainer and breeder . . . Just as each citizen at one moment or another can be called, urged to arms either by example of his fellow soldiers, or to earn glory; or by incitement of commanders[;] actions which are traditional and shared . . . cannot be done without teaching by the knowledgeable and certainly without diligent study. This is also true for horses.[21]

The *De re aedificatoria* does propose the triumphal arch (of the kind that supported the Este horse) as one of the three major types of antique commemorative monument worthy of emulation. Such a public celebration of leadership should be erected, Alberti advised, by the community rather than by the individual to be honoured, to avoid charges of self-aggrandisement. The monument to Niccolò suggests that we ought to read *De equo animante* alongside the discussions of public commemorative monuments in *De re aedificatoria* to understand humanistically inspired thinking about equestrian representation and its function. Once again, this means placing a treatment of 'actual' horses and their form alongside one of built form and its representational functions, thereby eliding the 'real' and the 'representational' in one highly specific case.

On the end of the arch supporting the Niccolò monument was a marble plaque bearing the following inscription: '[This monument of the] Marquis Niccolò d'Este, son of Albert, three times creator of peace in Italy, was decreed by Leonello, marquis and legitimate successor [to Niccolò].'[22] Surviving drawings show that Niccolò was depicted in ceremonial clothing, wearing the distinctive high beret of Este office and a cape. The marquis's raised right hand held a baton of office; the horse had one foreleg raised and a knotted tail. Thus the monument combined military achievement (which may have included a reference to the Council of Florence as one of the three occasions when Niccolò achieved peace in Italy)[23] with an image associated with the marquis's triumphal ride through the city (in civilian dress) to 'take possession' of it as part of his investiture ceremony.

Charles Rosenberg has suggested that Leonello commissioned the monument to Niccolò III at the moment when controversy surrounded his legitimacy as Este heir: 'The new marquis deemed it necessary to make a swift and public declaration of his sovereignty. With two legitimate half brothers waiting in the wings, Leonello may well have wished to leave no doubt as to his right to rule.'[24] The year 1443 was also when Leonello married his second wife, Maria d'Aragona, illegitimate daughter of Alfonso, King of Naples, with the expectation of raising the status of the Este family.

Work on the statue all but ceased in 1444 and was not properly reactivated until 1451 by Borso d'Este, following Leonello's death.[25] According to an anonymous seventeenth-century chronicle, a foundry was set up in the courtyard of the *palazzo ducale*. A mould for the statue was made and then set in a *basa profonda* – a deep pit – and buried there for two days. Next the bronze was melted and poured. The form was allowed to cool for four days and then drawn out of the earth. Much to everyone's dismay, when the figures emerged the horse was found to be missing one of its legs up to the middle of the hip (presumably the raised leg, the difficulty of whose casting was later to concern Leonardo da Vinci). A new form was made and the process repeated, the distressed bronze caster Ippolito Bindelli (who had been specially brought from Verona with his son and two assistants) praying to God that this time it would be successful. A litany to the Virgin was recited over the buried mould before pouring, and the statue was indeed perfect.[26]

Here, then, is a successful episode in the saga of equestrian statues projected and attempted. The monument to Niccolò performed an important function as part of a vigorous programme by the insecurely placed Leonello to establish his legitimacy and entitlement to rule, a programme that was completed by his equally insecurely placed brother Borso immediately after his own seizure of power.[27] History has judged Leonello to be a pre-eminently civilized and humane prince, his claim to urbanity validated by the association with his court of the great humanist Guarino Veronese – ignoring the awkwardness of his legitimacy and preferring to concentrate on his lasting reputation as a patron of art and learning.[28]

We should recall that it was Leonello who pioneered the revival of the portrait medal as a 'currency of fame' – he was credited with having over ten thousand such medals struck and distributing them as a sophisticated public relations exercise on behalf of the Este family.[29] In the present context, we might note the occasion for one such medal, now generally regarded as a masterpiece in the genre, Pisanello's rendering of Leonello (illus. 59) to celebrate his marriage to Maria d'Aragona. Scholars tend to refer to this medal as 'one of the most charming and delightful of any produced in the Renaissance'[30] and 'one of the least self-aggrandizing images' of its type.[31] We suggest that, circulated as part of the largesse surrounding the wedding, it astutely deflected attention from the dynasty-securing tactics of the marriage (a second marriage between two individuals of questionable, if elevated, parentage), presenting a dubious, hard-nosed power alliance as a sentimental love match.[32]

There is irony in the fact that Niccolò III's legitimate son Ercole, who finally succeeded Borso in 1471, is represented by the scholarly literature as more 'pushy' about his right to rule (as well he might

59 Antonio Pisanello, Portrait medal showing Leonello d'Este (obverse and reverse), 1444, bronze. National Gallery of Art, Washington, DC.

have been) and as developing a 'more aloof and "regal" air and a more grandiose form of patronage'.[33] The planning for the equestrian monument for Ercole, to be located prominently in the piazza of the costly city extension and fortifications he had added to Ferrara, was begun in 1499 (illus. 60). Like the monument to Niccolò, the surviving documents show that although the project was publicly represented as sponsored by the citizens of Ferrara (according to Alberti's advice that such an arrangement avoided charges of personal ostentation), it was in fact Ercole himself who was in charge of the commission. In 1501, he exchanged letters with his ambassador in Milan, suggesting that difficulties had arisen with the equestrian image for the monument and inquiring after an enormous clay horse that 'uno M.o Leonardo, quale è buono maestro in simile cosa' (one Master Leonardo [da Vinci], who is a masterly exponent of a similar thing) had made as the form for a Sforza bronze equestrian monument. The ambassador replied five days later that the French ambassador in Milan was quite amenable to Ercole's having the clay model, but that he would have to obtain the permission of the King of France.

Nothing further is heard of this inquiry. As far as it goes, however, it tells us that Ercole knew of the Leonardo project for the Sforza horse (and, incidentally, that the story of its destruction by French

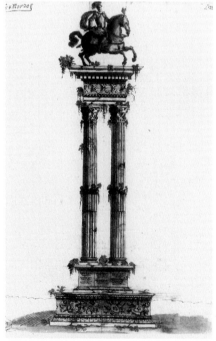

60 Monument to Ercole I d'Este, 17th century, drawing. Biblioteca Apostolica Vaticana.

soldiers is, as one might expect, a literary embellishment on the story of the demise of the clay horse).³⁴ Ercole's monument fared no better than Sforza's, however. Following a chapter of accidents with the enormous marble column, or possibly columns, that were to support the statue, the project was abandoned with the death of 'Ercole Augustus', as he liked to be known, in 1505.³⁵ Following the French invasion of Ferrara (and the destruction of all bronzes associated with Este rule) in 1810, a marble statue of Napoleon Bonaparte was briefly erected on the column, and in the location, originally intended for Ercole's equestrian memorial.

III

In addition to the kind of symbolic meanings we have examined so far, the horse inevitably carried powerful associations with the East which are largely lost to us today. Just as we think of the tulip as a quintessentially European flower despite its Asian origins, so too we find it hard to recognize the foreignness of the breeds of horses we see everyday in televised equestrian events – familiarity has de-exoticised them for us, and we can no longer retrieve their highly specific 'orientalism'.³⁶

From its earliest history, the domestication of the horse was inextricably bound up with cultural and commercial transactions between East and West. The famous Bactrian or Turanian horse emerged from Bactria on the northern slopes of the Afghan mountains at the midpoint of the Silk Road. It is recorded that Alexander the Great remounted his cavalry on Bactrian horses en route to India.³⁷ By the sixth century, the breed seems to have developed into the more recognizable Turkmenian horse of neighbouring Turkestan.³⁸ When the Arabs conquered Turkestan and Bactria in the eighth century, Arabic writers extolled the virtues of the horse and the importance of its export from these regions.³⁹ The Crusades led to a transfusion of Turcoman stock with western European stock, coinciding with the production of the much-prized Andalusian in Spain, the result of the introduction of Turcoman, Arabian and Spanish blood.⁴⁰ However, the commercial centre for the breeding, training and distribution of well-bred horses remained the territories to the East controlled by the Ottoman and Persian empires. Merchants and travellers from all over Europe travelled throughout the East, extolling the virtues of the horses they saw, admiring their numbers and the sophistication with which they were traded.⁴¹

The story of the emergence of coveted breeds or 'races' of horses out of the East-West exchange of bloodstock types runs uncannily close to the stories we have been telling of attempts at political and doctrinal bonding between the two territories. For instance, Heraclius I, the Byzantine Emperor whose military prowess re-established the Eastern Church in Constantinople and whom legend credited with returning the True Cross to Jerusalem, also played a key part in developing the breeds for which Byzantium became renowned:

The Emperor Heraclius . . . wrote a tactical manual which was the basis of the later and better-known work by Leo the Wise, dealing mainly with the reorganization of cavalry units . . . [his] reforms proved so effective that the Byzantines were at last able to vanquish and destroy the Persians.[42]

By the fifteenth century, both military and commercial dominance could be correlated with control of the means to move horses in large numbers over long distances. In 1471, Venice sent military aid to Uzun Hassan, ruler of Persia, in an attempt to prevent the growing power of the Ottomans. Josefa Barbaro, dispatched to Corfu to assist Hassan, gave a vivid account of the movement of the horses under his command: 'They were ninety and nine galeys. On which there were ccccxi horses of ours with their *stradiotte* [Albanian mounted mercenaries], viij in every galey, v galeys excepted, which had no horse.'[43] By the late fifteenth century, Portuguese commercial intervention in Asia and the Indian Ocean sought to establish a monopoly in the purchasing and distribution of horses in the area as one of the most lucrative and prestigious aspects of trade activity.

The Portuguese incursion into Indian Ocean trade had a profound effect upon the area's commerce, especially on the trade in horses – one of its most lucrative aspects. Indian courts had been importing Arabian horses for many years prior to the arrival of the Portuguese. However, the fall of Goa in 1510, followed by Hormuz in 1515, radically shifted the balance of commercial power in the region and was particularly decisive in affecting the movement of horses throughout the Indian Ocean littoral. In his highly influential account of Asian trade, *Suma Oriental* (1513), the Portuguese diplomat Tomé Pires offered a detailed description of the traffic in horses throughout the area. In his description of Aden, he comments that 'it trades with the kingdom of Goa, and takes there all sorts of merchandise and horses both from itself and from Cairo.'[44] Discussing Ormuz (Hormuz), Pires notes:

Ormuz trades with Aden and Cambay and with the kingdom of the Deccan and Goa and with the ports of the kingdom of Narsinga and in Malabar . . . Horses are worth a high price in the kingdoms of Goa, of the Deccan and of Narsinga, so the Ormuz [merchants] go to these kingdoms with them every year. A horse may be worth as much as seven hundred xerafins – coins worth 320 *reis* each – when it is good. The best are the Arabians, next are the Persians and third are those from Cambay.[45]

This accurate depiction of the horse trade had its correlative in Portugal's increasingly aggressive control of these activities. In 1513, Affonso de Albuquerque wrote to King Manuel to inform him that he had created 'stables for your horses in Goa' whilst playing off the friendly Hindu kingdom of Vijayanagar against the hostile Muslim state of Bijapur.[46] Having effectively monopolized the trade in horses, Albuquerque proceeded to indulge in his own form of horse-trading. In 1514, the Vijayanagar court offered him a substantial sum to establish their own monopoly on the import of horses. Desperate counter-offers from the court at Bijapur placed Albuquerque in a particularly powerful position:

. . . he wrote first to Vijayanagar saying that he would give the Râya the refusal of all his horses if he would pay him 30,000 cruzados per annum for the supply, and send his own servants to Goa to fetch away the animals, and also that he would aid the King in his war [against Bijapur] if he was paid the expense of the troops; and he wrote afterwards to Bîjapûr promising the Sultan the refusal of all horses that came to Goa if he would surrender to the king of Portugal a certain portion of the mainland opposite the island [of Goa].[47]

In November of the same year, Albuquerque wrote to King Manuel to sanction the importation of two thousand horses from Arabia and Persia to support the Hindu kingdoms, but Vijayanagar's titular monopoly was put on indefinite hold due to Albuquerque's death in December 1515.[48] However, the apparent Portuguese monopoly was often undermined by the complex transactions undertaken by the Indian rulers and merchants. Travelling into the heart of the sultanate around 1520, the Portuguese factor Fernão Nuniz recorded the ways in which the Rai of Vijayanagar was manipulating the Portuguese restrictions to his own financial benefit:

The king every years buys thirteen thousand horses of Ormuz, and country-breds, of which he chooses the best for his own stables, and he gives the rest to his captains, and gains much money by them; because after taking out the good Persian horses, he sells those which are country-bred, and gives five for a thousand *pardaos*, and they are obliged to pay him the money for them within the month of September; and with the money so obtained he pays for the Arabs that he buys of the Portuguese, in such that his captains pay the cost of the whole without anything going out of the Treasury.[49]

The Rai had originally paid a thousand *pardaos* for twelve to fifteen horses, so he broke even on his investments, as well as building up his personal holding of valued stock, one that reflected Tomé

Pires's equine hierarchy – Arab, then Persian, then local 'country-bred' horses.

The portrayal of the movement of precious exotic livestock in the *Voyage to Calicut* tapestries (illus. 44) is a vivid reminder of the ways in which the Portuguese laid claim to the ability to transport substantial numbers of horses from one side of the Indian Ocean to the other. This ability illustrated their power as commercial brokers in such exchanges between kingdoms and also signified their military strength; the ability to ship horses[50] displayed an ability to influence their deployment in future military engagements. In this context, it is useful to reconsider the ways in which virtually all the tapestries we have examined carefully delineate massed cavalry of readily identifiable horses, from the *Alfonso* tapestries to the *Tunis* series (illus. 70).

The practical requirements for transporting such large numbers of horses on a regular basis led to a significant development in Portuguese ship design. The *Nau Taforeia*, a heavy, round-bottomed ship carrying around 30 guns, was specifically designed to carry horses in its hold as humanely as possible for long voyages. Two such ships were used by Albuquerque in his conquest of Hormuz in 1515 and, subsequently, to ferry horses between Hormuz, Aden and Goa.[51]

What this brief excursus into the trade and transportation of horses tells us is that access to and possession of finely graded horses in considerable numbers was an index of political, military and commercial power, and that the supply and quality-control centre was located in the heart of the territories of the Ottoman and Persian empires.[52] Portuguese involvement in this arena tended to be limited to acting as a lucrative intermediary between the Hindu and Muslim states of India. The logistics of long-distance travel to and from India via the Cape of Good Hope made the potentially lucrative scenario of importing Arabian horses into Europe unfeasible.[53]

The need to develop more regulated transportation and breeding of horses in Europe was quickly appreciated and became a developed specialism under the patronage of noble enthusiasts. As early as 1329, the Gonzagas of Mantua were crossbreeding Arabian and local horses, thus establishing distinguished Mantuan bloodlines.[54] By 1488, the Mantuan ducal stud held 650 horses, including breeds from Spain, Barbary, Sardinia, Ireland and England. If we look more closely at the lifestyle of this famously 'horsy' dynasty, we begin to see how East-West two-way exchange of horses contributed to a shared cultural environment, as well as how a passion for the technical beauty of actual highly bred horses modulated into a sophisticated aesthetic of horse-related art objects.

In the 1490s, Francesco Gonzaga, Marquis of Mantua, carried on a cordial correspondence with the Ottoman Emperor Beyazit II, successor to Mehmet II, conqueror of Constantinople, sustained by their shared passion for breeding horses. Francesco collected and raced pure Arab and Persian horses, and was as expert about these as his wife, Isabella d'Este, was about her collection of antiques. 'We understand horses and arms better than engraved gems,' he once confessed.[55]

By 1492, Francesco had sent Alexis Becagut to Istanbul to negotiate the purchase of bloodstock horses. In 1525, Francesco's son Federico II also attempted to establish a horse-trading relationship with the Ottoman Sultan, sending his personal chamberlain Marcelli Anconitano to Istanbul with gifts and a request to buy a significant number of bloodstock Arab mares. Anconitano left Ancona on 15 November 1525, but took 23 days to reach Ragusa (where an Italian agent reported his safe arrival) because of violent storms. An Italian agent in Istanbul reported his arrival there on 6 March 1526: 'An emissary from the Marquis of Mantua has arrived here. He has brought presents for the Sultan of armaments for footsoldiers and for cavalry, saddles, falconets [small artillery pieces] and other things. He wants to negotiate for some horses.'

On 14 March, Süleyman responded to Anconitano's approach with a cordial letter to Federico in Turkish, sent with an accompanying Italian translation (three years later, the household of the Gonzagas boasted a Turkish 'interpreter', retained specifically for purposes of correspondence with Turkish horse contacts). Süleyman was preoccupied with impending hostilities against Hungary, and three months later Anconitano was still waiting for a final decision. On 18 July, he wrote to Federico from Ragusa to say that he had failed to acquire any horses from the Sultan, describing in minute detail the seventeen mounts he had managed to buy from other sources.[56] In the Mantuan Filippo Orso's album of finely executed drawings of horses and armour, dated 1554, the drawing of a horse labelled *Turcho d'Italia* (illus. 61) gives some idea of the outcome of this carefully controlled crossbreeding.[57]

Federico Gonzaga's enthusiasm for fine horses was matched by his enthusiasm for incorporating them into the lavish art decorating his Mantua palaces. In his summer palace, the Palazzo del Te, he had portraits of his favourite horses incorporated into the *trompe l'oeil* fresco decoration of one of the ceremonial receiving rooms (illus. 72). In the *palazzo ducale* in central Mantua, the great dining-room was also decorated with portraits of horses – this time concealed ingeniously behind *trompe l'oeil* curtains, which appear to have blown aside to reveal a hoof and fetlock here, an ear and neck there. Dinner guests could try to identify particular horses from these glimpses, presumably earning their host's approval if they did so.

Gonzaga art of all kinds is rich with horse imagery over which our 21st-century eyes tend to slide without recognition. There is some irony in the fact that we know of the Gonzagas' taste for horse-inspired art in part because of their passion for horses. They tended to commission wall paintings in place of the more fashionable and expensive tapestries favoured elsewhere in Europe by the beginning of the sixteenth century, because so much of their money was invested in the Mantuan stud and its valuable individual bloodstock horses. On ceremonial occasions, Isabella d'Este was even obliged to hire tapestries to decorate her receiving rooms with appropriate ostentation.

The fifteenth and sixteenth centuries saw an escalation in the commissioning of visual representations of horses in all media, from frescoes to statuary, by the princes of Europe. The resulting art objects laid vigorous claim to prestige on the part of European wielders of wealth and power. But nothing the European nobility could lay on could match the ostentatious displays of real horse-power arranged for

61 Filippo Orso, *Turcho d'Italia*, *c.* 1554, pen, ink and wash on paper. Victoria & Albert Museum, London.

visiting dignitaries by the Ottoman Sultan (illus. 62), who acquired one perfect bloodstock horse in tribute for every ten shipped through Istanbul. In 1544, an attendant to the French ambassador described the magnificent sight of Süleyman the Magnificent's horses lining the court through which the ambassadors passed on their way to pay their respects to the Sultan: 'The horses were very handsome turkish or barbary ones, of black, dark brown, bay, grey, dappled or white, each worth at least 200 ducats' (illus. 63).[58]

IV

We are arguing that representations of power and a vivid shared aesthetic combined in fine breeds of horses, and that their circulation and appreciation were integral parts of imperial bids for recognition. By the beginning of the sixteenth century, the English and also the French were on the lookout for pedigree stock to improve the quality of their native-bred horses. In the spring of 1514, Giovanni Ratto was sent by the Marquis of Mantua with a present of bloodstock horses to Henry VIII – progenitors in all likelihood of many of today's blood-stock English racehorses.[59] On 20 March, Ratto wrote to Mantua informing his master of the success of his mission. He reported that

62 Detail showing Süleyman the Magnificent from Pieter Coecke van Aelst, *Procession of Sultan Süleyman II through the Atmedan* (right-hand side), woodcut from *Ces Moeurs et fachons de faire de Turcz . . .*, 1533.

after presenting the horses to Henry that same day at Hampton Court, the English King was so pleased that, 'Had the marquis given him a kingdom he could not have been more delighted; and went from one nobleman to another saying, "What think you of these mares? They were sent to me by my cousin the Marquis of Mantua."'[60] The French Duke of Longueville, present at the gift-giving, told Henry that the horses exceeded the quality of anything possessed by the French King (although in fact Francis I possessed far superior horses at this time):[61]

Ratto offered the horses as a sign of his master's friendship with Henry, and added that the marquis had a stud of Barbary mares, of '*miche*' and of jennets, and of great mares, which he offered to the king, 'together with his territories and children, and his own person'. The queen was present during this conversation, which induced Ratto to put 'the bright bay' through his paces in the Spanish fashion, exhibiting the horse to the admiration of everybody. The king said to him, 'Is not this the best horse?' He answered in the affirmative, to the gratification of the king, who approaching the horse patted him, saying, 'So ho, my minion'.

This final horse 'was a Mantuan "barb" or race horse, and the Marquis had been offered for him his weight in silver, but preferred making a present of the animal to Henry VIII'. After this the king caused Ratto to be asked secretly what present would please the marquis, 'and he replied nothing but the king's love; though his intention was evinced of purchasing some hobbies, and three couples of staunch hounds.' Having put 'the bright bay' through his paces again, Ratto presented Henry with a further gift from the marquis: a scimitar. The king was delighted with that 'specimen of oriental workmanship'.[62]

The letter of thanks that Henry sent to the Marquis makes clear the careful manoeuvring for status and position effected by the choreographed moves in the gift-exchange of horses:

We have learnt from our intimate friend, Thomas Cene, with what affection, magnificence, and expression of singular favour and regard towards us he has been entertained by your Excellency; and that your very noble stables were thrown open to him, and that he was most earnestly requested to choose for us what horses he most approved of. When he refused to avail himself of this generosity, your Excellency's self selected the four most beautiful of them all for us, which we have received with your letters by your messenger, John Ratto, a man most circumspect and careful, and very well versed not only in horsemanship, but also in courteous behaviour, with which I have been marvellously pleased . . . And so many kind offices of yours towards ourself have at once presented themselves to us, that it is not very easy to determine for what we should first return thanks. But, foremost, we thank you most heartily for that your supreme good will towards ourself, which we cannot mistake; and for your exceeding desire of deserving well at our hands, as well as for those most beautiful, high-bred, and surpassing horses just sent for us. These we hold highly welcome and acceptable, as well because they are most excellent, as that they have been sent from the very best feeling and intention.[63]

In the autumn of the same year, Henry wrote to the Marquis thanking him for a further four horses and two jennets, dispatching 'our intimate friend and knight Griffith' with some English horses 'saddled and harnessed in their full trappings' and destined for Mantua.

Horses played a prominent part in the 'Field of the Cloth of Gold' meeting between Henry VIII and Francis I which took place in June 1520, between the villages of Guines and Ardres in the English 'pale' of Calais. The occasion was designed to show diplomatic amity between the two young sovereigns in the face of the growing political power of the new Roman Emperor Charles V. The ostentatious display of wealth and sophistication on the part of both sovereigns included the exchange and display of fine horses. In preparation for this, Sir Edward Guildford, Master of Henry's Armoury, was ordered to make extensive purchases of both arms and horses in early 1520.[64] Guildford and his officers went as far afield as the Hague, Brussels, Delft, Arras,

Lille and Zeeland in search of horses to be conspicuously displayed at the meetings. The price of purchasing and transporting the animals was considerable: the cost of ferry transportation exceeded that of a mass in Brussels (4d.). The horses purchased included a grey belonging to one Pierre de Lannoy and presented by Henry himself to his head of security at Guines, Sir Griffith Rice; a sorrel horse intended for the Queen's litter; and a black bald horse, bought at the Hague and presented to the Duke of Suffolk.

However, when it came to horses required for the dramatic and politically sensitive jousts and tournaments, Henry looked even further afield. As early as 1514, Sir Thomas Cheyney had acquired ten mounts on Henry's behalf in the Neapolitan kingdom; he was subsequently offered a selection from the Mantuan stud, whose owner, the Duke of Ferrara, volunteered to forward them to Henry along with one of his own servants. By 1519, Cheyney had returned to England with horses from Mantua – a highly significant exchange symbolic of the growing diplomatic amity between the two kingdoms.[65] Contemporary drawings of the Mantuan horses emphasize their highly selective breeding, and hence their 'racial' characteristics. Filippo Orso's 1554 album contains a drawing of a 'Corsier della Razza di Mantova' (illus. 64), the type presented to Henry.

The meeting at Guines signified an intensification of horse-trading based on the need not only for fine mounts for the King and his retinue but also for coursers of sufficient quality to present to Francis. On 9 June 1520, the two monarchs met and exchanged horses, Francis giving up his Mantuan mount, Henry surrendering his Neapolitan. On 18 June, Francis presented Henry with six coursers, four of which were from Mantua, including the dappled 'Mozaurcha' mare believed to be worth more than all those presented by Henry in exchange.[66] It seems safe to assume that when Henry established the first royal studs at Tutbury in Staffordshire (owing to the lack of space at Hampton Court), the bloodstock was made up of Barbary and Arabian lines drawn from sources like the Mantuan stud.[67]

The effect upon Henry's imperial bargaining power of this new-found ability to traffic in fine horses was significant. By 1526, he was able to send Francis I a gift of eighteen horses, whilst Charles V was also now prepared to offer his cousin in equine pursuits 25 Spanish mounts.[68] Nor did these exchanges end with Henry's death. In December 1551, the French court dispatched a gift of horses to Edward VI, who recorded in his diary: 'Paris arrived with horses, and shewed how the French king had sent me six cortalles, tow Turkes, a barbary, tow genettes, a sturring horse, and tow little muyles.'[69]

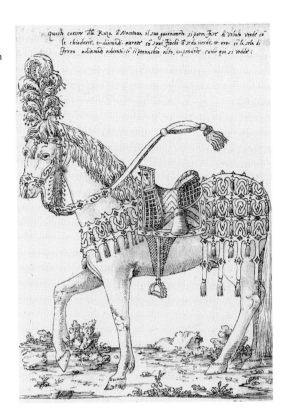

64 Filippo Orso, 'Corsier della Razza di Mantova', *c.* 1554, pen, ink and wash on paper. Victoria & Albert Museum, London.

Such exchanges reflected the claims of both the Tudor and Valois dynasties to imperial authority defined in both aesthetic and military terms through access to and possession of carefully selected and trained horses. However, as with the traffic in tapestries throughout this period, these relatively minor imperial courts found themselves wanting in their claim to equestrian pre-eminence in the face of the power of the Hapsburg empire of Charles V. As we shall see, in sharpening their ideological and aesthetic hold on territorial and religious authority in the latter half of the sixteenth century, the Hapsburgs were quick to deploy the 'flickering' equestrian image to devastating and terrifying effects.

V

In a letter written in March 1584, the Northern European educationalist and Reformer Johannes Sturm warned Queen Elizabeth I that a new, expensive style of warfare was becoming increasingly important in mainland Europe: a force of 'reiters' (riders) or light-horsemen, fast, manoeuvrable and armed with pistols, as illustrated by Dürer (illus. 65). The prudent ruler, he counselled, needed to forward-plan to take account of this phenomenon:

There is nothing which more weakens the strength of a kingdom than forces of foreign soldiers and especially horse, nor any Prince, however wealthy he may be, in our age, whose resources and treasury would not be exhausted, and

65 Albrecht Dürer, 'Soldier on Horseback', 1498, watercolour and pen on paper. Graphische Sammlung Albertina, Vienna.

his warlike strength weakened by the pay of these reiters; so that on account of want of money, a truce is frequently necessary, during which they may be able to recuperate, which interval is often harmful to the weaker party, and sometimes ruinous. And this evil in our century yearly grows greater, and is enlarged and confirmed.

The answer, Sturm continued, was for the Queen to invest in 'research and development' in horse-breeding in England, in the long-term interests of national security:

I know no kingdom more suitable for this equestrian business than your own; for in the supply of horses, England exceeds other countries. But because the horses are but weak, I advised that gradually a few stallions could be brought from Germany and Friesland, unknown to the enemy or to those who may be enemies in the future, which stallions would make the offspring of the English mare more robust.
  . . . one part of my advice was a stud [*equaria*] that England might in future have more robust and stronger horses and the supply of better horses might increase. Moreover I thought it would be well to invite secretly a few German saddlers and makers of greaves and shoes, not heads of households, who would need large pay, but their serving men, who, equally skilled, would come amongst us and be their own masters, for moderate pay. Also German tailors for making clothes and blacksmiths for making coats of mail, with a few saddlers.
  This should be done, not in show only, but in substance; not only that there might be a new form of saddle but the saddles themselves, with guns and engines of war, and also the anaphrates of the saddles, which some call stirrups [*stapedes*]; as also by the valour of the captains of horse and foot and the discipline and military exercise of the men, which is easy to effect if the law for the same be confirmed by the will and authority of your Majesty. [70]

Coming from a scholar and schoolteacher, this was well-informed counsel. Friesland horses, or 'Frizes' (illus. 66), were heavily built, tractable and sturdy, with good wind and stamina, but better suited for haulage than riding.[71] Crossing them with 'no-name' English stock could plausibly be expected to produce a fast, strong horse, suitable for modern military manoeuvres.
  Sturm's 'advice' raised an issue that had been on the English military agenda continuously since the 1540s.[72] Following a drastic depletion in horse stocks caused by their serving as literal cannon-fodder for the French military campaigns in the early decades of the sixteenth century, first Henry VIII and then Elizabeth I had introduced policies for increasing the number and improving the quality of English horses, specifically for military service.[73] This involved legislation to prevent English horses from being exported, requirements for landowners to re-allocate deer parks (hunting lands) as parks for the rearing of

horses and provide specified numbers for musters of national militia, and exhortations to the nobility to contribute to the national war effort and arrest 'the general decay of the generation and breeding of good and swift and strong horses, which heretofore have been bred in this realm'.[74]

Henry VIII had involved himself personally with an ambitious series of stud farms for horse breeding. Sir Edward Willoughby gave up his park at Henley for the King's stud in 1540; in 1545, Sir Nicholas Strelley, a Warwickshire gentleman, took 30 mares from the royal stud at Warwick Castle into his park for grazing at 4d. per week apiece.[75] In 1544, Henry bought two hundred Flanders mares and had to enter into delicate negotiations with the Hapsburg Queen Regent for permission to export them to England.[76] The French ambassador reported to Francis I in 1542 that Henry had two stables of a hundred horses which he had seen, and could draw 150 horses per annum from his stud parks in Wales and Nottinghamshire.

On the eve of his departure for the Low Countries in 1585, when Elizabeth finally authorized military assistance for the Netherlanders against the Spanish (immediately after the fall of Antwerp in August), Leicester toured the stud farms, including surveying 'the Quenes

66 Filippo Orso, *Frisone*, *c.* 1554, pen, ink and wash on paper. Victoria & Albert Museum, London.

great horses' at the Royal stud at St Albans, presumably looking at 'equipment' for the campaign.[77] He and other prominent figures at the Elizabethan court such as Walsingham owned stables of over a hundred horses apiece, including significant gift horses from great studs. Thus Walsingham's horses in 1589 included 'Grey Bingham' (a gift from Sir Richard Bingham), 'Bay Sidney' (from Sir Henry Sidney) and 'Pied Markham', from Robert Markham, whose son Gervase Markham wrote a notable book on horsemanship.

If we look more closely at Sturm's letter, there is something disturbing in its insistence on the superiority of all things 'German' where horses and horsemanship were concerned.[78] Native German 'blood' was to be surreptitiously introduced into England to strengthen both indigenous breeds and their 'management'. National character traits (which were assumed to be replicated in beasts and humans alike, born and bred in the Low Countries) and local skills were elided. Both animals and their keepers were to be covertly introduced into England to improve English horse stock: 'Gradually a few stallions could be brought from Germany and Friesland, unknown to the enemy or to those who may be enemies in the future, which stallions would make the offspring of the English mare more robust'; 'Moreover I thought it would be well to invite secretly a few German saddlers and makers of greaves and shoes.'

German stallions are to be crossed with English mares; German military suppliers and trainers are to be introduced alongside native English soldiers to produce a similar military 'cross'. Somewhat surprisingly, perhaps, crossbreeding of this kind was regarded as strengthening the bloodline. Yet at the same time, there is a clear implication that an influx of foreign matter polluted and weakened: 'There is nothing which more weakens the strength of a kingdom than forces of foreign soldiers and especially horse', wrote Sturm.

Where the visual imagery of breeding absorbs the idea of hybridization or 'crossing' with apparent ease – an applied science of improvement and refinement, which in the days before Mendelian genetics was of necessity approximate – texts betray an underlying anxiety. This suggestion that the crossbreeding that strengthens and improves a breed also sullies the pure national bloodline recurs in literature in and around horse breeding. In Shakespeare's *Henry V*, it is the basis for the Dauphin's outburst of humiliation after the French defeat at Harfleur and on the eve of Agincourt, faced with the formidable military men of England, with their mixed Anglo-Saxon and Norman blood:

O Dieu vivant! Shall a few sprays [bastards] of us,
The emptying of our fathers' luxury,
Our scions, put in wild and savage stock,
Spirt up so suddenly into the clouds
And over-look their grafters?

As we might expect, metaphors of animal crossbreeding overlap with a corresponding set of images drawn from horticulture and plant grafting. The Constable replies:

Dieu de batailles! Where have they this mettle?
Is not their climate foggy, raw, and dull,
On whom as in despite the sun looks pale,
Killing their fruit with frowns? Can sodden water,
A drench for sur-reined jades – their barley-broth –
Decoct their cold blood for such valiant heat?
And shall our quick blood, spirited with wine,
Seem frosty?

To which the Dauphin responds in a final explicit linking of animal crossbreeding and human miscegenation:

Our madams mock at us and plainly say
Our mettle is bred out, and they will give
Their bodies to the lust of English youth,
To new-store France with bastard warriors.[79]

The language is the same as Sturm's, as are the racial assumptions (as the reference to the Mantuan stock has already emphasized, breeds are *razze* in Italian). Cross a quick-blooded French stallion with a cold-blooded English 'sur-reined jade' and you'll get a tough, bastard warrior. But at what cost to national self-esteem?[80]

67 Barbary horse, engraving from The Duke of Newcastle, *Méthode de Dresser les Cheveaux* (London, 1737). The black groom indicates the assumption of shared otherness.

160

68 Andrea Mantegna, Detail of the *Camera Picta* fresco showing the portrait of a riderless horse with a groom, 1465–74. Camera degli Sposi, Castello San Giorgio (Palazzo Ducale), Mantua.

69 Paolo Uccello, *Painting of an Imaginary Equestrian Statue of the English Mercenary Sir John Hawkwood*, 1436, fresco. Duomo, Florence.

70 Jan Vermeyen, *Disembarkation off the Cape of Carthage*, *c.* 1548–50, charcoal and watercolour cartoon on paper. Kunsthistorisches Museum, Vienna.

71 Hans Holbein the Younger, *Portrait of Anne of Cleves*, 1539, oil on canvas.
Musée du Louvre, Paris.

72 Giulio Romano, Frescoes showing horses, *c.* 1527–30. Salone Cavalli, Palazzo del Te, Mantua.

73 François Clouet, *Portrait of Francis I on Horseback*, c. 1548, oil on panel. Galleria degli Uffizi, Florence.

74 Titian, *Charles V at the Battle of Mühlberg*, 1548, oil on canvas. Museo del Prado, Madrid.

75 Mark Wallinger, *Race Class Sex*, 1992, oil on canvas. The Saatchi Gallery, London.

This is a topic fraught with difficulties. We have indicated that the enthusiasm among the European nobility for horse breeding needs to be looked at alongside other competing strongly held beliefs about 'purity of blood'. In the sixteenth century, the same territory in southern Spain that bred Andalusian horses, whose pedigree was a known cross between Arab and Spanish stock, insisted that Muslims and Jews could never become 'true' Christians because of their 'blood'. When the Archbishop of Toledo was attempting to block the bestowing of a benefice on the *converso* Fernando Jiménez, he used the example of the practice of a horse dealer to deny Jiménez's pedigree as a Christian. If a horse dealer is offered an 'imperfect' horse, he wrote, even if he is offered it free, he will not accept it into his stable, because the first thing he will want to know is the animal's 'race'. Such is his concern in case the bloodline of his stud is polluted that he is bound to refuse, even if he is assured that the horse is of noble 'race' (illus. 67).[81]

One further fundamental assumption made about race and breeding in the sixteenth century is detectable in these passages, though more explicit elsewhere. It is the stallion alone, according to conventional breeding theories, that contributes the fundamental characteristics to the product of a reproductive union. As Shakespeare's Dauphin implies, nurture in all its aspects influences the outcome: the mother's temperament, the suitability of her womb as a receptacle, plus geographical location, climate, nutriment. But breed, type or race is determined by the breed, type or race of the stallion.[82]

Some 'receptacles' were considered likely to provide particularly successful incubators. Low Countries breeds were considered particularly strong, steady and manageable. After Charles V's acquisition of the Netherlands, he favoured local Flemish horses for breeding purposes.[83] Which (together with the negotiation for brood mares referred to above between Henry and the Hapsburg Regent in the Netherlands) casts a somewhat different light on Holbein's portrait of Anne of Cleves (illus. 71), and on Henry VIII's comments when he finally clapped eyes on her in 1540: 'The King found her so different from her picture . . . that . . . he swore they had brought him a Flanders mare.' 'A breeder, not a looker' was what he meant. In the event, of course, the 'breeding' was a failure, and the union lasted a mere six months. We do not, of course, have to take seriously the divorce testimony that the marriage was not consummated. Indeed, our current argument would suggest that quite the opposite was the case, and that the problem was Anne's inability to fulfil even her role as Flanders mare by failing to become pregnant.

We might note further implications for transnational relations here. This version of the suitability of Low Countries horses as 'receptacles' for bloodlines 'passing through' (as it were) – which we have taken from respectable sources on early horse breeding – is uncannily close to the contemporary version of the nation itself. In the opinion of sixteenth-century Europe and in the hierarchy of early modern states, the Low Countries were an *entrepôt* – a kind of receptacle, like the mare, which was crucial for the development of Empire, but not a global power in its own right.

As a Protestant reformer addressing the hoped-for (if reluctant) Deborah, leader of Protestant Europe, Sturm's advice on investing in military 'reiters' turned out to be prophetic. Lack of a clear under-standing of the appropriate use of new-fangled light-horsemen during the English campaigns in the Low Countries in the 1580s contributed to their poor performance against Philip II's Spanish forces. It also produced the symbolic nadir of those operations – the death of Sir Philip Sidney, champion and white knight of European Protestantism, at the Battle of Zutphen, in September 1586. It was while acting as an English 'reiter' (in a troop of 50 equally skilled young equestrian noblemen) that Sidney met his death. This dashed the hopes of European Protestants that the young man they thought of as the rising star of the English aristocracy might provide a lasting bridge between groups of Calvinists separated by the English Channel (illus. 76).

'Reiters' required quality horsepower – the equivalent of the modern-day highly manoeuvrable tank. Horses at the Leicester/ Norris campaign were from the Low Countries. Sir John Norris shopped around for his troops' equipment. On this occasion, having sounded out the English markets, he made an informal recommen-dation to Walsingham that it would be cheaper for the Crown to send horsemen unequipped, purchasing both mounts and armour in the Netherlands when they arrived.[84]

On 22 September 1586, Leicester's troops encircled Zutphen, isolating it and surrounding it with trenches manned by musketeers. Sir John Norris was on the east bank, while Leicester commanded the main force to the west. Their intention was to draw the Prince of Parma into battle when he attempted to resupply the city. As Parma approached Zutphen in dense fog, Leicester (not expecting a major military engagement) sent Norris to intercept the supply convoy, with a force of three hundred horse and two hundred foot. Meanwhile, he himself headed a 50-strong troop of light-horse 'lancers' (or 'reiters') to skirmish in and out again, leaving the field to Norris.[85] Just as Leicester's company (including Philip Sidney) swept down on the

76 Philip Sidney on horseback, woodcut from Geoffrey Whitney, *Choice of Emblems* (London, 1586).

convoy, the fog lifted, revealing a train of over five hundred carts escorted by three thousand Spanish troops. Behind them were Spanish muskets, well dug into their own trenches. Sidney was wounded by a musket ball in the thigh – a minor injury which became infected and proved fatal.[86]

Here again, our tendency to let our eye slide over the image of the horse as literally 'insignificant' damages our understanding of Sidney's reputation in his lifetime (as opposed to his posthumous hagiography). As he reminds us at the beginning of his *Apology for Poetry*, he was something of a skilled horseman by profession – a soldier-hero in the European power stakes of a highly specific and up-to-date kind.

VI

One of the reasons we overlook the highly specific nature of individual horses in this period is because of the familiarity of certain sorts of equestrian representation – a familiarity we have learned, through the work of scholars like Gombrich and Panofsky, to associate with 'the classical tradition'. From the statue of Marcus Aurelius in Rome to Leonardo's ambitious, unfulfilled dream of an immense statue of a horse for the Sforzas, we believe we recognize in monumental figures of horses, and in figures on horseback, a timeless, universal representation of power.[87] Precisely because there is a link between Leonardo's horse studies (illus. 77) and antique equestrian statues, we confidently identify the tradition in which the studies stand as both classical and Renaissance in its conception, setting aside any idea of the need to bring a specifically contemporary 'real' context to bear on these art objects as well.

For a moment, we should look at the way in which such images evolved during the early modern period, alongside growing expertise and understanding of horses as international goods (we do not believe we can call them a commodity).[88] Because in fact the equation 'horse = power' was both Eastern and Western, and this has implications for its use in representations of imperial might during the fifteenth and sixteenth centuries.

Some of the most successful equestrian power-promoting images

77 Leonardo da Vinci, Studies for the Sforza horse, *c.* 1490, silver-point on paper. Royal Library, Windsor Castle.

are not in fact large-scale at all. They are to be found on the reverses of the fifteenth- and early sixteenth-century portrait medals we looked at in our opening chapter. As the Christian West and Muslim East struggled for control of Constantinople, the gateway between them, in the first half of the fifteenth century, portrait medals of the contending figures competed with each other for ownership of the most resonating symbols of imperial rule. Costanzo da Ferrara's portrait medal of Mehmet II (illus. 78) shows with particular clarity the way in which a portrait head of the great ruler, accompanied by a reverse incorporating some iconographically compelling scene based around a horse, provided such objects with equal recognition value, and equal vigour, from West to East and East to West. As we put it in chapter 1, the Mehmet medal 'is a resolutely Ottoman artefact, yet in a strenuously Western European artistic tradition',[89] drawing as it does on Pisanello's medal of John Paleologus (illus. 79).

Our suggestion is that the circulation of portrait medals traces with peculiar clarity a sequence of key iconographic 'moments' as images of power, consolidating their symbolic effectiveness and contributing to

78 Costanzo da Ferrara, Portrait medal of Mehmet II (reverse) showing the Sultan riding, c. 1481, bronze. National Gallery of Art, Washington, DC. See also illus. 10.

our sense that these narratives and images are 'timeless'. Medals crossed and recrossed the invisible ideological boundaries supposedly isolating Christian from Muslim, European from Turk. As is familiar in our own day, the urge to acquire transcends boundaries, and trade percolates where embargoes – Papal or otherwise – insist it should not.

The exchange of portrait medals with their 'art horses' mirrors that of the animals on which they were modelled. Horses were traditional gifts exchanged between heads of state; Arab horses were particularly coveted or, failing pure Arabs, Andalusian or southern Spanish horses derived directly from Arab stock. When Henry VIII married Katherine of Aragon, he promptly requested horses of good Spanish-based breeds – a Spanish jennet, a Neapolitan and a Sicilian – from his new father-in-law.

The horse on the reverse of Pisanello's medal showing John Paleologus was drawn from life (illus. 80), and was the horse on which the Emperor pursued his enthusiasm for hunting during the Council of Florence. Whether the medal was commissioned by John himself or by his Este or Medici hosts, it was intended to be legible as a symbol by both Eastern and Western audiences. Both the Mehmet medal and Sperandio of Mantua's medal of Giovanni Bentivoglio (illus. 81) are later, and were probably directly influenced by Pisanello as well as by the Paleologus medal. In the case of the latter, the transaction was between Eastern and Western Christian powers.[90] The fact that real horses were enthusiastically exchanged between them – as symbols of magnificence and courtly generosity – only went to amplify the resonance and claims to global importance of such public announcements in artistic form.

79 Antonio Pisanello, Portrait medal showing John VIII Paleologus (reverse), 1438, lead (see also illus. 8). Staatliche Museen zu Berlin – Preußischer Kulturbesitz.

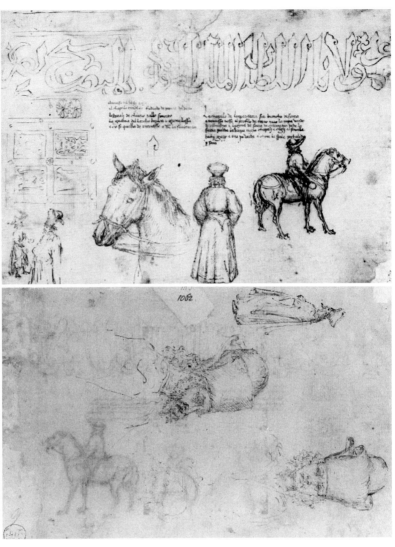

80 Antonio Pisanello, Preparatory drawings for the horse on the reverse of the John Paleologus medal (illus. 79), *c.* 1438, ink on paper. Musée du Louvre, Paris.

VII

Where horses are concerned, we are arguing, the real and the representational converge, competing for meaning in early modern graphic and plastic imaging of imperial power. The more 'realistic' the horse, the more convincingly captured in the moment of surging strength, mastered by the horseman, the more certain we are that our response is 'natural' and inevitable. The real animal, controlled by his noble

81 Sperandio of Mantua, Portrait medal of Giovanni II Bentivoglio (obverse and reverse, the latter showing him on horseback), *c.* 1480, lead. University Art Museum, University of California at Santa Barbara.

master, converges with the fantasized (and sometimes allegorized) representation of the imperial figure on a rearing mount, crushing his idealized adversary, graphically emphasized in Leonardo's designs for the Sforza monument (illus. 82).

By now, we hope, the reader will have grasped the carefully contrived process by which these equestrian images were executed, and their meaning manipulated, in the period we are examining. It is interesting, in this light, to contrast an equestrian image by an accomplished artist which, we would argue, set out to achieve a different response on the part of the onlooker.

At the end of Francis I's reign, in the 1540s, the court painter François Clouet produced a small panel portrait of the King on horseback (illus. 73). No such equestrian image had hitherto been executed (although one had been part of the temporary decorations for the *entrée* into Rouen in 1517, as an image of imperial grandeur following the King's military victory at Marignano). Janet Cox-Rearick has convincingly associated this portrait with the equestrian statue of Louis XII above the main entrance at Blois, where the image of the *roi-chevalier* (knightly king) is placed against a blue background decorated with fleur-de-lis.[91] Clouet's background is also bright blue. Francis, metamorphosed from ageing monarch into iconic knightly king, is armoured and bejewelled, rider and horse made virtually indistinguishable in the elaborate decorative programme. The horse is 'himself a kind of royal icon', as Cox-Rearick observes, as 'ostentatious and formalized' as the King. The animal's delicate, decorative caparison features the same personal emblem of the knotted double-eight

82 Leonardo da Vinci, Study for the Sforza monument, *c*. 1488–90, metalpoint on paper. Royal Library, Windsor Castle.

that decorates Francis's costume in the state portrait of him by Jean and François Clouet from the 1520s.[92]

Here, we suggest, we have horseman as emblem, iconically saturated with superimposed meanings (the Louis XII allusion, the decorative court elegance, the deliberately youthful stance of the ageing King).[93] In reality, Francis had a reputation as an accomplished horseman – stories of the Battle of Pavia, at which he was humiliated and taken captive, describe him as acquitting himself brilliantly on horseback, while the gout-stricken Emperor Charles V fell from his mount on two occasions. The reverse of Benvenuto Cellini's medal of Francis I shows just such a proficient horseman, though the figure is an allegorical one (illus. 17). With the likelihood in mind to which we alluded in chapter 1 of viewers' flipping the medal over in their hands, Francis and the horseman on his rearing horse are run together; hope for a 'victory of virtue over fortune' and the King of France are elided.[94]

The weakness of Francis I's political position in the international arena meant, as we have emphasized repeatedly, that his bids for symbolic cultural power were bound to be unconvincing. No such reservations restricted Charles V's self-promotion as the leading imperial figure – except, perhaps, the lurking figure of the Ottoman Sultan Süleyman (illus. 83).

We draw our argument to a close with one of the most lastingly imposing of sixteenth-century horse-centred graphic representations of imperial power: Titian's *Charles V at the Battle of Mühlberg* (illus. 74). We argue that this work is in a direct line of descent, and that in the cultural representations we have been discussing, we are hampered today in our understanding of, and ability to 'read' or interpret, a painting like this by our lack of sensitivity to horses themselves and to the East-West figurative tradition associated with them.

The painting is typically Hapsburg in its celebration of a crucial military and political victory in high-art form. Mühlberg was the decisive triumph of Charles as self-styled defender of the true Catholic faith against the forces of Reformed Christianity led by the Lutheran Philip of Hesse. Titian's painting is also, we suggest, a striking example of the kind of 'convergence' we have been describing between the real and the figurative in equestrian representations, and one that asks to have read back into it imputations of dominion whose more sinister contours are no longer immediately accessible to us.

In the painting, the horse Charles V rides is identifiably his own and recognizably an Andalusian (illus. 84) – a highly covetable example of the Spanish-type cross between an Arab and a European 'race'.[95] Both horse and rider are dressed, we are told by contemporary sources,

83 Charles V's medal showing Süleyman the Magnificent, *c.* 1530, bronze. British Museum, London.

84 Filippo Orso, *Gianetto natural di spagna* (Spanish or Andalusian), *c.* 1554, pen, ink and wash on paper. Victoria & Albert Museum, London.

exactly as they were for the battle itself.[96] Since Charles wears all the accoutrements of a 'modern' soldier in the field, including his pistol at his belt, there is therefore the confusing possibility of seeing him as a 'real' soldier in action, in spite of the obvious appeal to antique proto-types of power like the statues of Marcus Aurelius or Constantine.[97]

At the same time as it simulates a 'real' battle situation, therefore, this is patently a triumphalist work, broadcasting Hapsburg power and support for the Church of Rome (the Papacy were financial backers of the Mühlberg expedition). In this guise, horse and rider revert to timeless 'types'.[98] There is little doubt that this was deliberate on Titian's part, an effect carefully built into the composition. Avila's contemporary account of the battle already lined Charles up icono-graphically as he crossed the Elbe with Caesar crossing the Rubicon. Later in the same description, Avila has Charles recall a remark by Scipio; finally, he contrasts Caesar's 'I came, I saw, I conquered' with Charles's Christian purpose: 'I came, I saw and God conquered'.

Art historians commenting on the painting's composition have tended to seize confidently upon this Rome-related, ostensibly human-istic symbolism. This approach validates in suitably benign terms the ruthless crushing of the German Protestant League by Hapsburg Imperial armies in the name of the Holy Roman Church. With equiva-lent confidence, it discards Aretino's suggested programme for the work, whereby Charles was to have been depicted in the armour he wore, and on the horse he actually rode, in the battle; the vanquished were to be shown trampled under the horse's hooves, alongside which would be shown allegories of Religion and Fame, 'on foot and in motion (keeping pace with the horse and its rider) . . . the one with crucifix and communion chalice in her hands, pointing to the heavens, the other with wings and a trumpet, with which she offers him the earth'.[99]

Recent X-rays of Titian's equestrian portrait of Charles V (illus. 85) have revealed that the pose of horse and rider here was altered significantly in the course of painting. Originally, the horse was indeed rearing, as Aretino had suggested – a classic compositional arrangement in which infidels are routinely shown being crushed beneath stallions' hooves.[100] By the mid-sixteenth century, Muslim and Protestant had become interchangeable in European iconography, with the unfaithful, the non-believer and the 'infidel' substituting racial type and nationality as required. Titian here adjusted his equestrian figure so as to make Charles into a 'Christian Prince', riding into actual battle with set lance, while his horse settled down to the steady gait required.[101]

Superficially, the alteration might suggest a moderated, perhaps more considered version of dominion on the part of the Spanish at this moment. As we have seen, a contemporary account of the battle seized upon and emphasized the telling symbolic parallel between Caesar's crossing the Rubicon and Charles's crossing the Elbe. Several subsequent commentators have insisted that this was precisely what Charles is shown doing in Titian's painting. If we compare Titian's horse and rider with a contemporary engraving of the battle, however, it is apparent how calm and detached Titian's horse and rider are, how unbroken the horse's gait and the horseman's gaze, unlike the *mêlée* of plunging horses and riders shown struggling across the river in the engraving.[102]

So let us keep our attention focused explicitly on the rider and his horse, as we have done throughout this chapter. As contemporary documents stress, the Emperor's mount, painted as if from life, is 'A deep chestnut Spanish horse, which had been presented to the Emperor by monsieur de Ri, knight of the order of the Golden Fleece,

85 X-ray of
Titian's *Charles V
at the Battle
of Mühlberg*
(illus. 74).

and his first Chamberlain'.[103] Here, then, is a 'real' rather than a
humanistic or symbolic representation of imperial mastery. Into the
figure of the deep brown/dark chestnut Andalusian horse mastered
by the serenely controlling Spanish Prince are rolled up the converging
topoi of early modern horse breeding. The hot blood of the Arab
horse has been tamed and controlled by an intermingling of indigenous
Spanish blood.[104] The crushed infidel has gone from under the horse's
hooves, but the potent symbol of Spanish imperialism is still there.
Under the heel of the Hapsburg master lie crushed, together, the
hopes and aspirations of Protestant Europe and the Muslim East.
Eastwards and westwards, circulated to Muslim, Jew and Lutheran
alike in the early modern global community, this image and its threat
were provocative and unmistakable.[105]

Our re-reading of Titian's powerful yet disturbing painting is given
its ultimate confirmation once we locate the picture in relation to the
two groups of objects with which we have been concerned to frame
this study: the portrait medal and the tapestry.

In 1548, shortly after Titian completed his portrait, a portrait medal was struck in celebration of Charles V (illus. 86, 87). On the obverse of this large, silver medal is a bust of the Emperor, dressed in armour and wearing the Order of the Golden Fleece. The profile recalls Titian's *Battle of Mühlberg*. The reverse, however, features the outline of the harbour of Tunis and a skirmish between Ottoman and Hapsburg riders, with soldiers falling beneath the hooves of rearing mounts. Thirteen years after Charles's conquest of Tunis, captured so vividly in the tapestries that meticulously record the campaign against the infidel Turk, the medal conflates Charles's victory over the Protestants at Mühlberg (captured in Titian's portrait) with the Emperor's earlier conquest of Tunis (graphically portrayed in the *Conquest of Tunis* tapestries).[106]

As with the display of the tapestries six years later at the wedding

86, 87 After Giovanni Bernardi, Portrait medal of Charles V (obverse and reverse), *c.* 1548, silver. Kunsthistorisches Museum, Vienna.

of Philip and Mary Tudor, this medal brings together infidel Protestant and Turk in a terrifying image of Hapsburg conquest projected within a territorial, religious context and, finally, on a global scale.

We have argued that art objects from the Renaissance originally carried powerful associations with the East whose impact is now lost to us. Both the content and the forms of Renaissance art reflected a vigorous two-way process of recognition and development in which what we have called East and West played their parts. The pressure of commercial competition on style and taste in the period, the shaping influence of the market on our artistic heritage, has begun to be acknowledged more generally. Here we have taken a step further, pointing out that

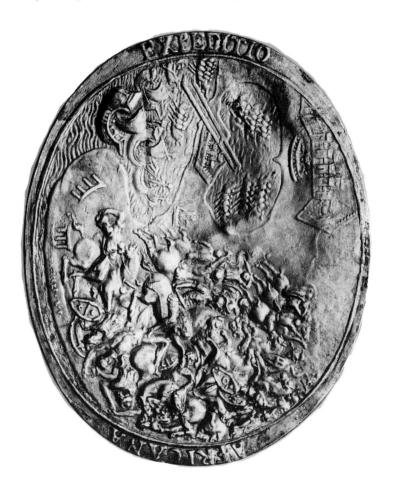

entrepreneurial competition is rarely one-directional and rarely involves one entirely passive partner. Once we recognize that the Ottoman Empire confronted the Hapsburgs on an equal footing at the end of the fifteenth century, and that each empire recognized the might of the other, it is only to be expected that Western art around that date should be shot through with considered responses to the artistic output of Europe's trading partners to the east.

We are signalling the need for a shift in mentality on the part of art historians and cultural historians. The ground has already been prepared by recent changes in Europe's understanding of itself. Gradually, over the last twenty years or so, the East has begun to come back into Europe's line of vision. In an age that talks constantly of a global village, we suggest, the cultural meanings we have been excavating are beginning to be registered again.

Mark Wallinger's four equestrian images, entitled *Race Class Sex* (illus. 75), appeal directly to the submerged meanings we have explored in this chapter. The perfect realism of the horses jars against the highly charged suggestions of purity, blood, sex and status for which their title is a catalyst. What is shocking to us is how perfectly Wallinger's horses seem to understand the tale we have been unfolding – how knowing he is about the implications of any appreciation of blood-stock, or the aesthetics of race and breeding. Why, though, are we so taken aback? Consult any present-day horse-racing enthusiast, for instance (and we have done so on more than one occasion), and it rapidly becomes clear that oriental bloodstock lines, exotic owners, commercial incentives and strenuous competitiveness between nations and ethnicities remain part of the heady mix that draws people to the sport. These factors are also clearly understood to play their part in decisions about 'beauty' and 'performance' where fine, expensive horses are concerned.

We believe that at this moment of the communal revisiting of a set of relationships with the East and of discovery of future possibilities for East-West understanding and collaboration, it is vital that we understand that this is not the first cultural encounter between the two. There is a dangerous suggestion in some of what is said, however affirmatively, about our Eastern neighbours that we come to them as the inevitable senior partner in any cultural transaction. European civilization, it is suggested, will finally offer its benefits to the barbarian.

We have shown that in the fifteenth and sixteenth centuries, East and West met on much more equal terms. Indeed, at the beginning of our story, in the 1430s, it was the East that provided Europe with some of its most enduringly potent symbols and images. Over the succeeding century, East met West in strenuous and constructive competition, from which many of the most familiar and perhaps reassuring elements of our modern cultural currency are derived. Yet in Bosnia and Kosova – to take the most obvious recent examples – the rediscovery of the historical intermingling of Eastern and Western cultures, mentalities and ways of life has resulted in a tragic emergence of crude, Burckhardtian ethnic essentialism.

The discovery of shared histories weaving Eastern and Western idioms deep into European culture must not lead to a clarion call to 'cleanse' European civilization of its barbarous other. That is not the reality, but a short-lived misprision, traceable, as we showed at the outset of this study, to a particular cast of mind at a particular historical moment – a moment we would characterize as one of inattention rather than of bigotry. Our shared histories mean that we inhabit a cultural environment rich with possibilities for future fruitful collaborations and contestations. That, in the end, is the lesson we hope the reader will have learned from this book.

References

Preface

1 *New York Times*, 25 December 1999.
2 Jill Dunkerton *et al.*, *Giotto to Dürer: Early Renaissance Painting in the National Gallery* (London, 1991), p. 91.
3 'Cultural mobility' is Stephen Greenblatt's coinage for the kind of trans-actability of cultural currency to which we are referring (Greenblatt in answer to questions following a lecture delivered at Queen Mary, University of London, December 1999).
4 Michael White, *Leonardo: The First Scientist* (London, 1999). For details of Leonardo's involvement in projects associated with the Ottoman court, see Franz Babinger, 'Vier Baurorschlage Lionardo da Vinci's am Sultan Bajezid II (1502/3)', *Nachrichten der Akademie der Wissenschaften in Göttingen*, Philol.–hist. Klasse, 1 (1952).
5 See also Lisa Jardine, *Worldly Goods: A New History of the Renaissance* (London, 1996).

1 *Exchanging Identity: Breaching the Boundaries of Renaissance Europe*

1 Jacob Burckhardt, *The Civilization of the Renaissance in Italy* (London, 1892), p. 181. For the traditional version of Ciriac of Ancona as an erudite traveller recording ancient Greek and Roman ruins, see E. W. Bodnar, *Cyriacus of Ancona and Athens* (Brussels, 1960); Bernard Ashmole, 'Cyriac of Ancona', reprint in G. Holmes, ed., *Art and Politics in Renaissance Italy: British Academy Lectures* (Oxford, 1993), pp. 41–57; Rudolf Pfeiffer, *History of Classical Scholarship 1300–1850* (Oxford, 1976), p. 51.
2 F. Babinger, *Mehmed the Conqueror and His Time* (Princeton, 1978), pp. 112, 496–8 (although the assertion that Ciriac was at the siege of Constantinople as Mehmet's secretary in 1453 is now regarded as a misreading of one of the sources; see F. Babinger, 'Notes on Cyriac of Ancona and Some of His Friends', *Journal of the Warburg and Courtauld Institutes* 25 [1962], pp. 321–3). On Ciriac's travels in both East and West, in particular his attendance at the courts of the Ottoman sultans Murad II and Mehmet II, see J. Colin, *Cyriaque d'Ancône: Le Voyageur, le marchand, l'humaniste* (Paris, 1981). On Mehmet's Western reading and library, see J. Raby, 'East and West in Mehmed the Conqueror's Library', *Bulletin du bibliophile* (1987), pp. 297–321. Ciriac was in the train of John VIII Paleologus on the mission to Italy to seek support for Constantinople in 1438 (Biblioteca

Nazionale Centrale, Florence, MS. II, IV, 128, fols 108v–110r = Bibl. Magliabecchiana, VI, 132, cited in K. M. Setton, 'The Emperor John VIII Slept Here . . .', in *Europe and the Levant in the Middle Ages and the Renaissance* [London, 1974], pp. 222–8). An autograph letter survives from Ciriac to Pope Eugene IV, dated 18 October 1441, in which he asks for support for an expedition to explore Ethiopia (see J. Rykwert and A. Engel, eds, *Leon Battista Alberti* [Milan, 1994], pp. 455–6).

3 Sigmund Freud, *Civilization and Its Discontents* [1930], in The Penguin Freud Library Volume 12, *Civilization, Society and Religion* (Harmondsworth, 1985), pp. 282–3.

4 Although the word *Renaissance* can be found in seventeenth-century sources, its use to describe this re-emergence of the high culture of antiquity in Western Europe derives from the nineteenth century. Burckhardt's *Die Kultur der Renaissance in Italien* was first published in 1860; it was republished with an important new introduction in 1930. Jules Michelet is supposed to have been the first modern historian to apply the term *Renaissance* to the whole epoch, so while Burckhardt did not coin it, he did make it popular, and his essay was the starting point for all subsequent discussions about the beginning and concept of the Renaissance (Pfeiffer, *The History of Classical Scholarship*, p. 18).

5 Freud, *Civilization and Its Discontents*, p. 338.

6 Stephen Greenblatt, *Renaissance Self-Fashioning from More to Shakespeare* (Chicago, 1980), pp. 174–5. Ten pages earlier, Greenblatt puts Burckhardt in place to anchor historically the Freudian discussion of consciousness that follows: 'Despite its age and its well-documented limitations, one of the best introductions to Renaissance self-fashioning remains Burckhardt's *Civilization of the Renaissance in Italy*. Burckhardt's crucial perception was that the political upheavals in Italy in the later Middle Ages, the transition from feudalism to despotism, fostered a radical change in consciousness: the princes and *condottieri*, and their secretaries, ministers, poets, and followers, were cut off from established forms of identity and forced by their relations to power to fashion a new sense of themselves and their world: the self and the state as a work of art' (*Ibid.*, pp. 161–2).

7 Greenblatt, *Renaissance Self-Fashioning*, p. 175.

8 The phrase 'continued allegory' is Spenser's own choice of description contained in the prefatory 'Letter to Raleigh'. See A. C. Hamilton, ed., *Edmund Spenser: The Faerie Queene* (London, 1977).

9 We use the terms *East* and *West* here as convenient shorthand. In fact, 'East' refers to territories eastwards and southwards across the Mediterranean, including the Mamluk Empire in North Africa.

10 Hamilton, *Edmund Spenser*, p. 737.

11 *Ibid.*

12 Una meets the 'goodly knight' Arthur in Bk I, canto vii, stanza 29. She identifies herself to him as 'th'only daughter of a King and Queene, / Whose parents deare, whilest equall destinies / Did runne about, and their felicities / The fauourable heauens did not enuy, / Did spread their rule through all the territories, / Which Phison and Euphrates floweth by, / And Gehons golden waues doe wash continually.' Although Hamilton identifies this location as 'Eden', it is, of course, more properly 'the Holy

Land' – the contested location of Eastern and Western cults. Arthur is identified by name (by Una) in the text (as opposed to the verse summary) in Bk I, canto ix, stanza 6. Shortly afterwards, he and Redcrosse exchange gifts before parting – a 'box of Diamond' from Arthur, containing 'few drops of liquor pure' to cure wounds and a book written in gold (the New Testament) from Redcrosse to Arthur.

13 Bk I, canto viii, stanza 27; Hamilton, *Edmund Spenser*, p. 113.

14 Bk I, canto ix, stanza 14; Hamilton, *Edmund Spenser*, p. 121. Arthur having confessed that he is committed elsewhere, Redcrosse observes to Una: 'Thine, O then . . . / Next to that Ladies loue, shalbe the place, / O fairest virgin, full of heauenly light, / Whose wondrous faith, exceeding earthly race, / Was firmest fixt in my extremest case' (*Op. cit.*, stanza 17, 122). Syntactically, it is not at all clear whether Redcrosse here is installing the Queene of Faeries above Una in his own affections, or whether he is advising her that she will rank second only to the Queen in Arthur's. Perhaps this ambiguity further indicates the possibility of eliding Arthur and Redcrosse as required.

15 Bk I, canto x, stanza 60; Hamilton, *Edmund Spenser*, p. 141.

16 For a convenient summary of the critical literature on this point, see Hamilton, *Edmund Spenser*, pp. 23–6.

17 This account is based on Michael H. Collins's website entitled 'Saint George in English History'. The Latin narrative tradition follows that of the Greek, but Diocletian becomes Dacian, Emperor of the Persians, with dominion over 72 kings. George lives and dies in Mitilene in eastern Cappadocia. His tortures continue for seven years and are considerably more extensive. They result in the conversion of the Empress Alexandra and 40,900 others, some of whom are first raised from the dead. As George dies, a whirlwind of fire carries off the wicked Dacian. Early accounts of the deeds, martyrdom and miracles of St George are to be found in Greek, Latin, Syriac, Arabic, Coptic, Ethiopic, Armenian and Turkish.

18 See W. G. Ryan, trans., *Jacobus de Voragine, The Golden Legend: Readings on the Saints* (Princeton, 1993), vol. I, pp. 238–42. Collins has suggested that the prominence in the St George legend of the knight on horseback, with the Crusader's red cross on his shield and pinioning a dragon with his long lance, can be traced back to Constantine the Great: 'At the tomb of George in Lod (Lydda), there is a bas-relief of Constantine trampling on a dragon and piercing it with his *labarum* or spear. (The use of the sword although known in the early centuries was commonly depicted only in the late Middle Ages.) According to Eusebius, *De vita Constantini*, III: 3, Constantine ordered that he be widely portrayed thus overcoming the evil of paganism. One of his bronze coins dating from 326–330 shows him surmounted by the chi-rho monogram and transfixing a serpent with his labarum. A gold solidus of Valentinian III struck at Rome 424–5 shows the emperor bearing a long cross and transfixing a serpent with a human head. A similar motif has been found on terra cotta icons unearthed in Macedonia in the 1980's and dated to the 6th or 7th centuries. One depicts St George and St Christopher side by side each impaling with a long lance a human-headed serpent. Similar icons have been found in Tunisia. It is impossible to say when or how the dragon motif became attached to

St George, except that it was much earlier than often claimed. Possibly the legend of George and the Dragon originated when the imperial image on the bas-relief was mistaken for that of St George.'

19 On the fifteenth-century cult of St George and its allegorical relationship with Trebizond, see G. Didi-Huberman, R. Garbetta and M. Morgaine, *Saint Georges et le dragon: Versions d'une Légende* (Paris, 1994). See also L. Olivata, 'La principessa Trebisonda: Per un ritratto di Pisanello', in P. Castelli, ed., *Ferrara e il Concilio 1438–1439: Atti del Covegno di Studi nel 5500 Anniversario del Concilio dell'unione delle due Chiese d'oriente e d'occidente* (Ferrara, 1992), pp. 193–211.

20 See also Cosimo Tura, *St George and the Princess of Trebizond*, 1469. Museo del Duomo, Ferrara.

21 Bk I, canto ii, stanzas 10–11; Hamilton, *Edmund Spenser*, p. 46.

22 The violent encounters with 'saracens' with dismembered bodies, like the human body parts that litter the landscape in Carpaccio's fresco of St George fighting the dragon, seem to invoke the second story of George's many dismembering tortures at the hands of Diocletian, while we attend as viewers/readers to the dragon-slaying version of the legend.

23 Bk I, canto ii, stanza 12.

24 The claim made in Bk I, canto x, stanza 60 that George is an 'ymp, sprong out from English race', born 'of Saxon kings . . . in Britane land' and then 'exchanged' and planted in a furrow 'in this Faerie lond', where a plough-man finds him and names him 'Georgos', rests on a piece of etymology used by Voragine to support the story of George's being born in Cappadocia and martyred at Lydda (stanzas 65–6; see Hamilton, *Edmund Spenser*, n. 142).

25 Bk I, canto x, stanza 61; Hamilton, *Edmund Spenser*, p. 141.

26 *The Currency of Fame* is the title given by S. K. Scher to his comprehensive book on Renaissance portrait medals (New York, 1994).

27 See E. Corradini, 'Medallic Portraits of the Este: Effigies ad vivum expressae', in N. Mann and L. Syson, eds, *The Image of the Individual: Portraits in the Renaissance* (London, 1998), pp. 22–39.

28 See L. Syson, 'Circulating a Likeness? Coin Portraits in Late Fifteenth-century Italy', in Mann and Syson, *The Image of the Individual*, pp. 113–25. As Syson points out, the act of placing one's portrait head on a coin could be used to assert authority: 'Ludovico [il Moro] had no real claim to power while his nephew, Gian Galeazzo Sforza, was alive, but he . . . used the introduction of his portrait onto the Milanese coinage as part of a well-orchestrated campaign, having taken over the regency, to become the duke. The French ambassador, Philippe de Commynes, who was in Lombardy in 1494 with Charles VIII of France, wrote: "Lord Ludovico soon made it evident that he very much wanted to keep his authority; and he had money coined with the duke [Gian Galeazzo's portrait] on one side and himself on the other, which made many people murmur." Only the use of a naturalis-tic portrait image allowed him to make his point so effectively' (p. 116).

29 See Corradini, 'Medallic Portraits of the Este', pp. 23–5. Pisanello (who is of particular interest to us here) copied the portrait heads from antique coins (*Ibid.*, p. 23); he collected such coins himself, several of which were found in his lodgings at his death (Scher, *The Currency of Fame*, p. 44).

30 The acquisition of the Constantine medal from 'Italian merchants' can be dated precisely to November 1402; it is generally assumed that the Heraclius medal was acquired at the same time or shortly thereafter. For a full account of the two medals and their afterlife, see Scher, *The Currency of Fame*, pp. 32–7. For an example of the direct influence of the Heraclius medal on East-West representations of power of the sort discussed in detail in this chapter, see Lisa Jardine, *Worldly Goods: A New History of the Renaissance* (London, 1996), chap. 8.

31 Our interpretation of the iconography of the two Berry medals (which does not correspond to Scher's) is based on Carlo Ginzburg, *The Enigma of Piero: Piero della Francesca* [1981], trans. M. Ryle and K. Soper (London, 1985). Although Ginzburg does not discuss the medals, his close treatment of the story of the True Cross in the context of Piero's Arezzo cycle leads us directly to the conclusion expressed above (see Ginzburg, *The Enigma of Piero*, pp. 36–43). In 1400, Manuel Paleologus (John VIII's father) and his family were in Europe seeking the aid of the Western princes against the Muslim threat to Constantinople (see J. Gill, *Personalities of the Council of Florence and Other Essays* [Oxford, 1964], pp. 104–5).

32 Thus the 'otherness' of the portrait medal tends only to obtrude itself where the subject is explicitly oriental; see, for example, Bertoldo di Giovanni's medal of Mehmet II, probably commissioned by Lorenzo de' Medici in the late 1470s (Scher, *The Currency of Fame*, pp. 126–8). The inscription on its obverse (around a portrait head borrowed from Bellini or Costanzo da Ferrara) reads 'Mehmed, emperor of Asia and also Trebizond and Magna Graecia'. The reverse shows a young nude male, brandishing a statuette and driving a triumphal chariot drawn by two prancing horses and led by a groom whose pose resembles that of the groom on the Heraclius medal. On the chariot are three nude women, bound by a rope held by the charioteer and labelled 'Greece', 'Trebizond' and 'Asia'. 'Relations between Florence and the sultan were especially close in these last two years of the Turk's life', observes Scher. 'In 1480, [Lorenzo] sent the sultan a letter thanking him for the gift of a saddle. According to the elaborate thesis of Emil Jacobs, this message would have been accompanied by Bertoldo's medal' (*The Currency of Fame*, p. 40).

33 Scher, *The Currency of Fame*, p. 15.

34 *Ibid.*

35 For a list of later works of art that use the medal portrait of the Emperor as a prototype for all kinds of Eastern emperors and sultans, see R. Weiss, *Pisanello's Medallion of the Emperor John VIII Paleologus* (London, 1966).

36 Scher, *The Currency of Fame*, pp. 44–6.

37 M. Vickers, 'Some Preparatory Drawings for Pisanello's Medallion of John VIII Paleologus', *Art Bulletin* 60 (1978), pp. 419–24.

38 Murad II ruled the Ottoman Empire from 1421 until 1444, and again from 1446 until 1451. Mehmet II ruled from 1444 to 1446, then from 1451 to 1481.

39 See J. Gill's two studies, *The Council of Florence* (Cambridge, 1959), and *Personalities*.

40 Gill, *Personalities*, pp. 186–203.

41 Setton, '"The Emperor John VIII slept here . . ."', pp. 222–8. See also

K. M. Setton, *The Papacy and the Levant (1204–1571)*, (Philadelphia, 1976–84), vol. 3.

42 Vickers, 'Some Preparatory Drawings', pp. 417–18.

43 Gill, *Personalities*, p. 113.

44 Vickers, 'Some Preparatory Drawings', p. 417.

45 See Olivata, 'La principessa Trebisonda', pp. 193–211.

46 If, as Olivata has suggested, there existed a second version of the medal, with two pairs of praying hands held towards a cross on the reverse, this would seem to corroborate the moment that is captured iconographically.

47 Ginzburg, *The Enigma of Piero*.

48 'Panofsky defined iconography as "that branch of the history of art which concerns itself with the subject-matter or meaning of works of art, as opposed to their form". He distinguished between two levels, iconography in the strict sense, which involves identifying a painted figure of a woman, say, as "Venus", "Judith" or "Clio", and iconology, a less precise term. It might be rendered as the art of grasping the meaning of the whole, whether that whole is an individual picture; the "programme" or unifying theme of a pictorial cycle; the oeuvre of a particular artist; or the distinctive quality of the art of a given period. Iconography proper depends very largely on the evidence of texts, but iconology, as Panofsky admitted, requires intuition or . . . the art of divination' (Ginzburg, *The Enigma of Piero*, p. 2).

49 Ginzburg, *The Enigma of Piero*, p. 3.

50 This is a simplified version of Ginzburg's interpretation, which conveys the elements relevant to the present argument.

51 The identification as Bessarion was considered tenuous by subsequent art historians, but there is no doubt that the figure is a Byzantine. Although Ginzburg did not make the explicit connection, the figure's hat and dress closely resemble one of the assembled Eastern Church figures in the *Raising of the Cross* section of Piero's Arezzo cycle. See A. Paolucci, *Piero della Francesca: Notizie sulla conservatione di Margherita Moriondo Lenzini* (Florence, 1989), pp. 179–80.

52 Ginzburg argues convincingly that both Piero's *Baptism of Christ* and the Arezzo cycle are referenced to the attempted unification of the Eastern and Western Churches in 1438/9.

53 For the general phenomenon of uninterrupted cultural exchange during this period, see Jardine, *Worldly Goods* (esp. chap. 5 for the exchange of letters between Mehmet and Sigismondo Malatesta of Rimini concerning the loan of portrait medallist Matteo de' Pasti in 1461).

54 See J. Raby, 'Costanzo da Ferrara', in Scher, *The Currency of Fame*, pp. 87–9; his entry in J. A. Levenson, ed., *Circa 1492: Art in the Age of Exploration* (New Haven, 1991), pp. 210–13; and his 'Pride and Prejudice: Mehmed the Conqueror and the Italian Portrait Medal', in J. G. Pollard, ed., *Italian Medals: Studies in the History of Art* (Washington, DC, 1987), pp. 171–94.

55 See Raby, in Levenson, *Circa 1492*, pp. 212, 78.

56 See, for instance, Bertoldo di Giovanni's 1490s medal of Mehmet (Scher, *Currency of Fame*, p. 127). Descriptions of the frescoes in one of the pavilions of the Topkapi Saray suggest that his profile there was also based on the portrait profile. See G. Necipoğlu, *Architecture, Ceremonial, and Power: The Topkapi Palace in the Fifteenth and Sixteenth Centuries*

(Cambridge, MA, 1991), p. 224.

57 See J. Raby, *Venice, Dürer and the Oriental Mode* (London, 1982).

58 For this image, see G. Necipoğlu, 'Suleyman the Magnificent and the Representation of Power in the Context of Ottoman-Hapsburg Rivalry', *Art Bulletin* (1989), pp. 401–27. The 'alla turchesca' horse and rider in the Mantuan Filippo Orso's mid-sixteenth-century manuscript book of horse types (Victoria and Albert Museum, London) is also closely related to both the Dürer drawing and the Ibrahim Pasha drawing based upon it.

59 In 'Süleyman the Magnificent and the Representation of Power', Necipoğlu tells a directly comparable story of the circulation of an ornamental helmet, commissioned from Venetian goldsmiths for Süleyman by Ibrahim Pasha, to a model based on a portrait medal of the sixth-century Byzantine Emperor Heraclius. Süleyman had the helmet paraded outside the gates of Vienna during its siege in 1532. See Jardine, *Worldly Goods*, chap. 8.

60 According to Raby, the inscription in Persian confirms Costanzo's authorship of the drawing (in Levenson, *Circa 1492*, p. 212).

61 On this drawing, see D. T. Rice, *Islamic Art* (London, 1975), pp. 224–6.

62 See, for example, the portrait of Riza-i Abbasi by his pupil Muin Muzaffar, dated 1676, in Rice, *Islamic Art*, p. 253.

63 Art historians continue, however, to maintain that the frescoes are based around a traditionally and uncomplicatedly religious programme. See, most recently, C. A. Luchinat, ed., *The Chapel of the Magi: Benozzo Gozzoli's Frescoes in the Palazzo Medici-Riccardi Florence* (London, 1994).

64 Recent Pisanello scholars have been happy to maintain a relationship between that artist's drawings of horses, oriental figures and animals and the Gozzoli frescoes, suggesting that pattern-books might well have been shared by the circles in which both artists moved.

65 M. Hollingsworth, *Patronage in Renaissance Italy from 1400 to the Early Sixteenth Century* (London, 1994), p. 211.

66 Gill, *Personalities*, p. 51.

67 Luchinat, *The Chapel of the Magi*, p. 7.

68 Hollingsworth, *Patronage in Renaissance Italy*, p. 168.

69 *Ibid.*, pp. 53–4.

70 In 1461, Ludovico Gonzaga's seventeen-year-old son was made a Cardinal by the Pope in gratitude for his hospitality. See Jardine, *Worldly Goods*, chap. 1.

71 Hollingsworth, *Patronage in Renaissance Italy*, pp. 212–13.

72 See J. Cox-Rearick, *The Collection of Francis I: Royal Treasures* (New York, 1995), p. 5.

73 *Juvenal and Persius* (Loeb edn), p. 206.

74 For a compelling study of another French king's 'self-fashioning' via his public images, see P. Burke, *The Fabrication of Louis XIV* (New Haven, 1992). In terms of our own argument, we would suggest that by the late seventeenth century, when, according to Burke, Louis XIV and his advisors were manipulating his images of power in medals, paintings and tapestries, the 'currency of fame' had descended into a gratuitous peddling of self-regarding contrivance. It nevertheless derived from the more vital transactions of the fifteenth and sixteenth centuries.

75 Cox-Rearick, *The Collection of Francis I*, pp. 14–16.

76 For a full discussion of the painting and its fortunes, see *ibid.*, pp. 248–51.

77 See chap. 3 in this volume.

78 Here the point is to use a familiar kind of critical analysis of high culture to trigger questions that we then begin to answer with the help of less familiar material and methodology, not to engage in art-historical investigation per se. We therefore acknowledge but do not address the considerable specialist literature on Holbein's *Ambassadors*.

79 James Gairdner, ed., *Letters and Papers, foreign and domestic, of the reign of Henry VIII* (London, 1880), vi [1531–32], #110. On resident ambassadors, see K. Hamilton and R. Langhorne, *The Practice of Diplomacy: Its Evolution, Theory and Administration* (London, 1995), chap. 2.

80 He was given leave to return by Francis on 6 September 1533 (*Letters and Papers*, vi, #1086] and left on 18 November (*Letters and Papers*, vi, #1435, 1445, 1481/10).

81 Georges de Selve left England before 23 May. Anne was crowned in Westminster Abbey on 1 June 1533.

82 Eric W. Ives, 'The Queen and the Painters: Anne Boleyn, Holbein and Tudor Royal Portraits', *Apollo* (July 1994), p. 39. We are grateful to Glenn Richardson for directing our attention to this article. Jean de Dinteville played a prominent part in Anne's coronation, representing the French Crown (the only major foreign power apart from Venice thus represented) in processions and ceremonies and contributing lavishly to the spectacle. See E. W. Ives, *Anne Boleyn* (Oxford, 1986), p. 22: 'The procession was headed by twelve servants of the new French ambassador, Jean de Dinteville, Francis I's *maître d'hôtel*. They wore [French colours] blue velvet with yellow and blue sleeves, and had white plumes in their hats, while their horses had trappers of blue sarcenet, powdered with white crosses. (In December, Francis would reimburse the ambassador for his outlay with a gift of 500 gold *écus* [£100]).' Whilst the French King's public endorsement of Anne's coronation was of considerable political importance to Henry, however, we should remember that the attitude of Henry's subjects was entirely different: Charles V's ambassador Chapuys (keeping a close eye on the royal divorce and remarriage from the Hapsburg point of view) reported that Dinteville and his retinue, leading the coronation procession with the Archbishop of Canterbury (*Letters and Papers*, vi, #584), were booed and insulted by the crowd (#585).

83 Writing to Francis I on 23 May, Dinteville informed him that the Archbishop of Canterbury was going to pronounce on the legitimacy of Henry's marriage to Anne in the following three days. Dinteville had asked for a delay until the Pope and the French King had met. Henry, however, was adamant that an announcement must be made, as the coronation was to take place at Whitsuntide, and insisted that if the baby was a boy it would be his sole heir (*Letters and Papers*, v, #524). The French King was to have been godfather to the baby if it had been male (Mary F. S. Hervey, *Holbein's Ambassadors, The Picture and the Men: An Historical Study* [London, 1900], p. 94); Dinteville would have held the baby at the font (*State Papers*, vi, #1076, #1135).

84 23 May, the same day as the much more explicit ambassadorial letter to Francis I mentioned above. In fact, the announcement that Henry's marriage was legitimate was made that very day (presumably after

Dinteville's carrier had left with his letters). It is probably because he knew that the impending decision would seriously hamper the French brokering negotiations in Rome that Jean hinted to his brother that he should find someone else to return there to negotiate with Clement VII concerning the royal divorce. See R. J. Knecht, *Renaissance Warrior and Patron: The Reign of Francis I* (Cambridge, 1994), p. 299.

85 Hervey, *Holbein's Ambassadors*, p. 80 (our translation).

86 In another letter, again pleading for recall, Dinteville writes: 'If I stay here much longer I greatly fear I'll leave my skin and bones here. I have only enjoyed one week of good health in the whole time I've been here' (Hervey, *Holbein's Ambassadors*, p. 90). Because their symbolic significance remains easily accessible to us, the two skulls are extensively explicated in the secondary literature on *The Ambassadors* as a *vanitas* emblem, or variant on the theme of the humbling reminiscence of death even amidst splendour. Other objects depicted in this heavily programmed painting which have lost their symbolic currency are treated as real. It is these so-called real items that interest us here.

87 For a clear reproduction of the globe and a detailed account of precisely which places and other markings differ from the Nuremberg globe (which it otherwise replicates), see Hervey, *Holbein's Ambassadors*, pp. 210–18.

88 On the struggle between Portugal and Spain for the Moluccas, see B. L. de Argensola, *The Discovery and Conquest of the Molucco Islands* (London, 1708). See also Jerry Brotton, *Trading Territories* (London, 1997), chap. 4.

89 For the way in which textbooks on arithmetic of the period were explicitly framed around commercial and territorial problems (on which their worked examples were based), see, for example, the translation of the 1478 *Treviso Arithmetic* in F. J. Swetz, *Capitalism and Arithmetic: The New Math of the 15th Century, Including the Full Text of the Treviso Arithmetic of 1478 Translated by David Eugene Smith* (La Salle, IL, 1987).

90 See John D. North, 'Nicolaus Kratzer – The King's astronomer', *Studia Copernicana XVI: Science and History: Studies in Honor of Edward Rosen* (Warsaw, 1978), p. 228. North suggests that the cylinder dial (C) is set for the equinox, and that the celestial globe is very roughly set for the autumnal equinox, with the sign of Scorpio rising. The future Queen Elizabeth was born on 7 September 1533, a few days from the equinox. Ives has calculated that on the pillar dial immediately alongside the globe, the date shown is Good Friday, 11 April 1533 ('The Queen and the Painters', p. 40), and believes that this was the date on which Anne Boleyn was accorded full royal honours. A recent X-ray of the painting, however, shows that the instrument still life was rendered as a piece onto the painting, suggesting that it was transferred from an existing drawing, most likely made at the same time as Holbein's portrait of Nicolaus Kratzer, painted five years earlier on Holbein's first visit to England. We are extremely grateful to Susan Foister and the National Gallery, London, for making it possible for us to see the painting in the act of restoration and the X-ray.

91 It has been pointed out by Hervey and others that the reckoning instruments in our painting appear to be identical with those in the portrait of Kratzer, an astronomer, mathematician and instrument maker associated with the German merchant community in London: 'Kratzer's interest in land

measurement and mapping is well documented, and he came from southern Germany, an area that had been associated since the 1480s with the production and publication of relatively sophisticated maps . . . It could well have been Kratzer who awakened an awareness of the utility of maps in the circle associated with More and in the king [Henry VIII] himself' (P. Barber, 'England I: Pageantry, Defense, and Government: Maps at Court to 1550', in D. Buisseret, ed., *Monarchs Ministers and Maps: The Emergence of Cartography as a Tool of Government in Early Modern England* [Chicago, 1992], p. 29).

92 The arrangement of instruments lies directly between the eye-level of the two sitters and their carefully posed resting hands (Dinteville's left, Selve's right). Their lower hands direct our attention to the mundane objects on the bottom shelf.

93 Mary W. Helms, *Ulysses' Sail: An Ethnographic Odyssey of Power, Knowledge, and Geographical Distance* (Princeton, 1988), p. 5.

94 The Order of St Michael was the French equivalent of the Order of the Garter. A coveted honour in the gift of the King, it was limited to 36 members at any one time. Francis I awarded it to the dukes of Norfolk and Suffolk as part of the ceremony associated with the signing of the Treaty of Calais in October 1532; contemporary accounts testify to its being remarkable for someone not a Frenchman to obtain the honour. Norfolk and Suffolk played prominent parts in Anne Boleyn's coronation in May/June 1533 alongside the French ambassador, symbolically confirming the French King's assent to and co-operation with the second marriage.

95 Hervey, *Holbein's Ambassadors*, p. 208.

96 Helms's point is that *many* cultures use the figure of the traveller to represent generalized leadership abilities (p. 152) – access to esoteric knowledge elsewhere connotes power. Holbein showed Dinteville as the archetypal ambassador rather than as a centre of oppression against the colonial Other. For a reading of *The Ambassadors* that picks up on the diplomatic frame and questions its relevance to modern versions of international relations, see Costas Constantinou, 'Diplomatic Representations . . . or Who Framed the Ambassadors?', *Millennium: Journal of International Studies* 23 (1994), pp. 1–23.

97 Nuremberg was the home of the geographer Johann Schöner, who by the late 1520s had established a virtual monopoly on the production of printed globes, woodcut gores printed on paper and mounted on solid wooden balls. Early analyses suggested that Schöner was directly responsible for the so-called 'Ambassadors' Globe' (see Hervey). More recent historians of cartography have questioned this attribution; see Rodney Shirley, *The Mapping of the World: Early Printed Maps, 1472–1700* (London, 1983); Peter van der Krogt, *Globi Neerlandici: The Production of Globes in the Low Countries* (Utrecht, 1993). However, as with the instruments borrowed from Kratzer and the undisputed reproduction of Schöner's celestial globe, the painting is clearly indebted to the southern German states for its apprehension of learning, science and exploration.

98 See R. A. Skelton, ed., *Magellan's Voyage: A Narrative Account of the First Circumnavigation* (New York, 1969), pp. 30–31.

99 The long-standing diplomatic negotiations over the contested possession of

the Moluccas, which dragged on throughout the 1520s, were primarily carried out through recourse to terrestrial globes rather than flat maps. See Jerry Brotton, 'Terrestrial Globalism: Mapping the Globe in Early Modern Europe', in Denis Cosgrove, ed., *Mappings* (London, 1999), pp. 71–89.

100 In January 1523, one of Charles's advisors noted that he had presented the Pope with 'a globe where the whole voyage has been painted' (Carlos Quirino, ed., *First Voyage Around the World by Antonio Pigafetta* [Manila, 1969], p. 43).

101 Robert Haardt, 'The Globe of Gemma Frisius', *Imago Mundi*, 9 (1952), pp. 109–10.

102 See Lawrence Wroth, ed., *The Voyages of Giovanni da Verrazzano* (New Haven, 1970).

103 See Knecht, *Francis I*, pp. 332–3.

104 *Ibid.*, p. 333.

105 The double portrait keeps the negotiative quality of Dinteville's occupation fully in focus. The Selve portrait is less minutely detailed than that of Dinteville, and we might indeed consider the possibility that he represents Jean's absent brother (the other partner in his then current negotiations). In a painting that hung alongside *The Ambassadors* at the Dinteville château at Polisy, both brothers are represented (Constantinou, 'Diplomatic Representations').

106 Eugene Rice Jr and A. Grafton, *The Foundations of Early Modern Europe, 1460–1559*, second edn (New York, 1994), p. 125.

107 Although France did not enter into a formal alliance with the Ottoman Empire until 1535, Francis's envoy, Antonio Rincón, was engaged in diplomatic negotiations with Süleyman in Istanbul, and with his trusted interpreter Yunus Beg in Venice, throughout the period with which we are concerned. See Knecht, *Renaissance Warrior and Patron*, pp. 295–305. For the details of Rincón's movements, see Setton, *The Papacy and the Levant*, chap. III.

108 Holbein's meticulous representation has allowed specialists to identify it as a particularly valuable Turkish carpet (known now as a Holbein). Fragments of such rugs survive in Istanbul. See Oktay Aslanapa, *One Thousand Years of Turkish Carpets* (Istanbul, 1988), pp. 86–8.

109 S. Shaw, *History of the Ottoman Empire and Modern Turkey* (Cambridge, 1976), vol. I, pp. 87–94; André Clot, *Suleiman the Magnificent: The Man, His Life, His Epoch* (London, 1992).

110 Knecht, *Renaissance Warrior and Patron*, p. 296.

111 Recent shrewd reading of texts by Erasmus and Rabelais that invoke the Ottomans as a focus for verbal violence has detected this tension between the fictional version of Christian/Muslim relations and occluded historic versions. See Timothy Hampton, 'Turkish Dogs: Rabelais, Erasmus, and the Rhetoric of Alterity', *Representations* 41 (1993), pp. 58–82.

112 E. Charrière, *Négociations de la France dans le Levant* (Paris, 1840–60), vol. I, p. 214.

113 Francis's ambassador Jean La Forêt concluded a commercial treaty with Süleyman in 1536, but by that time the agreement between Francis and Henry had broken down (Shaw, *History of the Ottoman Empire*, pp. 97–8).

114 Clot, *Suleiman*, pp. 137–8. Thus Selve could have been conveying

intelligence on Ottoman affairs between Venice, Rome and London. In December 1533, he was appointed French resident ambassador in Venice (Hervey, *Holbein's Ambassadors*, p. 154).

115 *The Ambassador* [Hotman] (London: James Shawe, 1603), fol. I2r (126). We are grateful to Alan Stewart for drawing Hotman's treatise to our attention. In the same spirit, Jean de Dinteville, though of Reformed sympathies, gave gifts of gold chains to Nicholas Carew and William Fitzwilliam (neither sympathetic to the Reformed church) (Glenn Richardson, personal communication).

116 During the same period, Francis also had an envoy in Istanbul building closer relations with Süleyman, as well as envoys in the non-aligned German states which also leaned towards an anti-Charles alliance.

117 This interpretation of the configuration (a missing central figure) is proposed on art-historical grounds in an early comment on the painting by Roy Strong (*Holbein and Henry VIII* [London, 1967], pp. 48–9). Strong suggests that the arrangement of the figures in *The Ambassadors* echoes (reversed) that of Henry VII and Elizabeth of York in Holbein's later (lost) Privy Chamber wall painting. There the figures may have stood either side of a window, or may have had between them an inscription or a coat of arms (and, in one near-contemporary copy, the figure of Prince Edward). In any of these cases, the implication for *The Ambassadors* is that the objects on the table substitute for a figurative absence. According to Strong, the model is a Madonna enthroned minus the Madonna.

118 In Holbein's standing portrait of Erasmus, the emblems of Jerome's church are represented behind a similar curtain, and a pilaster representing Renaissance Italy stands in front and to Erasmus' right. The crucifix in the painting (often trimmed out of reproductions) lies on a line running from Dinteville's right hand, firmly placed on his ornate dagger, up his arm and over his shoulder.

119 The *Letters and Papers, foreign and domestic, of the reign of Henry VIII* are full of open and easy discussion of Turkish matters. Katharine of Aragon, however, writing (in November 1532 from Artford [Hertford]) to the Emperor Charles V asking him to intercede on her behalf to reinstate her marriage to Henry (London, British Library, Additional 28,586, fol. 47), refers to the proposed divorce as the second Turk: 'I call it the second Turk, – because the ills which have followed, and still follow every day, owing to his Holiness not putting an end to this cause in time, are of so great and such evil example, that I do not know which is the worst, this business or that of the Turk.' We are grateful to Alan Stewart for drawing this letter to our attention.

120 In her excellent recent study of Ottoman commerce and seapower in the early sixteenth century, Palmira Brummett argues for an analysis of 'the Ottoman state as inheritor of Euro-Asian trading networks and participant in the contest for commercial hegemony in the economic space stretching from Venice to the Indian Ocean' (*Ottoman Seapower and Levantine Diplomacy in the Age of Discovery* [Albany, 1994], p. 175).

121 See chap. 2 in this volume.

122 Edward Said, 'East Isn't East', *Times Literary Supplement*, February 1995, p. 6.

123 This is the procedure suggested by the historical ethnography practised by Jean and John Comaroff, who have stressed that such analyses 'must always go beyond literary traces, beyond explicit narrative, exegesis, even arguments. For the poetics of history lie also in mute meanings transacted through goods and practices, through icons and images dispersed in the landscape of the everyday' (*Ethnography and the Historical Imagination* [Boulder, 1992], p. 35). This is not to reject the analysis of the textual as such; that carried out here is clearly based on material that is *read*, like a text. However, we are in broad agreement with the Comaroffs concerning the need to interrogate the movement of material cultural artefacts such as (within their own work) cattle, in the same way that we are concerned to articulate the cultural processes that produce the movement of objects such as maps, porcelain or even rugs. See Arjun Appadurai, 'Introduction', in A. Appadurai, ed., *The Social Life of Things: Commodities in Cultural Perspective* (Cambridge, 1986), pp. 3–63.

124 In his original account of the discourse of orientalism, Said argued that 'Orientalism depends for its strategy on this flexible *positional* superiority, which puts the westerner in a whole series of possible relationships with the Orient without ever losing him the relative upper hand . . . The scientist, the scholar, the missionary, the trader, or the soldier was in, or thought about, the Orient because he *could be there*, or could think about it, with very little resistance on the Orient's part' (*Orientalism* [London, 1978], p. 7).

125 As Said has remarked: 'Studying the relationship between the West and its dominated cultural others is not just a way of understanding an unequal relationship between unequal interlocutors, but also a point of entry into studying the formation and meaning of Western cultural practices themselves . . . [T]he persistent disparity in power between West and the non-West must be taken into account if we are accurately to understand cultural forms like that of the novel, of ethnographic and historical discourse, certain kinds of poetry and opera, where allusions to and structures based on this disparity abound' (*Culture and Imperialism* [London, 1993], p. 230).

126 For an account that fully endorses this myth, see Robert Schwoebel, *The Shadow of the Crescent: The Renaissance Image of the Turk, 1453–1517* (Nieuwkoop, 1967).

127 The other painting commissioned by the Dinteville brothers, which hung as partner to *The Ambassadors* at Polisy – a representation of them as Moses and Aaron – can still be 'read' because the elements in the signifying representations have not gone cold for us (or we can at least retrieve them); see above, n. 105.

2 *Telling Tapestries: Fabricating Narratives of Conquest*

1 See, for example, J. Gill, *Personalities of the Council of Florence* (Oxford, 1964), pp. 50–51.

2 On the *Acts of the Apostles* tapestries, see John Shearman, *Raphael's Cartoons in the Collection of Her Majesty the Queen and the Tapestries for the Sistine Chapel* (London, 1972).

3 Quoted in Barty Phillips, *Tapestry* (London, 1994), p. 58.

4 On this series, see Antonio Domínguez Ortiz *et al.*, eds, *Resplendence of the Spanish Monarchy: Renaissance Tapestries and Armor from the Patrimonio Nacional* (New York, 1991), pp. 27–39.

5 Some of the enthusiasm for moral instruction for the young Emperor may have derived from the fact that Charles's successful election had depended on large cash payments to the international electors rather than on any suggestion of merit or ability. See Lisa Jardine, *Worldly Goods: A New History of the Renaissance* (London, 1996), pp. 104, 287.

6 On the iconography of the whole series, see Guy Delmarcel, 'The Dynastic Iconography of the Brussels Tapestries *Los Honores* (1520–1525)', in *España entre el Mediterraneo y el Atlantico: Actas del XXIII Congreso Internacional de Historia del Arte* (Granada, 1977), vol. II, pp. 250–59.

7 See Phyllis Ackerman, *Tapestry: The Mirror of Civilisation* (New York, 1933), pp. 120–30.

8 Most recently personified and reproduced by John Hale in *The Civilisation of Europe in the Renaissance* (London, 1993).

9 See Ortiz *et al.*, *Resplendence*, p. 27; Iain Buchanan, 'Designers, Weavers and Entrepreneurs: Sixteenth-century Flemish Tapestries in the Patrimonio Nacional', *Burlington Magazine*, CXXXIV/1071 (1992), pp. 380–84.

10 On this critical tradition, see E. Panofsky, *Studies in Iconology: Humanistic Themes in the Art of the Renaissance* (Oxford, 1939); J. Seznec, *The Survival of the Pagan Gods: The Mythological Tradition and Its Place in Renaissance Humanism and Art* (New York, 1953) (first published in French as *La survivance des dieux antiques*, 1940); E. H. Gombrich, *Symbolic Images: Studies in the Art of the Renaissance II* (Oxford, 1972).

11 Panofsky, *Studies in Iconology*, pp. 29–30.

12 Hale, *The Civilisation of Europe*, pp. 7–8.

13 *Ibid.*, p. 8. Dürer's drawing is reproduced on p. 9 of Hale's book.

14 See Denys Hay, *Europe: The Emergence of an Idea* (Edinburgh, 1957); Norman Davies, *Europe: A History* (Oxford, 1996), pp. xv–xvii.

15 Hale, 'Preface', in *The Civilization of Europe*, p. xix.

16 On the history of tapestry, with specific emphasis on the late medieval and Renaissance period, see W. G. Thomson's still invaluable study, *A History of Tapestry* (London, 1906; reprint 1930); Ludwig Baldass, *Die Wiener Gobelinssammlung* (Vienna, 1920), 3 vols; Heinrich Göbel, *Wandteppiche* (Leipzig, 1923–34); Edith Appleton Standen, 'Studies in the History of Tapestry', *Apollo*, CXIV/223 (1981), pp. 6–53; Roger d'Hulst, *Vlaamse wandtapijten van de Xvde tot de XVIIIde eeuw* (Brussels, 1960); Guy Delmarcel, *Flemish Tapestry* (London, 1999)

17 See Candace Adelson, *European Tapestry in the Minneapolis Institute of Arts* (New York, 1994), p. 2.

18 *Ibid.*, p. 16.

19 See Adelson, *European Tapestry*, pp. 9–10.

20 See Philips, *Tapestry*, pp. 22–4; Adelson, *European Tapestry*, pp. 11–12.

21 Thomson, *History of Tapestry*, pp. 53–69.

22 Delmarcel, *Flemish Tapestry*, p. 27.

23 Thomson, *History of Tapestry*, pp. 105–36.

24 Quoted in Clifford M. Brown and Guy Delmarcel, *Tapestries for the Courts*

of Federico II, Ercole, and Ferrante Gonzaga, 1522–63 (Washington, DC, 1996), p. 11.

25 See Jardine, 'Preface', in *Worldly Goods.*

26 See Edith Appleton Standen, *European Post-Medieval Tapestries and Related Hangings in The Metropolitan Museum of Art* (New York, 1985).

27 Delmarcel, *Flemish Tapestry*, p. 117.

28 Thomson, *History of Tapestry*, p. 97.

29 The Burgundian tapestries were inventoried according to the ritually sensitive locations they inhabited throughout the court, for instance chambers, halls and chapels – an indication of the extent to which the form of the tapestries matched their courtly domestic function. See Thomson, *History of Tapestry*, p. 92.

30 Quoted in Thomson, *History of Tapestry*, p. 98.

31 See Roy Strong, *Art and Power: Renaissance Festivals 1450–1650* (Woodbridge, 1973), illus. 2. The scene of Charles's entry into Bruges in 1515 shows him toppling Fortune from her wheel.

32 See Philips, *Tapestry*, p. 32.

33 Quoted in J. Cox-Rearick, *The Collection of Francis I: Royal Treasures* (New York, 1995), p. 378.

34 *Ibid.*, p. 381.

35 *Ibid.*, pp. 381–2.

36 *Ibid.*, p. 376.

37 Quoted in Thomas Campbell, 'Henry VIII and the Château of Écouen *History of David and Bathsheba* Tapestries', *Gazette des Beaux Arts*, CXXXVIII (1996), p. 130.

38 For Wolsey's tapestries, see Thomas Campbell, 'Cardinal Wolsey's Tapestry Collection', *Society of Antiquaries Journal*, 76 (1996).

39 Campbell, '*History of David and Bathsheba* Tapestries', pp. 121–38.

40 Delmarcel, 'Dynastic Iconography'.

41 Hendrick Horn, *Jan Cornelisz Vermeyen* (The Hague, 1989), vol. I, p. 256.

42 On the novelty of the precise realism of the *Battle of Pavia* tapestries, see Roger D'Hulst, *Tapisseries flamandes* (Brussels, 1960), pp. 147–56.

43 On the ways in which cartoon production worked in practice, see the case study by J. Farmer, 'How One Workshop Worked: Bernard Van Orley's Atelier in Early Sixteenth-century Brussels', in G. Clark *et al.*, *A Tribute to Robert A. Koch: Studies in the Renaissance* (Princeton, 1995).

44 Horn, *Vermeyen*, vol. II, p. 348.

45 *Ibid.*, vol. I, p. 181.

46 See William Stahl, *Commentary on 'The Dream of Scipio' by Macrobius* (New York, 1952). Macrobius' fifth-century commentary is based on Cicero's 'Somnium Scipionis', in *De Republica*, 6.22. We are grateful to Denis Cosgrove for bringing this allusion to our attention.

47 See Alex Sampson, 'The Marriage of Philip of Habsburg and Mary Tudor and Anti-Spanish Sentiment in England: Political Economies and Culture, 1553–1557', PhD thesis, University of London, 1999.

48 Horn, *Vermeyen*, vol. I, p. 114.

49 Rosaline Bacou and Bertrand Jestaz, *Jules Romain: L'Histoire Scipion: Tapisseries et dessins* (Paris, 1978), p. 7.

50 See Ortiz *et al.*, *Resplendence*, pp. 69–74; Colonel d'Astier, *La Belle Tapisserye*

de Roy (1532–1797) et les tenures de Scipion l'africain (Paris, 1907).

51 'The knack was to allow the three lines of the maniple (of which there were thirty in the legion) to act more or less on their own . . . Scipio also experimented in Spain with a unit combining three maniples, the cohort, which provided greater cohesion, but at the same time still allowed greater flexibility than the larger legion itself' (Michael Grant, *History of Rome* [London, 1979], p. 107).

52 Horn, *Vermeyen*, vol. I, p. 189.

53 Strong, *Art and Power*, p. 82.

54 *Ibid.*, p. 83.

55 *Ibid.*

56 Horn, *Vermeyen*, vol. I, p. 285. De la Vega's own hybrid Inca/Spanish heritage tellingly offers a further dimension to the 'global' dimension of our argument here.

57 Brown and Delmarcel, *Tapestries for the Gonzaga*, p. 166.

58 *Ibid.*, p. 167.

59 *Ibid.*, p. 163.

60 Quoted in Thomson, *History of Tapestry*, p. 199.

61 In his highly influential study of commodities and the politics of value, the economic anthropologist Arjun Appadurai argues that '[T]he economic object does not have an absolute value as a result of the demand for it, but the demand, as the basis of a real or imagined exchange, endows the object with value. It is exchange that sets the parameters of utility and scarcity, rather than the other way round, and exchange that is the source of value' ('Introduction: Commodities and the Politics of Value', in Arjun Appadurai, ed., *The Social Life of Things: Commodities in Cultural Perspective* [Cambridge, 1986], p. 4).

62 On this series, see J. A. Levenson, ed., *Circa 1492: Art in the Age of Exploration* (New Haven, 1991), pp. 138–40.

63 Bailey Diffie and George Winius, *Foundation of the Portuguese Empire, 1415–1580* (Minneapolis, 1977), p. 145.

64 On the pervasive influence of the representation of the Trojan War in fifteenth-century tapestries, see Scott McKendrick, 'The Great History of Troy: A Reassessment of the Development of a Secular Theme in Late Medieval Art', *Journal of the Warburg and Courtauld Institutes*, 54 (1991), pp. 43-82; William Forsyth, 'The Trojan War in Medieval Tapestries', *Metropolitan Museum of Art Bulletin*, 14 (1955), pp. 76–84.

65 Thomson, *History of Tapestry*, p. 210.

66 Phyllis Ackerman, *The Rockefeller McCormick Tapestries: Three Early Sixteenth Century Tapestries* (Oxford, 1932), p. 43.

67 Records of subsequent Portuguese voyages to India record that tapestries were often part of the cargo, presumably displayed in ways similarly significant to those in which the *Conquest of Tunis* tapestries were shown. This emphasizes our argument regarding the legible 'currency' of such objects between East and West, although we increasingly detect a hardening of this currency as the political and imperial contestation of the period escalates.

68 For a discussion and reproduction of the final tapestry in the *Spheres* series, see Jerry Brotton, *Trading Territories* (London, 1977), chap. 1.

69 See Horn, *Vermeyen*, vol. I, p. 42.

70 Brotton, *Trading Territories*, chap. 1.

71 Quoted in William Stirling Maxwell, ed., *The Turks in 1533. A Series of Drawings made in that Year at Constantinople by Peter Coeck of Aelst* (London and Edinburgh, 1873), pp. 5–6. Delmarcel has a slightly different but similarly suggestive account of the venture, claiming that a set of *The Hunts of Maximilian* (1531–3) was 'offered for sale by a German merchant to Sultan Suleiman the Magnificent in Constantinople, together with a set of seven tapestries depicting "the King of France's battle at Pavia"; one piece from each of the sets, which were in the possession of Willem Dermoyen and his partners in Brussels, was sent via Venice as a sample' (Delmarcel, *Flemish Tapestry*, p. 121). Delmarcel does not elaborate on his sources for this version of the story.

72 Stirling Maxwell, *The Turks in 1533*, p. 8.

73 Note Horn's careful comparison of the military tapestries, from the *Battle of Roosebecke* through the *Battle of Pavia*, *History of Scipio* and *Conquest of Tunis* (*Vermeyen*, vol. I, pp. 293–6). Horn tends to disassociate these 'military' works from the wider context of sixteenth-century courtly tapestries. We would argue that, on the contrary, they are in fact symptomatic of the function of tapestries of the period.

74 Following the sudden death of her husband Henri II in 1559 and the brief reign of Francis II, Catherine was appointed regent in 1562 in the light of the minority of the new king, Charles IX. See R. J. Knecht, *Catherine De' Medici* (London, 1998), pp. 59–88.

75 Frances Yates, *The Valois Tapestries* (London, 1959), pp. 61–7.

76 *Ibid.*, p. 66.

77 *Ibid.*, p. xvi.

78 *Ibid.*, p. 70.

79 See Mack P. Holt, *The Duke of Anjou and the Politique Struggle During the Wars of Religion* (Cambridge, 1986), pp. 166–7.

80 Yates downplays the extent to which Anjou was a deeply incompetent military leader. His entry into Antwerp was not the popularly acclaimed triumph that she suggests; Anjou immediately found himself dealing with a suspicious populace and an inflexible States-General. See Holt, *Anjou*, pp. 166–84.

81 See Strong, *Art and Power*, pp. 98–125.

82 Knecht, *Catherine De' Medici*, p. 244.

83 The movement of these tapestries is another significant dimension of their political status. Horn noted that Alva's father had died at Djerba 25 years earlier, and the Duke recovered his father's arms during the sacking of the city. Upon completion, the tapestries (also woven by Pannemaker) were shipped at great expense from Lareda to the Duke's residence in Alba de Tormes. In 1568, Alva was also taken with a composite tapestry of the Tunis campaign in the possession of Philip's counsellor Cardinal Antoine Perrenot de Granvelle (whose father had also fought at Tunis), from which he also ordered his own (now lost) version (Horn, *Vermeyen*, vol. I, pp. 130–31). The fact that Granvelle's tapestry still hangs in the city hall of Mechelen is testimony to the various locations within which such items were put to work – particularly in the Low Countries – as Alva placed his stamp on the region.

84 See Dora Heinz, *Europäische Wandteppiche I: Von den Anfängen der Bildwirkerei bis zum Ende des 16. Jahrhunderts* (Braunschweig, 1963), p. 223, figs 155, 156, 170.

85 Caron was responsible for a series of cartoons which were ultimately transformed into tapestries that explicitly glorified Catherine de' Medici. These included, most famously, the early seventeenth-century series *Stories of Queen Artemisia*. See Adelson, *European Tapestry*, pp. 161–288.

86 Cox-Rearick, *The Collection of Francis I*, pp. 78–81.

87 Cited in *ibid.*, p. 383. Knecht emphasized Brantôme's partiality in his accounts of the festivals (*Catherine de' Medici*, p. 237).

88 Displaying the *Scipio* tapestries was clearly no conciliatory gesture on the part of the Valois retinue, another dimension of the deployment of tapestries within this period that goes against the grain of Yates's argument.

89 Yates made no attempt to date the painting, although as Caron's drawings of festivals are from 1573, it can be assumed that the painting is of similar date (Yates, *Valois Tapestries*, p. 4).

90 The relationship between Caron and the *Scipio* tapestries suggests that the *Valois Tapestries* were probably much more of a French affair than Yates suggested. On Caron, see Adelson, *European Tapestry*, p. 186. It also seems very unlikely that the *Valois Tapestries* drew on the iconography of Anjou's entry into Antwerp and managed to incorporate it into other works produced, according to Yates's argument, within the same year. The tapestries' sheer size and quality suggest that completion would have taken at least two years, if not longer.

91 Yates, *Valois Tapestries*, p. 62.

92 The Caron drawing is reproduced in Yates, *Valois Tapestries*, fig. XI, b.

93 Nicola Sutherland has elaborated on the ways in which the Ottomans were part of the complex diplomatic negotiations that swirled around the Valois court prior to the massacre. See N. M. Sutherland, *The Massacre of St Bartholomew and the European Conflict, 1559–1572* (London, 1973), esp. pp. 166, 287–8.

94 Yates, *Valois Tapestries*, p. 121.

3 *Managing the Infidel: Equestrian Art on Its Mettle*

1 On the portable triumphs of Charles V and his son Philip, see Roy Strong, *Art and Power: Renaissance Festivals 1450–1650* (Woodbridge, 1973), pp. 75–97.

2 On the commissioning of these later versions of the *Tunis* tapestries, see Hendrick Horn, *Jan Cornelisz Vermeyen* (The Hague, 1989), vol. I, pp. 129–32.

3 *Ibid.*, p. 131.

4 In this respect, there is an obvious relationship (as cultural objects) between horses and human beings pressed into service. We are thinking in particular of slaves.

5 Our translation. 'Illustrissimo princeps et excellentissime domine genitor et domine me precolendissime. Havendome questa dì vostra Excellentia mandato uno cavallo, quale come respondendo alla lettera di quella scripsi, me parse e anche mi pare, sì per bontà, sì per belezza, degno d'uno re. De

quello ho preso tanto piacere, et per lo cavallo in se, ma senza comparatione molto più per reverentia de vostra Sublimità qual se dignata mandarmelo, che me parso farlo ritrare como in la tavoletta qual porta il presente cavalaro, vostra Excellentia potrà vedere. Parendomi con esso ritracto far due cosse laudabile mandandolo a vostra Excellentia. L'una demonstrarli ch'io anche, benchè sia stato infermo questi dì, pur ho havuto caro de intendere le vertute et exercitii si operano in questa città, aciò a bisogni sapesse dove ricorere e anche per intendere la conditione d'essa. L'altro aciò vostra Excellentia comprehenda in quanta reverentia ho le cosse de vostra Sublimità, qual nel vero per rispetto de quella non solo el cavallo in carne, ma etiam esso ritratto non mì è perso may sufficientemente potere contemplare et riguardare. In esso cavallo, non potendo, per la infermità, far ritrarmi, como seria stato mio desiderio, glio ho facto ritrare il mio famiglio,benchè per la bontà d'esso ritracto sicondo el giuditio mio non bisognaria gli ponesse il nome. Io me ho creduto con questo far cossa grata a vostra Celsitudine e a questo fine el mando a quella . . . devotissimum servitor et filius Ludovicus Maria Sfortia Vicecomes' (Paris, BN ms Ital. 1590, fol. 4, cited in E. Welch, 'Naming Names: The Transience of Individual Identity in Fifteenth-century Italian Portraiture', in Nicholas Mann and Luke Syson, eds, *The Image of the Individual* [London, 1998], pp. 214–15).

6   Welch, 'Naming Names', p. 94.

7   Milan to Cremona is 50 miles as the crow flies. Hyland estimated that in the late Middle Ages a *nuncius* (messenger) might travel 35 miles in a day, resting his horse every ten miles. In this case, the gift horse sent to Ludovico Maria Sforza would have taken at most two days in transit. See Ann Hyland, *The Horse in the Middle Ages* (Stroud, 1999), pp. 118–20.

8   See Lisa Jardine, *Worldly Goods: A New History of the Renaissance* (London, 1996).

9   J.-C. Frère, *Léonard de Vinci* (Paris, 1994), p. 75. See also D. C. Ahl, *Leonardo da Vinci's Sforza Monument Horse: The Art and the Engineering* (London, 1995).

10 A. Cole, *Art of the Italian Renaissance Courts* (London, 1995), pp. 100–101.

11 The statue is now identified as 'Marcus Aurelius on horseback'. It survived during the Middle Ages because the more than four-metre-high gilded bronze monument was believed to be a statue of Constantine, the first Emperor of Byzantium. It was explicitly associated with Marcus Aurelius by Pierre Dan in 1642 (J. Cox-Rearick, *The Collection of Francis I: Royal Treasures* [New York, 1995], p. 361).

12 This is probably the moment to note as well the inevitable association of monumental horses with the Trojan Horse, and thus again with memorable military victories.

13 Ahl, *Leonardo*, pp. 101–2.

14 Ann Hyland, *The Warhorse, 1250–1600* (Stroud, 1998), p. 4.

15 In the 1540s, Francesco Primaticcio made a cast of the 'horse of Marcus Aurelius' and transported it back to France, where a plaster cast was made for Francis I. The horse stood in the Basse Cour at Fontainebleau until 1626 (Cox-Rearick, *The Collection of Francis* I, pp. 360–61). A full-sized bronze version of the Sforza horse, to Leonardo's design, has recently been

completed, the realization of a project begun by an American, Charles Dent, in 1977. It was presented to the city of Milan as a gift from the people of the United States on 10 September 1999, five hundred years to the day after the French invasion put paid to the original undertaking. See *Independent on Sunday*, 6 June 1999.

16 See P. F. Brown, *The Renaissance in Venice* (London, 1997), pp. 50–51.

17 The following discussion is based closely on C. M. Rosenberg, *The Este Monuments and Urban Development in Renaissance Ferrara* (Cambridge, 1997).

18 'The French occupation of Ferrara had disastrous results for both statues [the equestrian monument to Niccolò II d'Este and the later seated-figure monument erected by Borso on his own behalf]. On October 10, 1796, as part of the Napoleonic civic reforms, all titles were abolished in Ferrara. In conjunction with the abolition of the city's aristocratic past, prominent examples of the Este coats of arms were desecrated . . . The two Este monuments suffered a worse fate. On October 19, 1796, in what must have been seen, at least in part, as a symbolic purging of the city's "pernicious" Este past, the statues were pulled down from their bases and destroyed. A few weeks later, the shattered remains of the statues were seen floating on a barge down the Po di Panora toward Modena, where they were to be melted down to make cannon' (Rosenberg, *The Este Monuments*, p. 109).

19 For an intriguingly full account of these events see Rosenberg, *The Este Monuments*, pp. 54–7.

20 Rosenberg writes: 'The extraordinary decorative quality of the arch, with its proliferation of wreathed rondels in both the spandrels and frieze and its somewhat diminutive scale, make it likely that the base reflects the style of an artist best known as an illuminator and designer of medals, like Matteo, as that of a humanist-artist like Alberti' (Rosenberg, *The Este Monuments*, p. 59).

21 Quoted in Ahl, *Leonardo*, p. 60.

22 Rosenberg, *The Este Monuments*, p. 68.

23 Rosenberg identified two plausible occasions on which Niccolò III d'Este was a notable peacemaker. We suggest that the Council of Florence might have been a third.

24 Rosenberg, *The Este Monuments*, p. 53.

25 Borso's succession was once again without legitimacy. Leonello's will had passed the succession to his own son Niccolò, once again passing over the two legitimate sons of his father Niccolò III. In 1450, however, Borso, Leonello's brother, simply set this aside and took power himself. See Rosenberg, *The Este Monuments*, pp. 80–81.

26 *Ibid.*, p. 76.

27 Francesco del Cossa's frescoes for Borso in the Palazzo Schifanoia in Ferrara, like those by Mantegna in the Gonzaga *palazzo ducale* in Mantua, make prominent use of horses – favourite mounts, scenes of hunting and horse racing – as their vocabulary of courtly rule. See Cole, *Renaissance Courts*, pp. 130–31.

28 See, for instance, L. Jardine and A. Grafton, *From Humanism to the Humanities: Education and the Liberal Arts in Fifteenth- and Sixteenth-Century Europe* (London, 1986).

29 Cole, *Renaissance Courts*, p. 122.
30 S. K. Scher, *The Currency of Fame: Portrait Medals of the Renaissance* (New York, 1994), p. 50.
31 Cole, *Renaissance Courts*, p. 123.
32 On the sentimental imagery of love on the medal's reverse, see Scher, *The Currency of Fame*, p. 50. On the politics of Leonello's right to rule and his marriages, see Rosenberg, *The Este Monuments*, pp. 50–53, 78–9.
33 Cole, *Renaissance Courts*, p. 132.
34 See Rosenberg, *The Este Monuments*, p. 155.
35 For the full, gripping story, see *ibid.*, pp. 153–81.
36 For the story of the absorption of the tulip into European cultural and horticultural life, see Anna Pavord, *The Tulip* (London, 1999).
37 See Miklos Jankovich, *They Rode Into Europe: The Fruitful Exchange in the Arts of Horsemanship between East and West*, trans. Anthony Dent (London, 1971), p. 29. There are numerous general histories of the horse; see in particular Hyland's excellent studies, *The Horse in the Middle Ages* and *The Warhorse* and R.H.C. Davis, *The Medieval Warhorse* (London, 1989).
38 Jankovich, *They Rode Into Europe*, p. 33.
39 *Ibid.*
40 Hyland, *The Warhorse*, pp. 54–5.
41 The *Travels of Marco Polo* are filled with references to horses and the horse trade. Entering Persia, the narrative records that 'The country is distinguished for its excellent breed of horses, many of which are carried for sale to India, and bring high prices, not less in general than two hundred *livres tournois* [1,500–2,000 rupees] (John Masefield, ed., *The Travels of Marco Polo* [London, 1908]). See also the discussion of the Chinese export and Indian import of horses in *ibid.*, pp. 84, 248, 356, 402.
42 Jankovich, *They Rode Into Europe*, p. 56.
43 *Ibid.*, pp. 65–6.
44 Armando Cortesão, ed., *The Suma Oriental of Tome Pires and The Book of Francisco Rodrigues* (London, 1944), p. 17.
45 *Ibid.*, p. 21. Discussing the Kingdom of Diu, Pires records that '[t]here are three hundred horses in its stable, which are kept out of the revenues of the land' (Cortesão, *The Suma Oriental*, p. 35). In discussing 'Bhatkal' on the west Indian cost, Pires notes that 'many horses were landed there, and much other merchandise. These horses were bought for the kingdom of Narsinga, and heavy dues were paid on them' (*Ibid.*, p. 62).
46 Cited in Ronald Bishop Smith, *The First Age of the Portuguese Embassies to the Ancient Kingdoms of Cambay and Bengal, 1500–1521* (Bethesda, 1969), p. 34.
47 Robert Sewell, *A Forgotten Empire* (London, 1900), pp. 127–8.
48 Ironically, the monopoly was only formally registered under the terms of João de Castro's peace established in 1547, which stipulated that 'The Governor of Goa [would] allow all Arab and Persian horses landed at Goa to be purchased by the king of Vijayanagar, on due notice and payment, none being permitted to be sent to Bîjapûr' (cited in Sewell, *Forgotten Empire*, p. 186).
49 *Ibid.*, pp. 381–2.
50 The tapestry depicts what seems to be a unicorn, but the exotic nature of

the menagerie being transported, and its comparisons with the portrayal of the movement of horses in later tapestries like the *Conquest of Tunis* series, emphasize that exactly the same technique was used for horses. Thus the hard-nosed trade in the latter was displaced onto the portrayal of the fabulous unicorn.

51 These boats are the kind that were infamously used to transport African slaves across the Atlantic to the Americas. The customary equation frequently quoted for the low valuation placed on slaves' lives was that one horse equalled eight slaves. This corresponded to the space allocation in the deep hull of a ship: eight slaves could be stowed in the space required for a single horse. Such boats were also lent to Charles by the Portuguese in his attack on Tunis in 1535.

52 Eastern horse breeders were consistently more ruthless than their European counterparts in destroying foals that failed to meet their exacting breed standards, thereby keeping their 'races' pure. Prior to the discovery of genetics, the implications of crossbreeding were, of course, not fully understood.

53 This was not of course the case with spices and similar commodities, due to their size and inanimate nature. This emphasizes our point as to the peculiar significance of horses.

54 Hyland, *Warhorse*, p. 54.

55 The nobility of Europe's enthusiasm for horse-racing, bordering on addiction, is a subject on its own (as is hunting). One of Francesco's financiers, Silvestro da Lucca, presented him with a beautifully illuminated manuscript book on vellum, produced at his own expense, containing 35 miniatures of the Marquis's prize-winning racehorses with their names and prizes. On the title page it showed 'Il Dainosauro', who had won the gold sash at Ferrara, Florence and Mantua. According to da Lucca, Francesco had mentioned several times that he would like to have an illustrated record of his Barbary racehorses and a list of the prizes they had taken. See David Chambers and Jane Martineau, eds, *Splendours of the Gonzaga*, exh. cat., Victoria and Albert Museum, London (1981), p. 147. Virgil's fascination with horse breeding in Book 3 of *The Georgics* also offers a tantalizing precedent for the Mantuan interest in horses.

56 Compare the story of Cantino, Ercole d'Este's agent, travelling to Lisbon in 1502 as a 'horse trader', in the course of which visit he stole a crucial Portuguese map listing the Portuguese discoveries. We suggest that there is frequently a link between the quest for bloodstock horses – desirable luxury items – and the pursuit of trade routes to the East (as shown on the Cantino planisphere). See Jardine, *Worldly Goods*, p. 107; Brotton, *Trading Territories*, pp. 22–3.

57 Orso's manuscript album is currently held in the Print Room of the Victoria and Albert Museum, London. We are grateful to Rachel Jardine for this reference. On the album itself, see Peter Ward-Jackson, *Italian Drawings* (London, 1979), vol. 1, pp. 101–5.

58 Jardine, *Worldly Goods*.

59 J. P. Hore, *The History of Newmarket*, (London, 1886), vol. I, p. 71.

60 *Ibid.*

61 *Ibid.*, pp. 71–2.

62 *Ibid.*, p. 72, cited from *Calendar of State Papers, Venetian*, II, 1509–19, p. 162.

63 *Ibid.*, pp. 73–5.

64 Joycelyne Russell, *The Field of Cloth of Gold* (London, 1969), p. 118.

65 *Ibid.*, p. 119.

66 Discussing the affection of princes in his third *Eclogue*, Alexander Barclay, one of the scholars in attendance on Henry, summed up the Henrician attitude towards horses: 'But if they loue any they loue him not as a frende, / Betwene like and like best friendship shall we finde. / For truely great lordes loue suche men with delite, / By them when they take some pleasour or profite, / As they loue horses, dogges, and mo such, / What saide I, I lye, they loue them not so muche: / More loue they a horse or dogge then a man, / Aske of Minalcas, the truth declare he can. / For commonly as sone as any man is dead / Another is soone ready for to fulfill his stead, / With mede and with prayer his place is dearely bought / So oft haue princes their seruice cleare for nought: / But then if it fortune a dogge or horse to dye, / His place to fulfill another muste they by' (Beatrice White, ed., *The Eclogues of Alexander Barclay* [Oxford, 1928], p. 119).

67 C. M. Prior, *The Royal Studs of the Sixteenth and Seventeenth Centuries* (London, 1935), p. 2.

68 Hore, *Newmarket*, p. 79.

69 *Ibid.*, p. 82.

70 *Calendar of State Papers, Foreign Series 1583–1584*, p. 406, # 484, 'Sturm to Elizabeth', 15 March 1584, Nordheim, Germany, States, 3/6: 'There is nothing which more weakens the strength of a kingdom than forces of foreign soldiers and especially horse, nor any Prince, however wealthy he may be, in our age, whose resources and treasury would not be exhausted, and his warlike strength weakened by the pay of these reiters; so that on account of want of money, a truce is frequently necessary, during which they may be able to recuperate, which interval is often harmful to the weaker party, and sometimes ruinous. And this evil in our century yearly grows greater, and is enlarged and confirmed. / I remember how some time ago, in a certain letter, I wrote, as in a riddle, how the cost of these reiters might be diminished, giving as an illustration the fable of Jason and Medea. / I know no kingdom more suitable for this equestrian business than your own; for in the supply of horses, England exceeds other countries. But because the horses are but weak, I advised that gradually a few stallions could be brought from Germany and Friesland, unknown to the enemy or to those who may be enemies in the future, which stallions would make the offspring of the English mare more robust. / But as I do not hear of this being done, either because my opinion was not pleasing or because the riddle was not able to be read, I have chosen by this letter to declare the matter more openly to your Majesty, rather than again speak in riddles [*ainittein*], if perchance this my (not advice but) cogitation may be approved and choose rather to repeat my folly than by silence to injure your kingdom and your Majesty, to whom I owe my life itself. / Therefore, one part of my advice was a stud [*equaria*] that England might in future have more robust and stronger horses and the supply of better horses

might increase . . . / Moreover I thought it would be well to invite secretly a few German saddlers and makers of greaves and shoes, not heads of households, who would need large pay, but their serving men, who, equally skilled, would come amongst us and be their own masters, for moderate pay. Also German tailors for making clothes and blacksmiths for making coats of mail, with a few saddlers. / This should be done, not in show only, but in substance; not only that there might be a new form of saddle but the saddles [406] themselves, with guns and engines of war, and also the *anaphrates* of the saddles, which some call stirrups [*stapedes*]; as also by the valour of the captains of horse and foot and the discipline and military exercise of the men, which is easy to effect if the law for the same be confirmed by the will and authority of your Majesty. / I remember to have heard of a certain number of horses having been ordered to be provided either according to old institution or new custom, by knights, chief ecclesiastics and bishops, barons, earls and dukes. This law, if renewed and observed, might be salutary. I reckon perhaps foolishly, nevertheless I reckon with great care, and whether for good or evil, it is for your Majesty and your kingdom. / If the German discipline were set up by someone in single companies, the explanation and undertaking of this art and faculty would be easy. And if all the horsemen would obey some one faithful and zealous personage, such as the Earl of Oxford, the Earl of Leicester or Philip Sidney, it might be more convenient, speedy and fitting to entrust this matter to him. If this plan should please your Majesty I will name both workmen and horsemen, able, skilful and taciturn. And if it should please your Majesty, with this supreme commander to put as legate or vicar a German man of war, prudent, experienced and accustomed to many fights, I have more than one whom by discipline and taciturnity would be very suitable. Nor would it be without use to add another deputy, an English citizen, to the end that German and Englishmen, without envy and with more authority might enforce discipline. / It would be more than sufficient to have fifty German artificers and the same number of horsemen, whose charges and wages would not be great. It would be better to have widowers or single men rather than fathers of families; for the expense would be much less, the obedience much greater, and they would more faithfully hold their tongues.'

71 By the end of the seventeenth century, a 'cheval de frise' was a mobile military barricade, suitable to place in the way of attacking troops to impede their progress. If we compare this with the tactic recorded by Roger Williams and assume that the Friesian was particularly bulky, the term's origin is clear: 'We had gotten some twenty or thirty jades or mares, which we trimmed up with old saddles, cushions and halters that we got in boors' houses as we passed. These we placed behind the ambush, who had commandment to lie close until the ambush discharged their volley, then charge with all resolution.' When the convoy was within the ambush, the mares and jades were driven at them to see off the horsemen, while footmen dispatched the convoy (D. W. Davies, ed., *The Actions of the Low Countries by Sir Roger Williams* [Ithaca, 1964], p. 69).

72 Actually, as is usual for these pieces of advice soliciting for royal service, his letter raises a safely appropriate bit of policy that had been offered before,

one calculated not to give offence to the recipient – besides, Sturm was in his 70s at the time of writing.

73 J. Thirsk, *Horses in Early Modern England: for Service, for Pleasure, for Power* (Reading, 1978), p. 11. Elizabeth set up a commission 'For the increase and breed of horses and for the keeping of horses and geldings for service' in 1580, under the impending threat of war with Spain. It was staffed by her most prominent noblemen, including Leicester, Hatton and Sir Henry Sidney. See P. Edwards, *The Horse Trade of Tudor and Stuart England* (Cambridge, 1988). On Elizabethan attitudes towards the rearing and maintenance of horses, see Thomas Blundeville, *The Four Chiefest Offices belonging to Horsemanship* (London, 1593).

74 Thirsk, *Horses in Early Modern England*, p. 12.

75 *Ibid.*, p. 13.

76 *Ibid.*, p. 12.

77 S. Adams, *Household Accounts and Disbursement Books of Robert Dudley, Earl of Leicester, 1558–1561, 1584–1586*, Camden fifth ser., vol. 6 (Cambridge, 1995), p. 314.

78 On the complexity of the use of the term *German* in the period, see L. Jardine, 'Penfriends and Patria: Erasmian Pedagogy and the Republic of Letters', *Erasmus of Rotterdam Society Yearbook* 16 (1996), pp. 1–18. In this context, however, it is not crucial to distinguish amongst the various Low Countries who termed themselves 'German'.

79 Shakespeare, *Henry V*, III. v. 5-31, in *The Norton Shakespeare* (New York, 1997).

80 In breeding parlance, European horses are 'cold-blooded', while the Arab and Barb horses used by the Moors are 'hot-blooded': 'There is no biological difference between a warm or cold-blooded horse. Horses descended from the smaller Arabian or Barb are considered "warm-blooded." All other horses are "cold blooded," including modern day draft horses descended from the medieval warhorse' ('Museum of the Horse' website).

81 See A. A. Sicroff, *Les Controverses des statuts de "pureté de sang" en Espagne du xve au xviie siècle* (Paris, 1960), p. 101.

82 This tradition is continued in the pedigree of thoroughbred racehorses, which is determined by their direct descent from three Arab stallions: The Byerly Turk, Darley Arabian and Godolphin Arabian.

83 Hyland, *Warhorse*, pp. 2–3.

84 See J. S. Nolan, *Sir John Norreys and the Elizabethan Military World* (Exeter, 1997), p. 89.

85 *Ibid.*, pp. 98–9. This is not quite how Nolan described the engagement, because he did not fully appreciate the significance of the skirmish tactic.

86 For a better account, see A. Stewart, *Philip Sidney: A Double Life* (London, 2000): 'Leicester decided to join Norris, and crossed the river with fifty or sixty men. Thick mist hindered them for a while, but eventually they found Norris' camp, where they were warmly welcomed. Unbeknownst to them the incoming force under Marques del Vasto, was now close by, and had thrown up their own entrenchments, waiting for a sally from the gates of Zutphen. Suddenly the fog lifted. Into view came the victual wagons surrounded by a Spanish force of three thousand-foot soldiers and at least fifteen hundred horse. There was no time to rethink: Leicester and his

men advanced. The English horsemen charged the Spanish cavalry, driving them over their line of pikeman and back over their own trenches. They could go no further, because musket shot from the Spanish trenches forced the English back. Quickly reforming, the English charged again, once again forcing the Spaniards back behind their musketry, once again being repelled by musket shot. Count Hannibal Gonzaga ('a man of great account' in Dr James' estimation) was mortally wounded by Perrot; the Albanian cavalry leader Captain George Crescia was unhorsed by Willoughby and taken prisoner. Stanley's horse was shot eight times, although its rider came through unscathed. Sidney's horse too was killed under him on the second charge. A third charge threw the Spanish cavalry into disarray, but once again the bullets proved too much. The battle lasted for some ninety minutes before Verdugo let two thousand more troops out from the gates of Zutphen, forcing the English across the river. Their losses were twenty-two foot soldiers, and twelve or thirteen cavalry. Spanish losses were estimated at 250–300. Again it was a hollow victory: after the exhilarating battle, the enemy convoy simply rolled into Zutphen. Among the wounded was Sir Philip Sidney. Unfazed by the loss of his horse, he had secured a replacement, and on the third charge rode right through the Spanish lines. As he turned to retreat, however, he was struck by a musketball from the trenches: it lodged three fingers above the left knee, and shattered the bone' (pp. 311–21).

87 In the Renaissance, the Roman statue of Marcus Aurelius was believed to be of Constantine – the ultimate power-figure whose 'ownership' was contested by East and West.

88 Economists have suggested to us that use of the term *commodity* is only justified when consignments of the goods (like wheat or copper) in question are identical and interchangeable. Horses, like other luxury goods, are sold on an individual basis (distinguished both by breed and named animal).

89 See chap. 1 in this volume.

90 Both sides of this medal, however, readily lent themselves to copying as images of non-Christian oriental exoticism. The profile head of John, as we pointed out in chap. 1, sometimes stands in for an Ottoman or Mamluk Sultan in later paintings.

91 Cox-Rearick, *The Collection of Francis I*, p. 19.

92 In Orso's album, discussed above, the horse drawing entitled 'corsier della razza di Mantova' (courser of Mantuan stock) and illustrated in this volume (illus. 64) appears to have been taken directly from the Clouet painting. This suggests that to the contemporary observer, Francis's mount was still recognizably a 'real' Mantuan in spite of the painting's iconic nature.

93 Compare Roy Strong's arguments for the iconic status of late portraits of Elizabeth I of England in *The Cult of Elizabeth* (London, 1977).

94 See chap. 1 of this volume.

95 If this return to 'race' as opposed to 'breed' seems like special pleading, note such signals in the secondary literature as Carlo Cavriani, 'Le razze Gonzaghesche di cavalli nel mantovano e la lora influenza sul puro sangue inglese', *Rassegna contemporanea*, 2 (1909).

96 See the contemporary account of the battle by Luis de Avila y Zuñiga, reprinted in F. Checa, *Tiziano y la Monarquia Hispanica* (Madrid, 1994), p. 40. We are extremely grateful to Professor John Elliott for this reference.

97 Comparisons with other images from the battle show how accurately Charles's armour and weaponry are represented in this picture. Nonetheless, there is a tension between the 'brutal', possibly unreliable and underhand imagery associated with pistols and 'reiters' and the painting's imperial iconography.

98 See the Spanish literature on Charles as the figure of a 'Christian soldier', for example, F. Checa, *Tiziano y la Monarquia Hispánica* (Madrid, 1994), pp. 39–42; *Felipe II, Un Monarca y su Epoca: Un Principe del Renacimento*, exh. cat., Museo del Prado, Madrid (1998), p. 285.

99 The advice is given in a letter from Aretino to Titian. See Checa, *Tiziano*, p. 42.

100 For a clear account, see Strong, *Art and Power*, p. 86, illus. 61. Discussing triumphal arches for Charles V, Strong writes: 'Attitudes are epitomised in the introduction, both in Siena and Florence, of that most significant of imperial images, the equestrian statue. This was an honour reserved in antiquity for the emperor alone . . . In 1541, the theme was repeated when Charles entered Milan in an arch designed by Giulio Romano with a Moor, a (Red) Indian and a Turk falling under his horse's hooves while its final form was Titian's great canvas celebrating the defeat of the Lutherans at the Battle of Mühlberg (1547).'

101 Spanish commentators on this painting insist that it represents Charles 'crossing the Elba river' and recalling Caesar crossing the Rubicon. There is, however, no sign of a river, nor is the horse's pose or gait appropriate to river crossing (one may compare the contemporary woodcut of the Battle of Mühlberg, in which the struggling horses, breasting the river, are clearly visible). See Checa, *Tiziano*, pp. 40–46.

102 For a reproduction of Enea Vico's engraving, see Checa, *Tiziano*, p. 43. See also the chalk drawing by Titian for the *Battle of Spoleto* (*c.* 1537), which shows a skirmish between soldiers on horseback across a river. Here once again the carefully observed poses of the horses bear no resemblance to that in the *Battle of Mühlberg* (reproduced in P. F. Brown, *The Renaissance in Venice* [London, 1997] p. 73).

103 Checa, *Tiziano*, p. 40: 'Iba el Emperador en un caballo español castaño oscira, el cual le habia presentado mosiur de Ri, caballero del orden del Tuson, y su primer camarero; llevaba un caparazon de terciopelo carmesí con franjas de oro, y unas armas blancas y doradas, y no levabo sobre ellas otra cosa sino la banda muy ancha de tafetan carmesí listada de oro, y un morrion tudesco, y una media hasta, casi venablo, en las manos.'

104 If, as Professor Elliott has also suggested to us, the de Ri whose gift the horse was came from the Netherlands, then yet another conquered territory is encompassed symbolically in the horse under Charles's spurred heel.

105 Titian went to Augsburg to paint the Emperor (Charles was there having recalled the Diet in 1548 to discuss the political and doctrinal situation in Europe). The painter is supposed to have been given accommodation adjacent to the Emperor, to allow him access to Charles at all times without formalities. We may therefore imagine that the composition of this highly

propagandistic work conformed to the Emperor's own ideas on how best to represent the iron grip with which he supposedly ruled Christendom and held off the forces of Islam and Protestantism. The completed painting went straight into the collection of Mary of Hungary, Charles's Regent in the Low Countries, where its imperial message of mastery of alien infidels was entirely appropriate in an image of the occupying Hapsburg power. See *Felipe II, Un Monarca y su Epoca*, pp. 282–4.

106 Horn also noted that in another earlier medal celebrating Charles's victory at Tunis, the Emperor is portrayed resting his foot on a vanquished prisoner, believed to be the Turkish corsair Barbarossa (*Vermeyen*, vol. I, p. 324, n. 306). As with Titian's equestrian portrait, the graphic image of subjection is here made explicit, whilst Titian offered a more over-determined image.

Select Bibliography

Ackerman, Phyllis, *The Rockefeller McCormick Tapestries: Three Early Sixteenth-Century Tapestries* (Oxford, 1932)
——, *Tapestry: The Mirror of Civilisation* (New York, 1933)
Adelson, Candace, *European Tapestry in the Minneapolis Institute of Arts* (New York, 1994)
Ahl, D. C., *Leonardo da Vinci's Sforza Monument Horse: The Art and the Engineering* (London, 1995)
Appadurai, Arjun, ed., *The Social Life of Things: Commodities in Cultural Perspective* (Cambridge, 1986)
d'Astier, Colonel, *La Belle Tapisserye de Roy (1532–1797) et les tenures de Scipion l'africain* (Paris, 1907)
Babinger, Franz, *Mehmed the Conqueror and His Time* (Princeton, 1978)
Bacou, Rosaline, and Bertrand Jestaz, *Jules Romain: L'Histoire Scipion: Tapisseries et dessins* (Paris, 1978)
Baldass, Ludwig, *Die Wiener Gobelinssammlung*, 3 vols (Vienna, 1920)
Blundeville, Thomas, *The Four Chiefest Offices belonging to Horsemanship* (London, 1593)
Bodnar, E. W., *Cyriacus of Ancona and Athens* (Brussels, 1960)
Brotton, Jerry, *Trading Territories: Mapping the Early Modern World* (London, 1997)
——, 'Terrestrial Globalism: Mapping the Globe in Early Modern Europe', in Denis Cosgrove, ed., *Mappings* (London, 1999)
Brown, Clifford M., and Guy Delmarcel, *Tapestries for the Courts of Federico II, Ercole, and Ferrante Gonzaga, 1522–63* (Washington, DC, 1996)
Brown, P. F., *The Renaissance in Venice* (London, 1997)
Brummett, Palmira, *Ottoman Seapower and Levantine Diplomacy in the Age of Discovery* (Albany, 1994)
Buisseret, David, *Monarchs Ministers and Maps: The Emergence of Cartography as a Tool of Government in Early Modern England* (Chicago, 1992)
Burckhardt, Jacob, *The Civilization of the Renaissance in Italy* (London, 1892)
Burke, P., *The Fabrication of Louis XIV* (New Haven, 1992)
Charrière, E., *Négociations de la France dans le Levant*, 4 vols (Paris, 1840–60)
Checa, F., *Tiziano y la Monarquia Hispanica* (Madrid, 1994)
Clot, André, *Suleiman the Magnificent: The Man, His Life, His Epoch* (London, 1992)
Cole, A., *Art of the Italian Renaissance Courts* (London, 1995)
Comaroff, Jean and John, *Ethnography and the Historical Imagination* (Boulder, 1992)

Cortesão, Armando, ed., *The Suma Oriental of Tome Pires and The Book of Francisco Rodrigues* (London, 1944)

Cox-Rearick, J., *The Collection of Francis I: Royal Treasures* (New York, 1995)

Davies, D. W., ed., *The Actions of the Low Countries by Sir Roger Williams* (Ithaca, 1964)

Davis, R. H. C., *The Medieval Warhorse* (London, 1989)

Delmarcel, Guy, *Flemish Tapestry* (London, 1999)

D'Hulst, Roger, *Tapisseries flamandes* (Brussels, 1960)

Didi-Huberman, G., R. Garbetta and M. Morgaine, *Saint Georges et le dragon: Versions d'une légende* (Paris, 1994)

Diffie, Bailey, and George Winius, *Foundation of the Portuguese Empire, 1415–1580* (Minneapolis, 1977)

Edwards, P., *The Horse Trade of Tudor and Stuart England* (Cambridge, 1988)

Felipe II, Un Monarca y su Epoca: Un Principe del Renacimento, exh. cat., Museo Nacional del Prado (Madrid, 1998)

Frère, J.-C., *Léonard de Vinci* (Paris, 1994)

Freud, Sigmund, *Civilization and Its Discontents* [1930], in The Penguin Freud Library Vol. 12, *Civilization, Society and Religion* (Harmondsworth, 1985)

Gill, J., *The Council of Florence* (Cambridge, 1959)

——, *Personalities of the Council of Florence and other Essays* (Oxford, 1964)

Ginzburg, Carlo, *The Enigma of Piero: Piero della Francesca*, trans. M. Ryle and K. Soper (London, 1985)

Göbel, Heinrich, *Wandteppiche*, 5 vols (Leipzig, 1923–34)

Gombrich, E. H., *Symbolic Images: Studies in the Art of the Renaissance II* (Oxford, 1972)

Greenblatt, Stephen, *Renaissance Self-Fashioning: From More to Shakespeare* (Chicago, 1980)

Haardt, Robert, 'The Globe of Gemma Frisius', *Imago Mundi*, 9 (1952)

Hale, John, *The Civilisation of Europe in the Renaissance* (London, 1993)

Hamilton, A. C., ed., *Edmund Spenser: The Faerie Queene* (London, 1977)

Hay, Denys, *Europe: The Emergence of an Idea* (Edinburgh, 1957)

Heinz, Dora, *Europäische Wandteppiche I: Von den Anfängen der Bildwirkerei bis zum Ende des 16. Jahrhunderts* (Braunschweig, 1963)

Helms, Mary W., *Ulysses' Sail: An Ethnographic Odyssey of Power, Knowledge, and Geographical Distance* (Princeton, 1988)

Hervey, Mary F. S., *Holbein's Ambassadors, the Picture and the Men: An Historical Study* (London, 1900)

Hollingsworth, M., *Patronage in Renaissance Italy from 1400 to the Early Sixteenth Century* (London, 1994)

Holmes, G., ed., *Art and Politics in Renaissance Italy: British Academy Lectures* (Oxford, 1993)

Holt, Mack P., *The Duke of Anjou and the Politique Struggle During the Wars of Religion* (Cambridge, 1986)

Hore, J. P., *The History of Newmarket*, vol. I (London, 1886)

Horn, Hendrick, *Jan Cornelisz Vermeyen*, 2 vols (The Hague, 1989)

Hyland, Ann, *The Warhorse, 1250–1600* (Stroud, 1998)

——, *The Horse in the Middle Ages* (Stroud, 1999)

Ives, E. W., *Anne Boleyn* (Oxford, 1986)

Jankovich, Miklos, *They Rode Into Europe: The Fruitful Exchange in the Arts of Horsemanship between East and West*, trans. Anthony Dent (London, 1971)

Jardine, Lisa, *Worldly Goods: A New History of the Renaissance* (London, 1996)

——, 'Penfriends and Patria: Erasmian Pedagogy and the Republic of Letters', *Erasmus of Rotterdam Society Yearbook* 16 (1996), pp. 1–18

Knecht, R. J., *Renaissance Warrior and Patron: The Reign of Francis I* (Cambridge, 1994)

——, *Catherine De' Medici* (London, 1998)

Krogt, Peter van der, *Globi Neerlandici: The Production of Globes in the Low Countries* (Utrecht, 1993)

Levenson, J. A., ed., *Circa 1492: Art in the Age of Exploration* (New Haven, 1991)

Luchinat, C. A., ed., *The Chapel of the Magi: Benozzo Gozzoli's Frescoes in the Palazzo Medici-Riccardi Florence*, trans. E. Daunt (London, 1994)

Mann, N., and L. Syson, eds, *The Image of the Individual: Portraits in the Renaissance* (London, 1998)

Masefield, John, ed., *The Travels of Marco Polo* (London, 1908)

Necipoğlu, G., 'Süleyman the Magnificent and the Representation of Power in the Context of Ottoman-Hapsburg Rivalry', *Art Bulletin* (1989), pp. 401–27

——, *Architecture, Ceremonial, and Power: The Topkapi Palace in the Fifteenth and Sixteenth Centuries* (Cambridge, 1991)

Nolan, J. S., *Sir John Norreys and the Elizabethan Military World* (Exeter, 1997)

Olivata, L., 'La principessa Trebisonda: Per un ritratto di Pisanello', in P. Castelli, ed., *Ferrara e il Concilio 1438–1439: Atti del Covegno di Studi nel 5500 Anniversario del Concilio dell'unione delle due Chiese d'oriente e d'occidente* (Ferrara, 1992)

Ortiz, Antonio Domínguez, *et al.*, eds, *Resplendence of the Spanish Monarchy: Renaissance Tapestries and Armor from the Patrimonio Nacional* (New York, 1991)

Panofsky, E., *Studies in Iconology: Humanistic Themes in the Art of the Renaissance* (Oxford, 1939)

Paolucci, A., *Piero della Francesca: Notizie sulla consevatione di Margherita Moriondo Lenzini* (Florence, 1989)

Pfeiffer, Rudolf, *History of Classical Scholarship 1300–1850* (Oxford, 1976)

Phillips, Barty, *Tapestry* (London, 1994)

Pollard, J. G., ed., *Italian Medals: Studies in the History of Art* (Washington, DC, 1987)

Prior, C. M., *The Royal Studs of the Sixteenth and Seventeenth Century* (London, 1935)

Raby, J., *Venice, Dürer and the Oriental Mode* (London, 1982)

——, 'East and West in Mehmed the Conqueror's Library', *Bulletin du bibliophile* (1987), pp. 297–321

Rice, Eugene, and A. Grafton, *The Foundations of Early Modern Europe, 1460–1559*, 2nd edn (New York, 1994)

Rosenberg, C. M., *The Este Monuments and Urban Development in Renaissance Ferrara* (Cambridge, 1997)

Russell, J. G., *The Field of the Cloth of Gold* (London, 1969)

Ryan, W. G., trans., *Jacobus de Voragine, The Golden Legend: Readings on the Saints*, 2 vols (Princeton, 1993)

Rykwert, J., and A. Engel, eds, *Leon Battista Alberti* (Milan, 1994)

Said, Edward, *Orientalism* (London, 1978)

——, *Culture and Imperialism* (London, 1993)

Scher, S. K., *The Currency of Fame: Portrait Medals of the Renaissance* (Washington, 1994)

Setton, K. M., *Europe and the Levant in the Middle Ages and the Renaissance* (London, 1974)

——, *The Papacy and the Levant (1204–1571)*, 4 vols (Philadelphia, 1976–84)

Sewell, Robert, *A Forgotten Empire* (London, 1900)

Seznec, J., *The Survival of the Pagan Gods: The Mythological Tradition and Its Place in Renaissance Humanism and Art* (New York, 1953)

Shaw, S., *History of the Ottoman Empire and Modern Turkey*, vol. I (Cambridge, 1976)

Shearman, John, *Raphael's Cartoons in the Collection of Her Majesty the Queen and the Tapestries for the Sistine Chapel* (London, 1972)

Shirley, Rodney, *The Mapping of the World: Early Printed Maps, 1472–1700* (London, 1983)

Sicroff, A. A., *Les Controverses des statuts de 'pureté de sang' en Espagne du xve au xviie siècle* (Paris, 1960)

Skelton, R. A., ed., *Magellan's Voyage: A Narrative Account of the First Circumnavigation* (New York, 1969)

Smith, Ronald Bishop, *The First Age of the Portuguese Embassies to the Ancient Kingdoms of Cambay and Bengal, 1500–1521* (Bethesda, 1969)

Stahl, William, *Commentary on 'The Dream of Scipio' by Macrobius* (New York, 1952)

Standen, Edith Appleton, *European Post-Medieval Tapestries and Related Hangings in The Metropolitan Museum of Art* (New York, 1985)

Stewart, A., *Philip Sidney: A Double Life* (London, 2000)

Stirling Maxwell, William, ed., *The Turks in 1533. A Series of Drawings made in that Year at Constantinople by Peter Coeck of Aelst* (London and Edinburgh, 1873)

Strong, Roy, *Holbein and Henry VIII* (London, 1967)

——, *Art and Power: Renaissance Festivals 1450–1650* (Woodbridge, Suffolk, 1973)

Sutherland, N. M., *The Massacre of St. Bartholomew and the European Conflict, 1559–1572* (London, 1973)

Swetz, F. J., *Capitalism and Arithmetic: The New Math of the 15th Century, Including the Full Text of the Treviso Arithmetic of 1478*, trans. David Eugene Smith (La Salle, IL, 1987)

Thirsk, J., *Horses in Early Modern England: For Service, for Pleasure, for Power* (Reading, 1978)

Thomson, W. G., *A History of Tapestry* (London, 1906)

Vickers, M., 'Some Preparatory Drawings for Pisanello's Medallion of John VIII Paleologus', *Art Bulletin*, 60 (1978), pp. 419–24

Weiss, R., *Pisanello's Medallion of the Emperor John VIII Paleologus* (London, 1966)

Wroth, Lawrence, ed., *The Voyages of Giovanni da Verrazzano* (New Haven, 1970)

Yates, Frances, *The Valois Tapestries* (London, 1959)

Photographic Acknowledgements

The authors and publishers wish to express their thanks to the following sources of illustrative material and/or permission to reproduce it (excluding sources credited in full in the captions):

Daniel Arnaudet: 18; Ashmolean Museum, Oxford (Reitlinger Bequest) – photo © Ashmolean Museum: 23; Bibliothèque Nationale de France, Paris (Cabinet des Médailles): 6, 7, 24; Gérard Blot: 36; Osvaldo Böhm: 2–4; British Library, London: 5, 51, 62, 67, 76; The Trustees of the Edward James Foundation, West Dean College: 49; Hervé Lewandowski: 71; Metropolitan Museum of Art, New York (Fletcher Fund): 30; Musée du Louvre, Paris (Département des Arts Graphiques): 9, 20, 52, 80; Museo del Prado, Madrid: 85; National Gallery of Art, Washington, DC (Samuel H. Kress Collection): 10, 78; Luciano Pedicini/Archivio dell'Arte: 31; photos © RMN, Paris: 9, 18, 20, 36, 52, 71, 80; Royal Collection Picture Library: 77 (Inv. 12321), 82 (Inv. 12358); Scala Group: 12–17, 33, 46, 47, 68, 69, 72, 73; Staatliche Museen zu Berlin – Preußischer Kulturbesitz (Münzkabinett): 8, 79; Studio Milar: 45; University Art Museum, University of California at Santa Barbara (Sigmund Morgenroth collection): 81; V&A Picture Library, © The Board of Trustees of the Victoria and Albert Museum, London: 61, 63, 64, 66, 84.

Index

Figures in *italics* represent illustration numbers.